TIME
LIFE ®
BOOKS

Other Publications:

*This volume is one of a series that explains and demonstrates
how to prepare various types of food, and that offers in each
book an international anthology of great recipes.*

Variety Meats

BY
THE EDITORS OF TIME-LIFE BOOKS

TIME-LIFE BOOKS/ALEXANDRIA, VIRGINIA

Cover: A large roll of braised stuffed tripe is basted with some of its reduced cooking liquid to endow it with a rich brown glaze (page 64). The tripe was first sewn into a cylindrical package and stuffed with a mixture of chopped meats and herb-flavored rice, then cooked for about eight hours with a calf's foot and aromatic vegetables in veal stock and wine.

THE GOOD COOK

The original version of this book was created in London for Time-Life Books B.V.
European Editor: Kit van Tulleken; Design Director: Louis Klein; Photography Director: Pamela Marke; Planning Director: Alan Lothian; Chief of Research: Vanessa Kramer; Chief Sub-Editor: Ilse Gray; Chief of Editorial Production: Ellen Brush; Quality Control: Douglas Whitworth

Staff for Variety Meats: Series Editor: Gillian Boucher; Series Coordinator: Liz Timothy; Text Editor: Jay Ferguson; Anthology Editor: Josephine Bacon; Staff Writers: Alexandra Carlier, Sally Crawford, Jane Havell, Nicoletta Flessati, Thom Henvey; Researchers: Nora Carey, Deborah Litton; Designer: Cherry Doyle; Sub-Editors: Sally Rowland, Charles Boyle, Kate Cann, Kathy Eason; Design Assistant: David Mackersey; Editorial Department: Steve Ayckbourn, Sarah Dawson, Judith Heaton, Theresa John, Lesley Kinahan, Stephanie Lee, Debra Lelliott, Linda Mallett, Sylvia Osborne, Debra Raad, Molly Sutherland, Julia West, Helen Whitehorn

U.S. Staff for Variety Meats: Editor: Gerry Schremp; Senior Editor: Anne Horan; Designer: Ellen Robling; Chief Researcher: Barbara Levitt; Picture Editor: Christine Schuyler; Text Editor: Sarah Brash; Researchers: Tina Ujlaki (techniques), Ann Ready, Katherine F. Rosen (anthology); Assistant Designer: Peg Schreiber; Copy Coordinators: Tonna Gibert, Nancy Lendved; Art Assistant: Mary L. Orr; Picture Coordinator: Alvin Ferrell; Editorial Assistants: Carolyn Bounds, Patricia Whiteford

CHIEF SERIES CONSULTANT

Richard Olney, an American, has lived and worked for some three decades in France, where he is highly regarded as an authority on food and wine. Author of The French Menu Cookbook and of the award-winning Simple French Food, he has also contributed to numerous gastronomic magazines in France and the United States, including the influential journals Cuisine et Vins de France and La Revue du Vin de France. He has directed cooking courses in France and the United States and is a member of several distinguished gastronomic and oenological societies, including L'Académie Internationale du Vin, La Confrérie des Chevaliers du Tastevin and La Commanderie du Bontemps de Médoc et des Graves. Working in London with the series editorial staff, he has been basically responsible for the planning of this volume, and has supervised the final selection of recipes submitted by other consultants. The United States edition of The Good Cook has been revised by the Editors of Time-Life Books to bring it into complete accord with American customs and usage.

CHIEF AMERICAN CONSULTANT

Carol Cutler is the author of a number of cookbooks, including the award-winning The Six-Minute Soufflé and Other Culinary Delights. During the 12 years she lived in France, she studied at the Cordon Bleu and the École des Trois Gourmandes, and with private chefs. She is a member of the Cercle des Gourmettes, a long-established French food society limited to just 50 members, and is also a charter member of Les Dames d'Escoffier, Washington Chapter.

SPECIAL CONSULTANTS

Richard Sax, who was responsible for many of the step-by-step demonstrations in this volume, was for two years Chef-Director of the test kitchens for The International Review of Food and Wine. Trained in New York and in Paris, where he served an apprenticeship at the Hotel Plaza-Athénée, he has run a restaurant on Martha's Vineyard, written articles for a number of publications and conducted cooking courses.
Joyce Dodson Piotrowski studied cooking while traveling and living around the world. A teacher, chef, caterer, food writer and consultant, she also demonstrated step-by-step techniques for this volume.

PHOTOGRAPHER

Tom Belshaw was born near London and started his working career in films. He now has his own studio in London. He specializes in food and still-life photography, undertaking both editorial and advertising assignments.

INTERNATIONAL CONSULTANTS

GREAT BRITAIN: Jane Grigson has written a number of books about food and has been a cookery correspondent for the London Observer since 1968. Alan Davidson is the author of several cookbooks and the founder of Prospect Books, which specializes in scholarly publications about food and cookery. FRANCE: Michel Lemonnier, the cofounder and vice president of Les Amitiés Gastronomiques Internationales, is a frequent lecturer on wine and vineyards. GERMANY: Jochen Kuchenbecker trained as a chef, but worked for 10 years as a food photographer in several European countries before opening his own restaurant in Hamburg. Anne Brakemeier is the co-author of a number of cookbooks. ITALY: Massimo Alberini is a well-known food writer and journalist, with a particular interest in culinary history. His many books include Storia del Pranzo all'Italiana, 4000 Anni a Tavola and 100 Ricette Storiche. THE NETHERLANDS: Hugh Jans has published cookbooks and his recipes appear in several Dutch magazines. THE UNITED STATES: Judith Olney, author of Comforting Food and Summer Food, received her culinary training in England and France. In addition to conducting cooking classes, she regularly contributes articles to gastronomic magazines.

Correspondents: Elisabeth Kraemer (Bonn); Margot Hapgood, Dorothy Bacon (London); Susan Jonas, Miriam Hsia, Lucy T. Voulgaris (New York); Maria Vincenza Aloisi, Josephine du Brusle (Paris); Ann Natanson (Rome). Valuable assistance was also provided by: Janny Hovinga (Amsterdam); Bona Schmid (Milan).

CONTENTS

A Trove of Unexpected Treasure

Any cook daring enough to experiment with variety meats is almost always pleasantly surprised. The choices are many: The term encompasses both the innards of an animal, such as its liver, heart and kidneys, and the extremities—head, feet, ears and tail. And each kind of meat can bring unique flavor and texture to a multitude of delectable dishes.

Although variety meats are now sometimes ignored or snobbishly dismissed as peasant fare, Roman epicures prized the livers of pigs that had been fed on ripe figs, honey and wine, and in Renaissance Italy, lamb's tongues and peacock's brains were delicacies that graced banquet tables. Most parts of the world have a repertoire of variety meat dishes, each reflecting a distinctive tradition. In the Middle East, tripe is shaped into a roll and stuffed with chopped meat and rice, flavored with coriander and mint (pages 64-65). In Indonesia tripe is simmered with ginger, chili peppers and tamarind, then cut into squares and fried; and in Spain strips of tripe are braised with garlic sausages in a highly seasoned tomato sauce (recipes, pages 129-130). Homely, rustic dishes—the Scots haggis, made by stuffing a lamb stomach with innards and oatmeal—contrast with truffled sweetbreads that would enrapture a boulevardier.

This book deals with beef, veal, pork, lamb and poultry variety meats. The guide overleaf provides information on selecting and storing these meats and includes suggestions on where to purchase them. Availability often differs by region: The South, for instance, has an abundance of pork variety meats, and the Southwest, of lamb. Ethnic markets provide a valuable resource. Butchers catering to a Chinese clientele generally will sell chicken feet, German butchers will carry pork liver and French ones can be counted on for tripe and brains.

The chart on page 7 summarizes appropriate cooking methods, and demonstrations on the following pages detail how to prepare each type of meat for cooking as well as how to make the essential stocks, court bouillons, sauces and garnishes. The basic cooking methods—frying, grilling, broiling, roasting, poaching and braising—are shown step by step in the subsequent chapters; the demonstrations conclude with a chapter on sausage making. The second half of the book contains an anthology of 204 recipes gathered from cookbooks old and new.

Abats rouges, abats blancs

The taste and size of innards and extremities reflect, of course, the kind of animal from which they come—lamb heart, for instance, has the unmistakable flavor and aroma of lamb and is about one half the dimensions of the milder veal heart. None-theless, by adjusting quantities and cooking times, similar parts often can be cooked similarly; a particularly attractive recipe for veal kidney, for example, will usually serve equally well for lamb kidney. Moreover, the French—who are second to none in putting variety meats to delicious use—have classified variety meats by a system that enables the cook to make further substitutions. The French designate each type of meat, on the basis of appearance, as abat rouge or abat blanc—a red variety meat or a white one—and divide each group into tender and tougher meats. In this system, all liver, kidney, heart and spleen are tender red meats; gizzard, oxtail and tongue are tougher. The meltingly tender brains, sweetbreads and fries constitute one group of white meats, while ears, feet, heads, pigs' tails, stomachs, chitterlings and tripe belong in the other.

Color and tenderness provide the guidelines that a cook needs in dealing with possibly unfamiliar ingredients. For example, naturally tender red variety meats such as the lamb kidneys and the fat-encased veal kidney shown opposite are at their juiciest when cooked quickly by straightforward methods such as broiling and sautéing. Morsels of tender white meats such as sweetbreads can be dipped in batter and deep fried to make fragile fritters (pages 30-31). White meats that need long, moist cooking are often served in rich sauces based on the cooking liquid—poached calf's feet in an egg-enriched velouté, for example (pages 52-53). But feet as well as ears and tongues also make spectacular cold dishes when poached and encased in a shimmering aspic decorated with vegetables (pages 54-55).

The choices of wine to accompany these meats are as diverse as the cooking methods. Young, relatively mild red wines—Beaujolais or a light-bodied Zinfandel—are generally welcome accompaniments. However, some of the meats or the ingredients with which they are combined may dictate a different choice. The delicacy of sautéed sweetbreads, for example, is complemented by a light, young, fruity wine, such as Sancerre or California fumé blanc; served in a creamy sauce, they are well matched by a more complex wine such as a Meursault.

The full-bodied flavor of oxtail or beef cheeks, by contrast, is best offset by a robust red wine—Châteauneuf-du-Pape, an Italian Barolo or one of the more intense California Zinfandels. Sturdy white wines from the South of France or Italy suit tripe, while roasted veal liver is ideally complemented by the intricate nuances of an Hermitage from the Côtes du Rhône or an old Médoc. As always in choosing wine, there are no hard-and-fast rules: The choice should be inspired by the same spirit of adventure that makes variety meat cookery itself so rewarding.

A Guide to Buying

The spectrum of variety meats available to the good cook ranges from the reassuringly familiar to the unexpected and adventurous—from liver and kidney to cheeks and spleen, tails and feet. The names of these cuts may vary from butcher to butcher, but usually innards are known by the name of the animal's meat while extremities go by the name of the animal itself—thus pork and veal liver, but pig's or calf's feet.

Whatever the terminology, these cuts of meat offer a truly enormous sweep of sizes and shapes, textures and tastes. Beeves yield the largest cuts; in calves, pigs, lambs and poultry, equivalent cuts become progressively smaller. Lamb innards are fine-textured and delicate compared to pork, while veal innards are milder than beef. By contrast, poultry variety meats—from chickens, turkeys, ducks and geese—taste much alike.

Though supermarkets sell many types of variety meats, some—as indicated in this guide—must be obtained from specialty butchers or ethnic markets and may have to be ordered a week or more in advance. Generally the only poultry variety meats sold separate from the fowl are those of chicken.

Freshness is always a desirable attribute, and brains, fries, spleen or sweetbreads are so fragile in structure that freezing ruins them. Other types of variety meat, however, can be safely bought frozen, salted, corned or smoked.

Variety meats purchased fresh should be kept tightly covered in the refrigerator and cooked within two days. Frozen meats can be kept in a home freezer at 0° F. [–18° C.] for up to three months, but must thaw fully in the refrigerator—allow about 24 hours—before they are used. Salted or corned meats can be kept refrigerated for two weeks; before being cooked, they should be parboiled to rid them of excess salt. Smoked meats can be refrigerated for four months.

Brains. Veal and lamb brains are available at many supermarkets; pork brains are sold at ethnic markets; beef brains can be ordered from a specialty butcher. A brain consists of a pair of deeply ridged lobes, which should be plump and symmetrical. The thin shiny membrane covering them should be intact. Because this membrane contains a network of blood vessels, the creamy white flesh of the lobes will appear pink and be blotched with red.

Cheeks. Pork cheeks, often sold as pork or hog jowls, are available fresh, frozen or smoked at ethnic markets and in some supermarkets. Beef cheeks can be ordered from a specialty butcher. The streaks of flesh in fresh pork cheeks should be pink, the fat white and firm, and the skin smooth and pale pink; smoked pork cheeks resemble bacon. Beef cheeks are skinned before they are offered for sale; they should have red flesh, generously marbled with fat.

Chitterlings. These are the large intestines of pigs. They are widely available slit, cleaned and cut into sections, and sold fresh or frozen. Whole cleaned chitterlings are obtainable from some ethnic markets or can be ordered from a specialty butcher. In either the cut or whole form, they should be pinkish beige.

Ears. Pig's ears are available fresh or frozen from some supermarkets and ethnic markets, and can be ordered from a butcher. They should be plump with smooth, pale pink skin. Fresh ears should look dry, not sticky.

Feet. Pig's feet are widely available fresh, frozen or salted from supermarkets, ethnic markets and butchers. Fresh calf's feet can be ordered from a specialty butcher; fresh lamb's feet are rare, but butchers may sometimes be able to obtain them. Chicken feet are available fresh from some ethnic markets and from poultry stores. Fresh pig's feet should be plump, pale pink and smooth—neither sticky nor dry. Calf's and lamb's feet are nearly white in color. Chicken feet usually are whitish yellow, but in some breeds the feet may be blue, black, green or white.

Fries. These are the testicles. Beef and veal fries, often called mountain or prairie oysters, are available fresh from some ethnic markets, and—like both pork and lamb fries—can be ordered from a specialty butcher. All fries should be firm, plump and pinkish beige, and their shiny skin should be intact.

Gizzards. The gizzard is the equivalent in a bird of an animal's stomach. Chicken gizzards are widely available fresh or frozen. They should be plump, shiny and reddish brown.

Head. Fresh pig's heads are obtainable at ethnic markets. Fresh calf's or lamb's heads must be ordered from a butcher. Pig's heads should have smooth, pinkish beige skin with only a few hairs; calf's heads should have smooth, almost-white skin. Lamb's heads are always sold skinned. As a rule, a head is sold with the brains, tongue and eyes intact; the butcher will discard the eyes on request. If you do not plan to bone a pig's or calf's head (pages 14-15), ask the butcher to remove the brains and tongue for you and to saw the skull into several pieces to simplify handling.

Heart. Veal and chicken hearts are widely available fresh or frozen. Most butchers can order fresh beef, pork or lamb heart. Veal heart is pink to rosy red; other types are red to reddish brown. Veal, lamb and chicken hearts are sold intact; pork and beef hearts are usually split open for government inspection.

Kidney. Beef, veal, pork and lamb kidneys are widely available fresh or frozen from supermarkets, ethnic markets and butchers. A pork or lamb kidney has a single lobe; beef and veal kidneys have many lobes. Lamb kidney is often sold encased in its fat, which should be creamy white. The surface fat is usually removed from beef, veal and pork kidneys at the slaughterhouse; if you want this fat, order the kidney in advance. Choose beef, veal or pork kidneys that are firm, plump and surrounded by thin, shiny membranes. Beef and pork kidneys are reddish brown; veal kidney is a lighter color. Avoid any kidney that has a disagreeable odor.

Liver. Beef, veal, pork and chicken livers are available fresh or frozen. Lamb liver usually must be ordered in advance from a specialty butcher. Chicken livers are sold whole; other livers are generally presliced—if you want a whole beef, veal, pork or lamb liver, you may have to order it. Select liver that is firm and shiny, with the surface membrane intact. Veal liver is pinkish brown; other livers are dark red or brown.

Spleen. This is an abdominal organ found near the stomach. Beef spleen is usually available from kosher butchers, who sell it as miltz. Both beef and lamb spleens may be ordered from specialty butchers. Spleen should have pulpy red flesh surrounded by a white membrane.

Stomach. Pig's stomach, often sold as hog's maw or sow's maw, is available fresh or frozen from ethnic markets or can be ordered from a butcher. It is usually sold whole. The stomachs of cows and calves are marketed as tripe (below). Whole lamb's stomach is sold as stomach and can be ordered from a butcher; when cut up, lamb's stomach is sold as tripe. Chicken stomachs are sold as gizzards (left).

Sweetbreads. This is the two-lobed thymus gland of a calf or lamb; the gland disappears in mature animals. The gland is usually called a pair of sweetbreads although one lobe is flat and elongated, the other rounded. In taste and texture the lobes are the same. Fresh veal sweetbreads are widely available at supermarkets; lamb sweetbreads must be ordered from a specialty butcher. In both kinds of sweetbreads, the lobes should be plump, pink and intact, and surrounded by a shiny membrane.

Tails. Beef tails, marketed as oxtail, are widely available fresh or frozen at supermarkets—usually already cut into sections at the joints. Pig's tails are sold intact, fresh or frozen, at ethnic markets. Fresh oxtail should have red flesh and firm white fat. Fresh pig's tails should be smooth, pink and neither wet nor sticky.

Tongue. Beef tongues are sold fresh, frozen, corned or smoked at many supermarkets. Veal, pork and lamb tongues are usually sold fresh; veal tongue is available at some supermarkets, but pork and lamb tongues must be ordered from a butcher. All tongues should be firm. Fresh tongue is grayish pink; corned tongue is deep rosy red; smoked tongue is reddish brown. Dark spots on the skin do not affect quality.

Tripe. Two of the four parts of the stomachs of ruminants—beeves and lambs—are sold as tripe: smooth blanket tripe (the first stomach, or paunch) and honeycomb tripe (the second stomach, named for its appearance). Beef tripe is available from supermarkets, ethnic markets and butchers; veal and lamb tripe must be ordered specially. All tripe is yellowish beige and has a rubbery texture. Tripe is always scalded before sale; ordinarily it is available cut into pieces, but you can order any kind of tripe whole.

Suitable Cooking Methods at a Glance

The chart below shows the kinds of variety meat available from different animals and indicates the cooking methods suitable for each of them. To use the chart, find the name of the cut that you wish to serve in the alphabetical listing across the top of the chart. Then read down that column to match the cut to the appropriate meat—as listed at left.

For easy reading, the entry for each meat includes the six basic cooking methods—sautéing, deep frying, grilling or broiling, roasting, poaching and braising. Wherever a cooking method is suitable, the box corresponding to that method will contain a dot; otherwise the box will be empty. As an example, for veal heart the dot in the box opposite roasting means that the heart can be cooked that way, whereas the absence of a dot opposite poaching means the method is not recommended. Where all six boxes are empty, that type of cut is not available from the animal: Pigs do not yield sweetbreads, but are the only source of chitterlings.

Any variety meat will, of course, require some preliminary trimming or cleaning and most require precooking before they are finished by another method (pages 8-15). In many cases, the meat also must be cut into pieces suitable for the method chosen. Heart, for example, should be sliced or julienned for sautéing, but cut into small cubes for deep frying.

		Brains	Cheeks	Chitterlings	Ears	Feet	Fries	Gizzards	Head	Heart	Kidney	Liver	Spleen	Stomach	Sweetbreads	Tails	Tongue	Tripe
Beef	Sautéing	•					•			•	•	•					•	•
	Deep Frying	•					•			•		•					•	•
	Grilling/Broiling	•					•			•	•	•				•	•	•
	Roasting	•					•			•		•	•				•	•
	Poaching	•	•				•									•	•	•
	Braising		•							•	•	•	•			•	•	•
Veal	Sautéing	•					•			•	•	•			•		•	•
	Deep Frying	•				•	•			•	•	•			•		•	•
	Grilling/Broiling	•				•	•			•	•	•			•		•	•
	Roasting	•				•	•		•	•	•	•	•		•		•	•
	Poaching	•				•	•		•			•			•		•	•
	Braising					•	•		•	•	•	•	•		•		•	•
Pork	Sautéing	•		•			•			•	•	•					•	
	Deep Frying	•		•	•	•	•			•	•	•					•	
	Grilling/Broiling	•			•	•	•			•	•	•				•	•	
	Roasting	•		•	•	•	•		•	•	•	•		•		•	•	
	Poaching	•	•	•	•	•	•		•			•		•		•	•	
	Braising		•	•	•	•	•		•	•	•	•			•	•	•	
Lamb	Sautéing	•					•			•	•	•			•		•	•
	Deep Frying	•				•	•			•	•	•			•		•	•
	Grilling/Broiling	•				•	•			•	•	•			•		•	•
	Roasting	•				•	•			•	•	•	•	•	•		•	•
	Poaching	•				•	•					•		•	•		•	•
	Braising					•	•			•			•	•	•		•	•
Poultry	Sautéing							•		•		•						
	Deep Frying					•		•		•		•						
	Grilling/Broiling					•		•		•		•						
	Roasting					•				•		•						
	Poaching					•		•										
	Braising					•		•		•								

Tailoring the Treatment to the Meat

The advance treatment required for all variety meats ensures that they will look and taste their best in the finished dish. For some of these meats, a little trimming will suffice; others need washing, soaking or even precooking.

The nature of the preparation depends both on the type of variety meat involved and on the animal it came from, as the livers, hearts and kidneys shown here demonstrate. Beef, lamb, pork and veal livers are usually sold sliced; the pieces sometimes contain blood vessels, which must be cut out, and often are sheathed in membrane, which must be peeled away. By contrast, poultry livers are sold whole, and the blood vessels are so small and the membrane so thin they can be left alone. However, the liver of a freshly killed bird may contain the gall bladder, which must be removed carefully to avoid spilling its bitter contents.

Poultry, veal and lamb hearts generally come intact, while most pork and beef hearts will have been slashed. In any case, the fat around the top of the heart must be trimmed away and the tubular blood vessels cut off. With beef and veal kidneys, both the outer membrane and the inner core of fat are removed; with lamb and pork kidneys, the inner fat may be left in place.

The demonstrations on pages 10-11 show how to clean nine more types of meats. A thorough washing is all that is needed for tripe, pig's and lamb's stomachs and pig's tails. Excess fat must be trimmed from oxtails and pulled off chitterlings. Loose portions of the membrane are trimmed from spleen, but brains are freed entirely of their membrane.

The gizzards of freshly killed poultry contain a gravel-filled sac that must be extracted or emptied. Poultry feet of all kinds must be skinned; calf's, pig's and lamb's feet only need a thorough cleaning, but may be partially boned.

The brief precooking technique called parboiling firms the flesh of sweetbreads and fries, and draws out scum from pig's ears (pages 12-13). To make them compact, sweetbreads may be pressed with weights after parboiling. Tongue needs both parboiling and extended poaching to loosen its tough skin and make it ready for peeling.

Peeling Liver

Removing the membrane. With a knife, cut away any blood vessels from the liver—here, a large piece of veal liver—taking care not to damage the flesh. To remove the surface membrane, gently loosen it at one edge and pull it away from the flesh. As you pull, hold the liver down with one hand to keep the flesh from tearing.

Trimming Poultry Liver

Removing the gall bladder. Trim off any bits of fat from the liver—a goose liver is shown. If the bird is freshly killed, the gall bladder may be attached. Cut around the base of the gall bladder and lift it off intact with the small section of liver attached to it. Discard the gall bladder.

Coring Beef or Veal Kidney

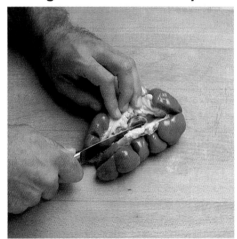

1 **Halving the kidney.** If the kidney —in this case, veal—is still encased in fat, pull it off with your fingers. Then make a shallow slit in the surface membrane of the kidney and peel it off. Cut the kidney in half lengthwise, slicing through its fatty core.

2 **Removing the core.** Using your finger tips and a sharp knife, pull or cut away from the flesh as much of the hard core of fat as possible.

Trimming Veal or Lamb Heart

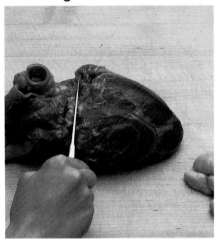

Slicing off the tubes. With a sharp knife, cut away the layer of fat from the top portion of the heart—a veal heart is shown. Slice off the large tubular blood vessels together with the fibrous tissue around them. Discard the trimmings.

Trimming Pork Heart

Cutting away the top. Lay the pork heart on a cutting board and trim the fat from around the top. Slice off the tubes and attached fibrous tissue. Inspect the heart for any blood clots and wipe them off with a paper towel.

Trimming Beef Heart

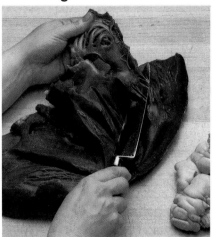

Removing membranes. Trim as much fat as possible from the outer surface of the heart. Slice off the tubes and fibrous tissue from the top. Spread the heart open to expose the tough membranes that line the chambers, then work the blade of a sharp knife under the membranes to cut them away.

Peeling Pork or Lamb Kidney

1 **Pulling away fat.** With a knife, slit the hard white fat that encloses the kidney. Here, lamb kidney is shown; pork kidney is handled in the same way if still sheathed in fat. With your fingers, pry the fat apart at the slit.

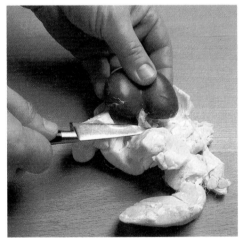

2 **Cutting off the fat.** Peel the fat away from the kidney. It will come off easily except for one small section in the center of the underside of the lobe where the fatty covering is attached to the kidney's core. Sever this section with a sharp knife and discard the fat.

3 **Removing the membrane.** With a knife, make a slit about 1/8 inch [3 mm.] deep in the rounded side of the kidney to split the thin, shiny membrane that surrounds it. Pull the membrane off the kidney and cut the membrane free where it is attached to the kidney's core. Leave the core fat intact.

Cleaning Stomach or Tripe

Rinsing. Fill a large bowl with cold water and repeatedly dunk the stomach or tripe—in this instance, honeycomb tripe—into the water to remove any particles of dirt. Pull off any bits of fat. Put the rinsed stomach or tripe into a colander to drain, then pat it dry with paper towels.

Cleaning Pig's Tail

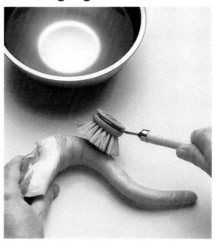

Scrubbing the tail. Grasp the tail near its base. Dip a brush into water and scrub the tail vigorously to remove any traces of scum or particles of dirt. Rinse the tail under cold running water and pat it dry.

Trimming Oxtail

Cutting off fat. With a knife, pare away excess fat from a whole oxtail; the fatty layer is particularly thick at the base of the tail. Leave only a thin layer of fat intact to help keep the meat moist during the cooking period.

Paring a Gizzard

1 **Slitting the gizzard.** Remove any fat that surrounds the gizzard—here, a turkey gizzard. If the bird is freshly killed, the gizzard may be intact. In that case, slit open one side, cutting through the flesh and the tough connective tissue that lines it. Pull apart the flesh at the slit to expose the gravel sac inside the gizzard.

2 **Cutting off the flesh.** If the gravel sac is intact, pull it out. Otherwise, discard the contents of the sac, rinse the gizzard well and peel away any loose sac membrane. A chicken gizzard is now ready for use. With any other fowl, cut the flesh away from the connective tissue and discard the trimmings.

Skinning Poultry Feet

Singeing the foot. To loosen the skin, pass the foot—in this case, a turkey foot—through a flame until the skin is blistered all over. Using a paper towel, pull off the pieces of parched skin and discard them. Trim off the nail from the base of each toe with kitchen shears or a sharp, heavy knife.

Cleaning Chitterlings

Removing the lining. Hold a piece of chitterling in one hand so its fatty membranous inner lining faces upward. With the fingers of your other hand, peel the lining off and discard it. Place the cleaned chitterlings in a large bowl of acidulated cold water and let them soak for one to two hours. Drain them well before using them.

Trimming Spleen

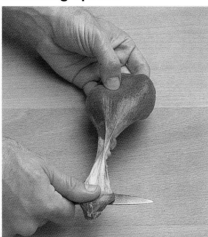

Pulling off the membrane. Using a sharp knife, cut away fat and any loose pieces of membrane from the spleen—lamb spleen is shown here. Leave the clinging membrane intact to avoid damaging the spleen's pulpy flesh.

Peeling Brains

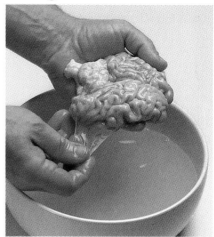

Removing the membrane. To remove excess blood, soak brains—here, veal brains—in several changes of cold water for 30 minutes, or until the water remains clear. Peel off the outer membrane, dipping the brains in water repeatedly to help loosen it. Soak the brains in fresh water for approximately one hour to whiten them.

Boning a Calf's, Pig's or Lamb's Foot

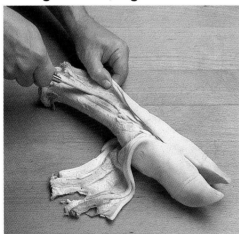

1 **Exposing the bone.** Scrape between the toes of the foot—here, a calf's foot—to remove any clinging tufts of hair. Scrape or singe off any other hairs on the foot. Starting at the point where the large bone joins the toes—just above the cleft of the foot—make a lengthwise incision through the skin and flesh to expose the large bone.

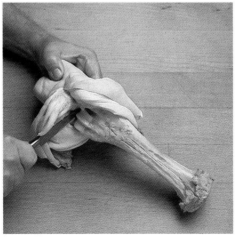

2 **Removing the bone.** Turn the foot over and make another lengthwise cut along the center of the underside. Cut the skin and flesh from the large bone, scraping downward against the bone with the knife blade. Sever the tendons that attach the toes to the large bone and remove the bone.

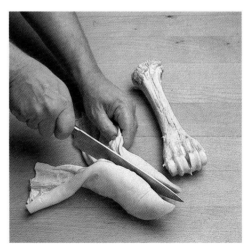

3 **Splitting the foot.** Trim away the ragged edges of skin, leaving neat flaps above the toes. If you like, split the foot in two: The halves will fit more easily into a pot and the gelatin they contain will be released sooner. Reserve the large bone for use in stock.

Peeling and Firming Sweetbreads

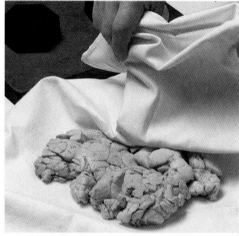

1 **Parboiling.** To remove excess blood, soak sweetbreads—in this case, veal—in several changes of cold water. When the water remains clear, place the sweetbreads in a pan. Cover them with fresh water and bring it slowly to a boil. Simmer veal sweetbreads for five to six minutes, lamb for two to three minutes.

2 **Removing membrane.** Cool the sweetbreads in a bowl of cold water. With your fingers, remove the membrane that covers each sweetbread and the fat and tubes attached to the membrane. Keep the peeled sweetbreads in a bowl of water while you prepare the rest. Lamb sweetbreads are ready for cooking after peeling.

3 **Weighting.** To press veal sweetbreads into a compact shape, put them on a dry towel on a tray and fold the towel over them. Set a board on top and put about 2 pounds [1 kg.] of weights or canned foods on the board, distributing the weight evenly. Refrigerate the sweetbreads for three hours, or until they are firm.

Poaching and Peeling Tongue

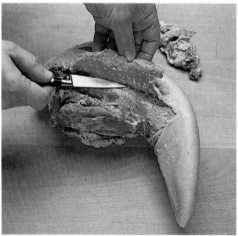

1 **Cleansing.** To remove blood from a fresh tongue or excess salt from a corned one, soak the meat in cold water for several hours. Then put the tongue—here, a corned beef tongue—in a pot and cover it with fresh cold water. Bring the water to a boil, reduce the heat and simmer for 10 minutes. Then pour off the water and rinse the tongue.

2 **Poaching.** Return the tongue to the pot; add carrots, onions, herbs and enough water to cover them. Bring to a boil, reduce the heat and simmer the tongue—one and one half to two hours for beef, 45 minutes for veal or pork, 30 minutes for lamb. Keep the tongue in the pot until it is just cool enough to handle (above).

3 **Trimming.** Transfer the tongue to a cutting board and use a small, sharp knife to trim fat and gristle from the base of the tongue. Remove the throat bones.

Peeling and Parboiling Fries

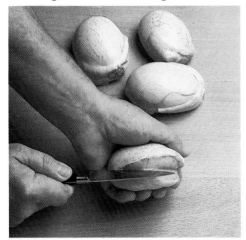

1 **Slitting the skin.** Hold a fry—in this instance, lamb—firmly in one hand and slit the skin with a small, sharp knife by making a lengthwise cut along one rounded side. Make sure the knife penetrates all three layers of the skin— the innermost layer is thin and clings tightly—but do not pierce the flesh.

2 **Removing the skin.** Pry the skin loose at the slit with your finger tips, then—gripping the flesh firmly—pull off the three layers of skin. Drop the peeled fries into cold water and soak them to remove all blood, changing the water several times.

3 **Firming the fries.** Transfer the fries to a pan and cover them with cold water, salting it lightly. Bring the water to a boil, reduce the heat and simmer the fries for six to seven minutes to firm them. With a slotted spoon, transfer the fries to a bowl of fresh cold water to rinse off any scum. Drain them and pat dry.

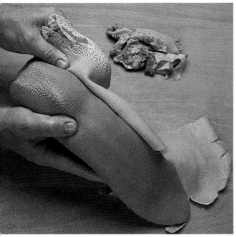

4 **Removing the skin.** Place the tongue upside down and slit the skin lengthwise from the tip to the base. Use the tip of the knife to loosen the skin at the slit. Then, with your fingers, work the skin free and peel it off the tongue. Discard the trimmings and the skin.

Cleaning and Parboiling Pig's Ears

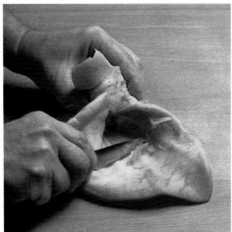

1 **Removing hairs.** Place each ear on a cutting board and scrape it with a small, sharp knife to remove all hairs. If necessary, pass the ear over an open flame to singe off any stubborn hairs. Use a small, stiff-bristled brush to rid the cavity of the ear of any particles of dirt.

2 **Parboiling the ears.** Put the cleaned ears in a pot of cold water and bring the water to a boil. Cook the ears for five minutes, then use a perforated spoon or metal skimmer to transfer them to a bowl of cold water to wash off any scum. Keep the rinsed ears in acidulated water until you are ready to cook them.

Freeing the Meat from a Whole Head

For the cook, the most challenging of variety meats is a whole calf's or pig's head. Although the head may be poached as is, it will require an enormous pot and at least six hours of cooking. To decrease the time and pot size, the butcher can be asked to saw the head into three or four pieces. But when the meat and skin of the head are poached on the bone, they will turn to tatters.

To achieve attractive as well as perfectly cooked meats, the best approach is to bone the head. As demonstrated here, the process requires more patience than skill and keeps the head meat and skin in a single neat piece that lends itself to diverse treatments. Left intact, the boned head can be used as a pouch for stuffing (pages 52-53) or it can be spread flat and wrapped jelly-roll fashion around stuffing to form a cylinder. Alternatively, the head can be cut into pieces for poaching, individually or with the brains and tongue (pages 46-47).

When ordering the head, specify that you want the butcher to take out the eyes. Before you begin the boning, rid the head of any remaining hairs: Singe them with a lighted match and then rub them off with a kitchen towel. To draw out blood, immerse the head in a pot of salted water, acidulated to prevent the skin from discoloring. Measurements do not need to be precise, but allow about 1 tablespoon [15 ml.] each of salt and vinegar or lemon juice for every quart [1 liter] of water. Change the water repeatedly until it remains clear. Then drain the head and pat it dry with paper towels.

As you cut the flesh free, keep the knife close to the bone to avoid piercing or tearing the skin. Be particularly careful when you are working on the top of the head and around the eyes. In both these places, only a thin layer of tissue separates the skin and bone.

When the head is boned, drop it into fresh acidulated water to cleanse it—and keep it soaking if you plan to use the head the same day. Otherwise, pat the head dry and enclose it in plastic wrap (not foil, which will react with the acid in the soaking water). It can be kept refrigerated for two or three days.

The Process of Boning

1 **Slitting the skin.** Soak the head—in this case, a calf's head—for two hours in several changes of acidulated salted water. Dry the head with a towel. Trim the fat from the base of the head and scrape the ears clean. Lay the head face down and cut through the skin from the neck to the chin.

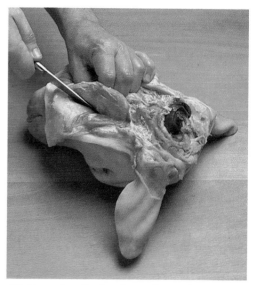

2 **Exposing the jawbone.** Insert the knife between the jawbone and one cheek just below the ear. Keeping the knife blade against the bone and following its outer contours, free the flesh from the bone. Then free the flesh from the outer surface of the other side of the jawbone in the same way.

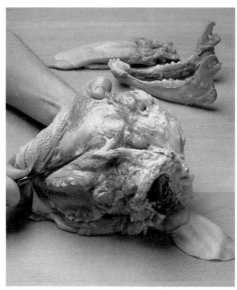

6 **Exposing the skull.** Lay the head on its side. Keeping the knife against the skull and following its contours, cut the flesh and skin away from the side of the skull. Pull the freed flesh and skin away from the skull as you work.

7 **Working around the eyes.** Free the flesh around the eyes carefully, keeping the knife tip in contact with the eye socket and taking care not to cut the eyelids. Turn the head over and cut away the skin and flesh to expose the skull on the other side.

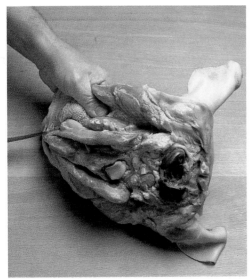

3 **Freeing the chin.** Scrape the flesh from the inside of the jawbone on both sides. To free the chin, insert the knife between the flesh of the lower lip and the jawbone and scrape the flesh away from the bone.

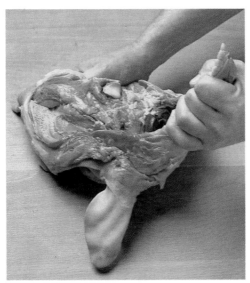

4 **Removing the jawbone.** When the jawbone is completely exposed, steady the head with one hand and use your other hand to grasp the jawbone at the chin end. Pull the bone backward to break the joints, then cut through the flesh and tendons around them to free the jawbone.

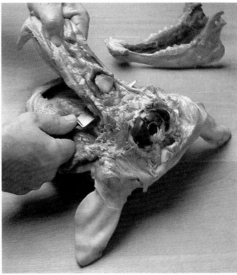

5 **Removing the tongue.** Grasp the end of the tongue firmly, holding it up and away from the head. Cut through the base of the tongue where it joins the throat. Reserve the tongue.

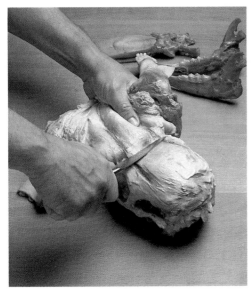

8 **Exposing the top of the skull.** Turn the calf's head face upward. Scrape the flesh free at the back of the skull where it is firmly attached. Continue to scrape the flesh free, working from the back of the skull toward the front and pulling the flesh toward the muzzle.

9 **Freeing the muzzle.** Continue to scrape and pull the flesh off the skull. Use the knife to free the flesh from the bone of the upper jaw at the tip of the muzzle. Turn the skull over and use a cleaver to split it open lengthwise down its center. Scoop out the brains and soak them in clear water (page 11).

10 **Soaking the head.** Reserve the jawbone and the skull for stock making. Soak the reserved tongue and boned head in acidulated water, changing the water several times until it stays clear.

Aromatic Liquids in Many Guises

A well-flavored cooking liquid can enhance variety meats in diverse ways. The paradigm of cooking liquids is a slowly simmered meat stock *(below; recipe, page 165)* that provides a rich medium for braising or for poaching red meats; a savory base for sauce making; and—with a little forethought—an aspic sheath or garnish. By contrast, a quickly prepared court bouillon *(bottom; recipes, page 165)* is most useful for poaching white meats; after the court bouillon takes on their fla-vor it also serves as a base for sauces.

Stock can be based on beef, veal, chicken or a combination of the three, and flavored with assorted aromatics such as onions, carrots and herbs. Beef stock is the strongest in taste, veal the most delicate. In any case, the best meat cuts are inexpensive and bony ones: beef or veal neck or shank, or chicken trimmings—necks, backs, wing tips and such. All bones supply some gelatin to give the stock body, but to produce an aspic, the stock requires pig's ears, pig's or chicken feet, or the calf's foot shown below.

Up to five hours of cooking are needed to extract the flavor and gelatin from meat and bones, and the stock must then be strained and degreased. Court bouillons, on the other hand, are flavored with vegetables, herbs and acid liquid. They are cooked just long enough to soften the vegetables—10 to 30 minutes—and can be used without being strained.

Wine, vinegar or lemon court bouil-

Slow Simmering to Develop Flavor

1 **Adding meat.** Put a rack in a pot and place a blanched, halved calf's foot *(page 11)*, veal neck and shank on the rack. Cover the meats with cold water. Heat slowly over medium heat, skimming off any scum.

2 **Adding aromatics.** To keep the water from boiling and dispersing scum, add a cup of cold water. Skim until no more scum rises, adding cold water as needed. Add carrots, a clove-studded onion, garlic and a bouquet garni.

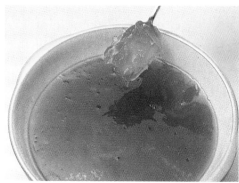

3 **Setting the stock.** With the lid ajar, simmer the stock for at least five hours. Strain through a colander lined with cheesecloth or muslin. Cool the stock and refrigerate it overnight. Scrape off the solidified fat from the clear aspic.

Quickly Assembled Court Bouillons

Vinegar court bouillon. Put leek, onion, carrot, celery, herbs, salt and water into a nonreactive pan. Bring to a boil, cover and simmer for 15 minutes. Add wine vinegar. Cook 15 minutes; add peppercorns for the last five.

Wine court bouillon. Bring salted water and aromatics to a boil in a nonreactive pan, as for vinegar court bouillon. Cover, simmer for 15 minutes, add red wine and cook 15 minutes, adding peppercorns for the last five.

White court bouillon. Put carrots, two clove-studded onions and a bouquet garni into a pot. Add water, and whisk in a thin solution of flour and water. Add beef suet and lemon juice. Bring to a boil and cook for 10 minutes.

lons lend piquancy to mild-tasting white meats, such as brains, that require only brief cooking. A white court bouillon is best for long-cooking meats such as ears or feet: The inclusion of flour and lemon juice keeps the meat white, while chopped suet forms a seal on the liquid's surface to help exclude air and thus inhibit discoloration.

Turning a stock or meat-imbued court bouillon into a sauce can be accomplished most easily by boiling the liquid to reduce it and concentrate its flavor, then whisking in a *beurre manié*—a paste that is made by kneading butter and flour together. Allow about 1½ tablespoons [22½ ml.] each of butter and flour for every cup [¼ liter] of liquid.

The more complex velouté sauce *(below; recipe, page 166)* needs long cooking to develop its smooth texture: "Velouté" means "velvety" in French. The stock or court bouillon is blended with roux—a cooked mixture of flour and butter—and simmered for at least 40 minutes to rid it of the taste of flour, to reduce it, and to let fatty particles in the sauce collect and form a skin that can be skimmed off.

A basic velouté sauce can be flavored by stirring in heavy cream or a puréed vegetable such as tomato, mushroom or spinach during the last few minutes of cooking. Or, to make a luxurious poulette sauce, velouté can be cooled slightly and augmented with egg yolks, parsley and lemon juice *(bottom; recipe, page 166)*.

Composing a Basic Velouté

1 **Adding stock.** Melt butter in a heavy saucepan and add flour. Cook for two to three minutes, stirring with a whisk until the mixture is smooth but not brown. Whisk in liquid—veal stock is shown—and bring the sauce to a boil.

2 **Skimming the sauce.** Reduce the heat and set the pan half off the burner so that the sauce boils gently on one side. After about 10 minutes, skim off the skin of impurities that will have formed on the cooler side of the pan.

3 **Cooking the sauce.** With the pan half off the heat, let the sauce simmer for about 40 minutes—periodically skimming off any skin that forms. If the finished sauce is thin, boil it until it lightly coats a spoon *(above)*.

Enriching a Velouté with Eggs

1 **Flavoring egg yolks.** Prepare a velouté sauce—here, with a white court bouillon poaching liquid—and let it cool slightly. With a fork, beat egg yolks with chopped parsley and lemon juice until smooth. Stir in a little cooled sauce.

2 **Enriching the sauce.** Whisking the pan of sauce continuously, pour the egg-yolk mixture into the velouté. When the egg-yolk mixture is well blended, place the pan over very low heat.

3 **Thickening the sauce.** Stirring with a whisk, simmer the sauce for three to five minutes—just long enough for it to heat through and thicken.

The Ever-Useful Tomato

The bright color and tangy flavor of tomatoes complement variety meats of all kinds—providing the form the tomatoes take is adapted to the way the meats are cooked. With a sautéed meat, for example, tomato halves are a welcome last-minute addition to the pan. To prepare them, the tomatoes are peeled, halved and seeded *(right)*, then sautéed in butter until they become tender without losing shape—about five minutes.

By contrast, for a braised meat, tomatoes should be peeled, then seeded and chopped. Added to the pan with the braising liquid, the tomatoes will reduce to tiny particles as the meat cooks.

Yet another option is to turn tomatoes into a thick puréed sauce *(below)* that can accompany roasted, grilled, deep-fried or poached variety meats. During cooking, the sauce can be imbued with fresh herbs: basil, parsley, dill, thyme, marjoram, mint, sage, bay leaf, oregano. Just before serving, the sauce can be enriched, if you wish, with heavy cream.

Eliminating Peel and Seeds

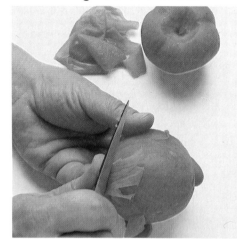

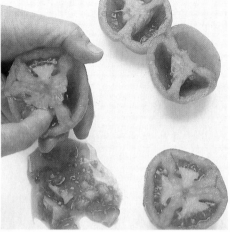

1 **Peeling tomatoes.** Cut a conical plug from the stem end of each tomato, and cut a cross in the top. Immerse the tomatoes in boiling water for about 10 seconds to loosen their skins. Drain and cool the tomatoes. To peel each one, slide a sharp knife under the edges of the cross and pull off the skin in sections, working toward the stem end.

2 **Seeding tomatoes.** Cut the peeled tomatoes in half crosswise to expose the seed pockets. Grasp each tomato half firmly in one hand and, with one finger of your other hand or the handle of a teaspoon, scrape out the seeds and juice from all the pockets.

Producing a Smooth Sauce

1 **Seasoning tomatoes.** In a nonreactive pan, sauté finely chopped onions in a little oil until they are soft. Quarter tomatoes and add them to the onions, along with coarse salt, a bay leaf, thyme and garlic cloves. Stirring occasionally, cook uncovered over low heat until the tomatoes disintegrate—about 30 minutes.

2 **Puréeing the tomatoes.** Set a strainer over a large bowl, and push the tomatoes through the mesh with a pestle or the back of a large wooden spoon. Discard the seeds, skins and seasonings left in the strainer. Pour the tomato purée back into the pan.

3 **Cooking the purée.** Simmer the tomato purée uncovered over low heat for 20 to 30 minutes until it is reduced to the consistency you wish. Stir it frequently to prevent scorching, especially toward the end of cooking. Season the sauce with pepper and, if you like, add chopped fresh herbs such as basil or parsley.

A Gallery of Garnishes

Sautéed or braised variety meats benefit from garnishes that add color, flavor and textural contrast. Wedges of tomato or lemon, chopped fresh parsley or sprigs of watercress will serve, of course. But the garnishes also may be more substantial, such as the four classics shown here.

The most versatile of garnishes is croutons—sautéed bread cubes that can be scattered over a fully cooked dish to provide a crisp counterpoint to tender meat. Sautéed bacon strips contribute a smoky note if added to a meat shortly before it is ready for serving. The bacon should be first blanched to remove excess salt, then cooked in oil until browned but not crisp.

Vegetables, too, should be precooked and added when the meat is almost done. Prime candidates for garnishes, aside from tomatoes *(opposite)*, are carrots or other root vegetables cut into little balls or ovals, and small whole mushrooms and onions. Simmering the mushrooms with lemon juice adds flavor and whitens them, while sautéing root vegetables or onions gives them a golden glaze.

Golden Cubes of Bread

Sautéing croutons. Remove the crusts from slices of white bread ½ inch [1 cm.] thick and cut the bread into cubes. In a skillet, melt butter with an equal volume of oil. Add as many of the bread cubes as will fit in one layer. Tossing them constantly, sauté them over moderately high heat until they are crisp and golden—about two minutes.

Bacon Sautéed in Oil

Sautéing bacon. Remove the rind from slab bacon, slice the bacon ¼ inch [6 mm.] thick and cut the slices crosswise into strips ¼ inch wide. Drop the strips into a pan of cold water, bring to a boil and simmer for two minutes; drain the strips. Sauté them in a skillet filmed with oil until lightly browned. Drain them on paper towels.

Mushrooms Stewed with Butter

1 **Adding butter.** Trim the stems from small button mushrooms. Wash and drain the mushrooms, then put them in a sauté pan with a little salt, the juice of a lemon and 1 or 2 tablespoons [15 or 30 ml.] of water. Add a generous chunk of butter to the pan.

2 **Cooking the mushrooms.** Bring the contents of the pan to a boil, then reduce the heat, cover and simmer for three minutes. Take the mushrooms off the heat; strain just before using them. The cooking liquid can be reserved and used as a flavoring for a velouté or poulette sauce *(page 17)*.

Onions with a Syrupy Glaze

Sautéing the onions. To loosen their skins, blanch boiling onions for one minute; peel them. Melt a large chunk of butter in a skillet and add the onions. Cook them, uncovered, over low heat until they are soft and lightly colored—at least 20 minutes. Shake the pan repeatedly and turn the onions over with a spoon to keep them from sticking.

1
Sautéing and Deep Frying
Strategies for Sealing In Succulence

The secrets of stir frying
Deglazing the pan for sauce
Cooking kidney in its mantle of fat
A choice of coatings for fritters

Whether it is done in a thin film of fat or in a layer several inches deep, frying endows meat with an appetizing appearance and a succulent taste. Just about any variety meat can be fried, providing it is prepared properly beforehand *(pages 8-13)*. Tender red variety meats such as liver or heart can then be fried from the raw state; tender white types including sweetbreads and brains need parboiling to be firm enough to handle; tougher meats must be softened by poaching.

The way in which the meats are cut for frying varies with the procedure selected. Sautéing, for example, employs just enough fat or oil to flavor the meats' surfaces and prevent them from sticking to the pan. Generally, sautéing is done over high heat in an open pan and the meats must be sliced or cut into small pieces so that they will cook quickly without drying out; the most notable exception to the rule is the whole veal kidney shown opposite, which is sautéed slowly in a covered pan to keep it juicy all through.

Stir frying, the Chinese version of sautéing, is always a quick process. But because the food is constantly being lifted, turned and tossed, the meats must be sliced especially thin or cut into matchstick-sized strips. In sautéing, meats are often dusted with flour to produce browner crusts; in stir frying, meats are coated with a slippery cornstarch mixture to help keep the pieces separate as they are turned.

For deep frying, meats are cut bite sized and transformed into fritters by a protective coating of batter or bread crumbs. At the ideal frying temperature of 375° F. [190° C.], the coating is instantly sealed and quickly crisps. Peanut and corn oil are the prime choices for deep frying; neither will burn at temperatures of less than 425° F. [220° C.] and their flavors are pleasantly bland. Peanut oil is also the medium Chinese cooks prefer, but sautéing may be done in olive oil or butter as well.

Stir-fried meats are cooked with vegetables, so garnishes are built-in; deep-fried meats are usually served with no more than a wedge of lemon or a spoonful of tomato sauce to counterpoint their richness. By contrast, sautéed meats invite imaginative garnishing. Colorful vegetables or bacon strips can be added to the pan before the meat is served, and croutons sprinkled over it at the table. And blending wine or stock and cream or butter with the pan juices will yield a delicate sauce *(pages 24-27)*.

A veal kidney, cooked whole inside its casing of fat, is sliced for serving from the sauté pan. The kidney is garnished with sautéed tomatoes, fried bacon strips and cepes that have been sautéed in butter with bread crumbs, parsley and shallots *(pages 28-29)*.

Simple Tactics for Tender Meats

When cut into thin slices or julienne, naturally tender red variety meats can be sautéed or stir fried to perfect succulence in four or five minutes. Because the heat used for both processes is high, the meat browns to a rich mahogany color so fast that it remains juicy within.

Here, veal liver is sliced and sautéed (*recipe, page 86*), whereas pork heart is julienned and stir fried (*recipe, page 98*). The meats are interchangeable with each other and with any beef, veal, pork or lamb liver or heart. Kidneys can be stir fried or sautéed similarly, but must be drained for a minute or so afterward to rid them of their acrid juices (*pages 26-27*). To reach the proper degree of doneness quickly, the slices should be about ¼ inch [6 mm.] thick for pork, ½ inch [1 cm.] thick for beef, veal or lamb; julienne should be about ¼ inch thick.

Before sautéing, the meat pieces can be dusted with flour to help ensure a brown crust. Flouring must be done at the last minute and the pieces positioned without overlapping lest the flour become soggy. For stir frying, the meat is marinated in a mixture containing cornstarch, which makes the marinade cling and keeps the pieces separated as they cook.

Appropriate mediums for sautéing include olive oil, for its fruity flavor; butter, for its sweetness; and bland vegetable oil. To counteract butter's tendency to burn quickly, add a little oil to it. For stir frying, peanut oil is classic.

Choose the pan with care. If a sauté pan or skillet is too broad, the fat covering the exposed areas between pieces of meat may burn. However, if the pan is too small, the meat will steam rather than brown. The traditional vessel for stir frying is a wok, designed to facilitate tossing and turning the food as it cooks. You may, though, substitute a large skillet, providing it has deep sloping sides.

Because both processes are fast, all ingredients must be prepared in advance. Garnishes for sautés should be ready to add to the pan as soon as the meat is done so that they can be browned or heated without letting the meat cool. The vegetables that are an integral part of a stir-fried dish should be cleaned and larger ones—carrots, celery or broccoli, for example—cut into julienne or thin slices.

Liver and Sage: A Natural Partnership

1 **Flouring the liver.** Remove the membrane (*page 8*) from the liver—in this case, veal liver—and cut the liver into slices ½ inch [1 cm.] thick; with pork, cut ¼-inch [6-mm.] slices. Spread flour on a plate. Coat both sides of each liver slice with flour, then shake it gently to remove the excess. As you flour them, set the slices on a tray.

2 **Sautéing the liver.** Film the bottom of a skillet with olive oil. Set the pan over high heat, add a crushed garlic clove and remove it when it browns lightly. Add the liver slices. Sauté them for two to three minutes on each side, or until pink juices appear on the upper surface of the slices. Pork is done when the juices are no longer pink.

Julienned Heart with a Spicy Tang

1 **Cutting the meat.** Prepare a marinade of soy sauce, sherry, peanut oil, cornstarch, pepper and sugar. Halve a heart lengthwise—a pork heart is shown here. Place each half cut side down and cut it crosswise into ¼-inch [6-mm.] slices. Cut each slice into julienne ¼ inch wide and 2 inches [5 cm.] long. Toss the julienne with the marinade.

2 **Preparing the vegetables.** Peel carrots and a piece of fresh ginger and cut them into julienne ¼ inch wide and 2 inches long. Cut scallions lengthwise and remove the stems and seeds from fresh green chilies. Cut the scallions and chilies into julienne that are of the same size as the carrots.

3 **Sautéing the sage.** Transfer the liver to a heated platter and set it in a warm place. Add a handful of fresh sage leaves to the oil remaining in the skillet.

4 **Garnishing the liver.** Sauté the sage leaves until they are slightly crisp—about one minute. Then remove the skillet from the heat and pour the sage leaves and any savory juices that remain in the pan over the liver slices. Serve the garnished liver immediately, accompanied, if you like, with wedges of lemon.

3 **Stir frying the meat.** Pour peanut oil into a wok and swirl the pan to coat it evenly with oil. Set the wok over high heat. When the oil is very hot, drop in a garlic clove, let it color, then discard it. Add the heart julienne and stir them constantly with a spoon or Chinese spatula until brown and slightly firm— about two minutes. Drain in a strainer.

4 **Stir frying vegetables.** Dissolve cornstarch in chicken stock and set it aside. Heat more oil in the wok and add the ginger. Stirring constantly, cook it for half a minute; add the carrots and stir fry for a minute more. Add the scallions and chilies and cook them for half a minute. Stir in the heart, then the cornstarch mixture.

5 **Finishing the dish.** Toss all of the ingredients together, reduce the heat slightly, and stir fry for about two minutes, or until the cornstarch mixture thickens and forms a glossy coating on the meat and vegetables. Dribble in a little sesame-seed oil, toss once more and serve the meat and vegetables immediately with plain boiled rice.

Making the Most of Pan Juices

When meat is sautéed, it leaves a residue of savory fragments and concentrated juices in the pan. To transform this natural resource into sauce, you need only deglaze the pan by adding liquid—wine, spirits, stock or water—and stirring the fragments and juices into it.

Deglazing can be accomplished midway through the sautéing process, as demonstrated with the chicken livers at right *(recipe, page 93)*. While the meat finishes cooking, the liquid absorbs the pan juices and reduces to a syrupy sauce that can be thickened with butter.

However, when meat has been floured —a variation shown below with sweetbreads *(recipe, page 115)*—it will keep its crisp surface best if fully cooked before the liquid is added.

Either way, the meat can be embellished by precooked vegetables, bacon or pieces of prosciutto added to the sauce at the last minute.

Chicken Livers in a Film of Butter and Brandy

1 **Preparing cucumbers.** Cut peeled cucumbers into 3-inch [8-cm.] lengths. With an apple corer, remove the seedy centers, then slice the cucumbers into rings. Parboil them for three minutes in lightly salted water to draw off excess moisture. Drain them on a towel. Sauté the rings in butter for three minutes; set aside in the skillet.

2 **Sautéing livers.** Trim chicken livers *(page 8)* and slice the two lobes of each liver apart. Melt butter in a sauté pan set over medium heat. Add finely chopped shallots and cook them for a few minutes to soften them, then add the livers. Sauté the livers until they are lightly browned on one side—about three minutes—then turn them over.

Sweetbreads Enhanced with Wine and Prosciutto

1 **Slicing the sweetbreads.** Soak and parboil sweetbreads—here, veal sweetbreads—then compact them by pressing them under weights for several hours *(page 12)*. As a garnish, melt butter in a skillet, add peeled small onions and glaze them *(page 19)*. Meanwhile, cut the sweetbreads into slices about ½ inch [1 cm.] thick.

2 **Flouring.** Season the sweetbread slices with salt. Put some flour on a plate and dip both sides of each slice into the flour, making sure that the slice is completely and evenly coated. Brush off the excess flour. Place the coated slices side by side on a tray.

3 **Sautéing the sweetbreads.** Melt butter with oil in a large skillet set over medium heat. Add a single layer of sweetbread slices and sauté them until browned and crisp—about five minutes on each side. Transfer the slices to a warmed plate and drape them loosely with foil to keep them hot while you sauté the rest and deglaze the pan.

3 **Deglazing the pan.** Pour liquid—in this case, brandy—over the livers. Without increasing the heat, let the brandy reduce to one third of its original volume; turn the livers occasionally with a wooden spatula. When the brandy has reduced to a sauce, remove the pan from the heat and season the livers with salt and pepper.

4 **Thickening the sauce.** Add a few of the sautéed cucumber rings to the pan of livers. Put small cubes of cold butter in the pan and stir them with the spatula until they melt and combine with the sauce to form a smooth emulsion. Reheat the remaining sautéed cucumber rings for a minute or so.

5 **Serving the livers.** Gently spoon the livers, cucumber rings and sauce from the sauté pan onto the center of a warmed platter. Arrange the rest of the cucumbers around the edge of the platter. Sprinkle the chicken livers with finely chopped fresh chervil and parsley, and serve them at once.

4 **Preparing the sauce.** Cut thinly sliced prosciutto into small pieces. Drain off the excess fat from the skillet and pour in dry white wine or a combination of wine and stock. Boil the liquid to reduce it to about half its original volume, stirring constantly to dislodge the brown fragments that will cling to the bottom of the skillet.

5 **Adding the garnish.** Toss the prosciutto in the sauce until the pieces are hot, then add the glazed onions, and fresh green peas that have been parboiled in salted water for four minutes. Stir in a few cubes of butter; add more wine if the sauce seems dry. Shake the skillet, tossing the ingredients until they heat through.

6 **Serving the sweetbreads.** Arrange the slices of sweetbread on a warmed platter and spoon the prosciutto-and-vegetable garnish over them. Strew croutons (page 19) over the sweetbreads and serve immediately.

Special Handling for Sliced Kidneys

Because they are naturally tender, kidneys are ideal candidates for sautéing. However, when they are sliced, halved or segmented for quick cooking, kidneys will release acrid juices into the pan and the pieces must be drained—as demonstrated here—after they are browned. Unlike the juices, the residue of fragments in the pan are savory and, while the kidneys drain, can be exploited by deglazing them to form a rich sauce.

In the demonstration at right, the pan is deglazed with stock and white wine: Chopped shallots lend aromatic support; butter thickens the sauce. Cider could replace the stock and wine, and brandy can be added for a more vigorous flavor. Bits of ham or bacon, sliced mushrooms, boiling onions and Dijon mustard are possible additions. For a richer sauce, substitute cream for the butter *(box below; recipe, page 97)*.

Just before serving, the kidney slices are reheated in the sauce. Do not let the sauce boil during the reheating. Intense heat will toughen the kidneys and make the sauce bitter if it includes mustard.

1 Segmenting kidneys. Remove the membrane from kidneys—in this case, veal kidneys. Cut the kidneys in half and remove the core fat *(page 8)*. Slice each kidney into pieces about ½ inch [1 cm.] thick; for veal or beef kidney, cut as nearly as possible along the natural divisions between the lobes.

2 Sautéing the kidneys. Put butter or a combination of oil and butter into a sauté pan and set it over high heat. Season the kidney slices with salt and pepper and add them to the pan. Turning the pieces frequently with a wooden spatula, sauté the kidneys until they lose all their surface pinkness—four or five minutes.

A Lavish Alliance of Mushrooms and Cream

1 Adding cream. Slice, sauté and drain kidneys *(Steps 1-3, above)*. Melt more butter in the sauté pan. Sauté finely chopped shallots over medium heat until they are soft; add sliced mushrooms and sauté them for a minute or two. Add a dash of brandy and let it come to a boil. Ladle in heavy cream.

2 Warming the kidneys. Increase the heat to high and stir the sauce until it has thickened and reduced to about half its original volume. Add prepared mustard and finely chopped fresh parsley. Then reduce the heat to low and add the drained kidneys.

3 Serving the kidneys. Season the sauce and allow the kidneys to heat through, taking care that the sauce does not return to a boil. Present the sauced kidneys alone or with boiled rice, as here, or noodles.

3 **Draining the kidneys.** Set a strainer over a bowl. With the aid of the spatula, tip the kidney slices and their cooking juices into the strainer. Let the kidneys drain while you make the sauce.

4 **Deglazing the pan.** Melt more butter in the pan, add chopped shallots and cook them until they are soft—about two minutes. Add a spoonful of stock *(page 16)* and a dash of white wine. Stirring continuously, simmer the mixture over medium heat until it becomes syrupy. Return the drained kidney slices to the pan.

5 **Enriching the sauce.** When the kidneys have warmed through, remove the pan from the heat. Sprinkle finely chopped fresh parsley over the kidneys. Add small cubes of cold butter and stir them into the sauce to thicken it.

6 **Serving the kidneys.** When the butter and sauce have blended and formed a fine coating over the kidneys *(left)* they are ready to be served. Present the kidneys alone in their sauce *(inset)* or accompanied by rice.

Gentle Cooking for a Whole Kidney

The nonpareil of sautéed variety meats doubtless is a whole veal kidney, cooked in its natural mantle of fat. Since this outer layer is usually removed from veal kidneys by the butcher and sold separately as suet, you may have to place a special order to obtain a kidney with its mantle intact. However, the extra effort you go to will be more than rewarded by the finished dish.

During the 30 or 40 minutes of gentle sautéing required to cook the kidney through, the mantle will render most of its fat to keep the meat moist. Because the process is so long, the inner core of fat will soften and the acrid juices of the kidney will dissipate. The result will be meltingly tender and delicately flavored: veal kidney at its finest.

The mild taste of its meat and fat make veal kidney uniquely suited to this presentation. The meat of beef and pork kidneys is too assertive in flavor, and the fat of lamb kidneys is too pungent.

Although most sautéing is done in an uncovered vessel, the kidney must be cooked under a lid so that it will heat through evenly in its whole form. Toward the end of sautéing, a precooked garnish can be introduced into the pan to exchange flavors with the kidney. Glazed onions, mushrooms *(page 19)* or rounds of cucumber sautéed in butter *(pages 24-25)* all could complement the meat.

In this demonstration, the kidney is surrounded by an elaborate garnish of sautéed tomato halves, bacon and cepes *(recipe, page 96)*. Cepes, which are wild mushrooms, are rarely available fresh in American markets, but are readily obtainable dried at specialty food stores. In most cases, the stems have been removed from the cepes before drying and both the caps and stems have been sliced. Soaking softens the dried cepes so that they can be treated like fresh mushrooms *(box, opposite)*. Here, the cepes are sautéed with bread crumbs, garlic, parsley and shallots. Cepes or other mushrooms cooked in this manner—a classic treatment that is known as *à la bordelaise*—would also make a delicious garnish for other sautéed variety meats, including liver, brains and sweetbreads.

1 **Sautéing the kidney.** With a small, sharp knife, pare away most of the fat from the outside of a whole veal kidney, leaving behind a layer ¼ inch [6 mm.] thick. Melt a little butter in a heavy sauté pan or casserole set over low heat. Add the kidney to the pan *(above, left)* and sprinkle it with salt and pepper. Cover the pan and sauté the kidney—turning it over from time to time *(right)*—for 30 minutes. Transfer the kidney to a plate and drape it with foil to keep it warm. Pour off the fat from the pan and set the pan aside.

2 **Sautéing bacon.** Peel, halve and seed ripe tomatoes *(page 18)*. Sauté the halves in butter for about five minutes; season them with salt and pepper. Prepare cepes *à la bordelaise*. Using the pan in which the kidney was cooked, sauté blanched bacon strips *(page 19)* for 10 minutes, or until they are crisp. Drain off the excess fat from the pan.

3 **Garnishing the kidney.** Return the kidney to the pan containing the bacon strips. Scatter the sautéed tomato halves around the kidney and spoon the cepes *à la bordelaise* over it.

A Classic Garnish from Dried Mushrooms

1 **Softening the cepes.** Pick over dried cepes and discard any small fragments. Add the cepes to a bowl of warm water and let them soak for about 30 minutes, stirring occasionally to be sure all the pieces are well moistened.

2 **Trimming the cepes.** Drain the softened cepes in a strainer set over a bowl. Trim the hard, knobby end from stem pieces and cut any unusually large pieces of stem or cap in half. Sauté the cepes in vegetable oil over high heat for two minutes, tossing them frequently to coat the pieces thoroughly with oil.

3 **Completing the garnish.** Reduce the heat to medium, and add chopped shallots, garlic, parsley, lemon juice and fresh bread crumbs to the cepes. Stirring constantly, cook the mixture until the shallots are soft and transparent—two to three minutes. Remove the pan from the heat.

4 **Slicing the kidney.** Cover the pan and cook the kidney with its garnish over low heat for eight to 10 minutes. Transfer the kidney to a board for carving; leave the garnish in the pan. Cut the kidney into slices ¼ inch [6 mm.] thick. Return the kidney to the pan, cover it and warm the slices through—still over low heat—for two or three minutes. Serve the kidney slices and garnishes directly from the pan.

Delicate Morsels in a Golden Crust

When morsels of variety meat are deep fried, their surfaces must be protected from the searing oil by a coating of batter or bread crumbs. The heat of the oil crisps the coating, which provides a contrasting texture to the tender meat. Most kinds of variety meat are suitable for deep frying *(chart, page 7)*, either individually or in combinations. In this demonstration brains, sweetbreads and fries are cooked and served together.

Each type of meat will require its own particular preparation *(pages 8-13)* before being cut into small chunks or slices for frying. Meats such as ears and feet that need long, moist cooking to tenderize them must be poached in advance; if the meats contain bones, these must, of course, be removed.

Once cut up, any meat can be endowed with extra flavor by marinating it for an hour or so. The marinade here includes oil, lemon juice, parsley and tarragon. Dry wine or wine vinegar could take the place of the lemon juice, and the herbs can be freely varied.

Whatever coating you choose, prepare it ahead of time. A fritter batter is made by whisking flour together with liquid—water, milk or beer; oil tenderizes the mixture and egg yolks bind it together *(recipe, page 167)*. Whisking develops the gluten in the flour, and the batter will be tough unless it is allowed to rest at room temperature for an hour or so. For greater airiness, beaten egg whites may be folded into the batter just before the pieces are coated and fried.

If you are coating the meats with bread crumbs, dip the pieces first in flour, then in egg beaten with a little water, and finally roll them in the crumbs. Dry the pieces on a rack for 30 minutes to ensure that the crumbs adhere during cooking.

For deep frying, the oil must be several inches deep to submerge the coated meat pieces completely. However, for safety's sake the pan should not be more than two thirds full. Preheat the oil to 375° F. [190° C.] and keep it as close to that temperature as possible. If the oil is hotter, the coating will brown before the meat cooks; if the oil is cooler, the coating will absorb it and become soggy. To help keep the oil's temperature constant, fry only a few pieces of meat at a time.

1 Preparing the meats. Soak, parboil, trim and weight sweetbreads *(page 12)*. Peel and soak brains *(page 11)* and poach them for 20 minutes in a vinegar court bouillon *(page 16)*. Peel, soak and parboil fries *(page 13)*. Cut the sweetbreads into small pieces and the brains and fries into even slices.

2 Marinating the meats. Place the pieces of meat in a dish large enough to hold them in one layer. Pour lemon juice over the meats and sprinkle them with chopped fresh parsley and tarragon. Pour in a little olive oil and add salt. Marinate the meats for one hour, turning them over two or three times.

6 Testing the oil. Heat the oil until it reaches a temperature of 375° F. [190° C.] on a deep-frying thermometer. If you are not using a thermometer, drop a small spoonful of batter into the hot oil: If the batter immediately sizzles, the oil is sufficiently hot.

7 Deep frying the meats. Lift the pieces of meat out of the batter with a perforated spoon—letting excess batter drip off before lowering them into the hot oil. Fry the meats in small batches until golden brown—about four minutes on each side. Remove the fritters with a skimmer, drain them on paper towels and keep them warm.

3 **Making the batter.** Combine flour and salt in a large bowl; make a well in the center and pour oil into it. Separate eggs, add the yolks to the oil and reserve the whites. Pour in beer in a steady stream, then whisk the ingredients together—working from the center outward. Cover the bowl and let the batter rest for one hour.

4 **Folding in egg whites.** Fill a large pan to a depth of 2 inches [5 cm.] with vegetable oil and set it over high heat. While the oil heats, beat the reserved egg whites until they form stiff peaks. With a wooden spoon, gently fold the beaten egg whites into the batter.

5 **Coating the meats.** Drain the pieces of meat well and pat them dry with paper towels. Then add the meats to the batter. Turn the pieces about to separate them and be sure they are all evenly coated with batter.

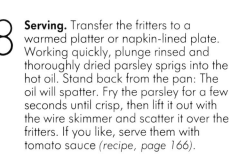

8 **Serving.** Transfer the fritters to a warmed platter or napkin-lined plate. Working quickly, plunge rinsed and thoroughly dried parsley sprigs into the hot oil. Stand back from the pan: The oil will spatter. Fry the parsley for a few seconds until crisp, then lift it out with the wire skimmer and scatter it over the fritters. If you like, serve them with tomato sauce *(recipe, page 166)*.

2
Grilling, Broiling and Roasting
The Searing Effect of Dry Heat

Quick cooking to keep meat rare
Butterflying kidneys
How to use caul as a wrapper
Crumbs for crusty gratins

In grilling and broiling, the heat comes from one direction—hot coals below or a broiler unit above—and food is exposed to it just one side at a time. In roasting, or oven baking, the heat is indirect and surrounds the food, penetrating from all sides simultaneously. What these methods have in common is that they cook food by dry heat instead of by using fat or liquid as a cooking medium. As a result, the surfaces of the food sear and brown while the interior remains tender and juicy.

Variety meats, being lean, need a coating of oil, of fat, or of egg and bread crumbs to prevent them from parching on the grill, or in the broiler or oven. With that single proviso, most kinds of variety meat can be cooked by dry heat. However, liver, kidney, heart and spleen are the only ones both tender and firm enough to be started from the raw state. Precooking is necessary to soften such tough meats as tripe, feet or ears and to firm sweetbreads, brains or fries.

The size and shape of the meat dictate the dry-heat method that is appropriate. The intensity of the heat used in grilling and broiling demands that the meat be cut into small and fairly flat pieces that will cook through fast, before the surfaces have a chance to burn. Thin slices of veal liver or butterflied lamb kidneys *(opposite)* seem made to order: In as few as six to eight minutes, they will be seared outside, but remain moist enough inside so that drops of pink juice will ooze through their top surfaces *(page 34)*. Cubes or chunks of variety meat packed onto skewers need only 15 minutes or so of cooking time *(pages 36-37)*. And if relatively thin poached meats—squares of tripe, for example, or pig's feet that have been pressed under weights to flatten them *(pages 38-39)*—are coated with bread crumbs, they will develop a crisp brown crust in approximately 20 minutes.

Large or irregularly shaped meats, on the other hand, are better suited to roasting. After the meats have been seared briefly at high heat, the oven temperature can be reduced to cook them through gently. Thick slabs of liver, whole veal kidneys and whole hearts of all kinds lend themselves to this treatment. So, too, do pig's ears that have been poached, filled with a creamy stuffing, coated with crumbs and drizzled with butter to become paradigms of the kind of elegance cooks can achieve with humble meats.

Butterflied for even cooking and skewered on sharpened rosemary twigs to keep them flat, lamb kidneys are coated with olive oil and finely chopped herbs before going under the broiler *(page 34)*. The oil will help to keep the kidneys from drying out as they broil.

Rapid Treatments That Conserve Juices

A thin slice of heart, liver or kidney exposed to the intense heat of a broiler or an open grill rapidly becomes beautifully brown outside and succulent inside. Lamb, beef and veal innards are best rare—after eight or nine minutes overall; pork must be well done for safety's sake and requires 12 to 15 minutes.

Heart, liver *(right)* and veal and beef kidneys all should be sliced ½ inch [1 cm.] thick. Pork and lamb kidneys *(below)* are too small for slicing, so they should be cut almost in half and spread open in a butterfly shape. Skewering keeps the butterflied kidneys flat enough to cook through evenly. The rosemary-branch skewers here contribute flavor to the meat, but metal skewers or bamboo skewers that have been soaked in water could be used instead.

Because these meats are low in fat and dry out easily, liver, heart and kidney benefit from a marinade based on oil, which also helps to keep them from sticking to the broiler rack or the grill. If you like, lace the marinade with herbs, but do not salt the meat until you are ready

to cook it: Salt draws out meat's juices. Both broilers and grills require preheating with the rack in place. Allow approximately 10 minutes for the broiler to reach its highest heat. The fire in an outdoor grill should be started at least 30 minutes ahead of time to allow the coals to burn down to white ashes.

Just before putting the meat on top, brush the broiler or grill rack with oil. The meat should be turned just once during cooking. Cook the rounded outer surface of a butterflied kidney first when you are using a broiler; after you turn the kidney over, its juices collect in the slightly concave cut surface. With an outdoor grill, this order is reversed.

In this demonstration, both meats are served with potatoes. For the liver, small potatoes are sautéed in their jackets. To accompany the kidneys, potatoes are first shredded and then cooked in butter to make a potato cake *(box, opposite)*. After the potato shreds are rinsed free of starch to prevent the cake from sticking to the pan, they must be dried: Too much liquid would result in a soggy cake.

Searing Liver over Coals

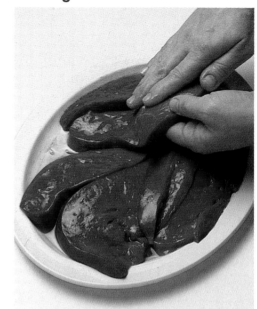

1 **Preparing the garnish.** Put whole small potatoes in a pan with unpeeled garlic cloves and butter. Add salt, cover, and cook over low heat for 30 minutes, shaking the pan occasionally. Remove the membrane from veal liver *(page 8)*; cut the liver into ½-inch [1-cm.] slices and rub them with olive oil.

Skewering Kidneys on Rosemary Branches

1 **Butterflying the kidneys.** Remove the outer fat and the membrane from lamb kidneys *(page 9)*. With a small, sharp knife, split each kidney lengthwise down its rounded back, taking care not to cut all the way through; then open out the kidney into a flat, butterfly-like shape.

2 **Skewering the kidneys.** Cut rosemary branches 6 inches [15 cm.] long. Starting 2 inches [5 cm.] below the tip of each branch, scrape off all the leaves; sharpen the end. Skewer each kidney crosswise, piercing through its fatty center. Put the kidneys in a dish and sprinkle with oil and dried herbs.

3 **Garnishing the kidneys.** Season the kidneys. Cook them, cut sides down, under a preheated broiler—about 4 inches [10 cm.] from the heat—for three minutes. Turn them over and broil for three minutes more. Arrange the kidneys around a potato cake; garnish with herb butter *(recipe, page 101)*.

2 **Grilling the liver slices.** Brush the rack of a preheated grill with oil to prevent sticking. Then season the liver slices on one side and lay them seasoned side down on the grill.

3 **Turning the slices.** After four to five minutes, season the upper surfaces of the liver slices and turn them over. Grill them for four to five minutes longer, or until drops of rose-colored meat juices begin to appear on their surfaces. Transfer the liver to a warmed platter.

4 **Serving the liver.** To brown the potatoes, uncover them and cook them for five minutes more. Stir in a handful of chopped fresh parsley, and arrange the potatoes and garlic cloves on the platter around the liver slices. Garnish with slices of peeled lemon and serve.

Shredded Potatoes Shaped into a Cake

1 **Adding potatoes.** Shred peeled potatoes into thin straws with a rotary shredder, food processor or mandolin. Drop the straws into cold water to remove surface starch; drain them, then rinse and drain again. Dry the straws well in a towel. Melt butter in a heavy skillet with a flat lid; tilt the pan to coat its sides. Add the potato straws.

2 **Adding butter.** With the back of a fork, gently pack down the potato straws into a flat cake. Sprinkle the cake with salt and put pieces of butter around the sides of the skillet. Cover the skillet, and cook the cake over low to medium heat for 15 to 20 minutes, until its edges begin to crisp and turn golden.

3 **Turning the cake.** Remove the lid and shake the skillet to free the cake. Holding the lid firmly on top, turn both lid and skillet upside down, unmolding the cake onto the underside of the lid. Add more butter to the skillet; slide the cake back in with its cooked side up. Add salt and cook, uncovered, for another 15 minutes.

Fashioning Kebabs from a Combination of Meats

Bite-sized cubes or chunks of meat are transformed into kebabs when threaded onto skewers and broiled. Sweetbreads, brains, fries, heart, liver, spleen and kidney are prime candidates for such treatment. To achieve textural and flavor contrast, meats can be mixed, but will combine best if all come from one kind of animal. In this demonstration, the mixture consists of chicken hearts, livers and gizzards—the giblets of the bird.

Sweetbreads, brains and fries require parboiling *(pages 11, 12 and 13)*; gizzards must be poached. The other meats need only be trimmed. Marinating adds tang and provides a basting liquid.

To keep the meats moist during broiling, the kebabs are wrapped in caul—the fatty membranous lining of a pig's stomach—available fresh or frozen at specialty butchers. As it cooks, the caul melts, forming a crisp skin around the meats.

Kebabs are traditionally served with rice. Plain boiled rice will do, but rice will provide a more colorful accompaniment if flavored with saffron and mixed with sautéed tomatoes as shown below.

1 Preparing the giblets. Trim the excess fat from the giblets and cut livers into pieces slightly larger than the whole hearts. With a sharp knife slice through the whitish membrane connecting the two halves of each gizzard. Poach the halves in salted water for 30 minutes, then drain them.

2 Marinating the meats. Combine olive oil and lemon juice with chopped fresh thyme, marjoram and tarragon in a shallow dish. Add the meats, stir, and let them marinate for 30 minutes. Meanwhile, drop bacon slices into cold water and boil them for two minutes to remove excess salt. Drain them.

Tomatoes with Golden-hued Rice

1 Adding saffron. In a large pan, sauté a finely chopped onion in butter until it is soft but not browned. Add long-grain rice and salt to the butter. Stir the rice until it becomes opaque— about five minutes. Add a pinch of powdered saffron and combine it with the rice-and-onion mixture.

2 Pouring in water. Add twice the rice's volume of boiling water to the pan. Stir, then cover the pan and reduce the heat to low. Simmer the rice until the water has all been absorbed— approximately 20 minutes.

3 Adding tomatoes. Peel and seed tomatoes *(page 18)*. Chop the tomatoes and sauté them in butter for a few minutes. Season the tomatoes with salt and pepper, and mix them gently into the rice along with cubes of cold butter.

3 **Skewering the meats.** Thread the meats alternately onto square or flat-bladed skewers, wrapping each piece of liver in a bacon slice as you proceed. Reserve the marinade.

4 **Preparing the caul.** Soak the caul in cold water for a minute or so to help separate the filmy sheets. Drain the sheets and pat them dry with paper towels. With a knife or kitchen scissors, cut the sheets into rectangles, each large enough to enclose the meats on a single skewer.

5 **Wrapping the meats.** Place a skewer on top of a rectangle of caul and wrap the caul around the meats; the caul will adhere to itself. Wrap the remaining skewers of meat similarly. Lay the ends of the skewers on the sides of a baking pan deep enough to keep the meats suspended above the fat that will drip from them during broiling.

6 **Broiling the kebabs.** Brush each skewer with marinade and place the pan under a preheated broiler, positioning it so that the meats are 4 inches [10 cm.] from the heat source. Basting them from time to time, broil the meats for about seven minutes on each side.

7 **Serving the kebabs.** Spoon saffron-and-tomato rice (box, opposite) onto a large warmed platter and lay the skewered meats alongside it. At the table, use a fork to push all of the meats together off each skewer.

Buttery Crumbs for a Crisp Finish

Coated in bread crumbs, moistened with butter and then toasted under a broiler or on a grill, poached or parboiled meats as various as pig's feet and tripe, or fries and brains, acquire a crisp, gilded finish. Whole or sliced tough meats—pig's feet in this demonstration—can be slathered with mustard and covered with crumbs before being broiled or grilled. For a milder flavor, the meats may be floured and dipped in beaten egg—like mustard it will make the surface sticky—then rolled in crumbs seasoned with herbs or grated Parmesan cheese.

The strategy that is best for tender white meats is to sieve them and shape the resulting purée into croquettes as shown below *(recipe, page 119)*. In this case, herbs and mushrooms contribute flavor, crumbs give the brain purée body and egg yolks bind the mixture. Caul holds the croquettes in shape. Because of their delicacy, the croquettes are best broiled on a baking sheet.

A Mustard-flavored Coating for Pig's Feet

1 **Weighting pig's feet.** Wrap cleaned pig's feet in cloth and poach them for four hours *(pages 54-55)*. Drain the feet, unwrap them and lay them on a tray. To press the feet into a compact shape, cover them with plastic wrap, place a heavy board on top, and put weights or canned foods on the board. Refrigerate the weighted feet.

2 **Coating the feet.** After four to six hours, transfer the compressed feet to a work surface. With a knife, trim off the ragged edges of meat to give each foot a neat shape. Using your fingers, cover each foot completely with mustard before rolling it in fresh bread crumbs.

Brain Croquettes in a Lacy Cloak of Caul

1 **Sieving brains.** Poach veal brains in a vinegar court bouillon until they are firm *(page 50)*. Drain them well and put them in a nylon or stainless-steel sieve set over a large mixing bowl. Using a wooden pestle, push the brains through the sieve. Alternatively, purée the brains in a food mill or processor.

2 **Adding flavorings.** Trim and wash mushrooms; chop them fine and sprinkle with lemon juice. Soak fresh bread crumbs in milk; squeeze almost dry. Add the mushrooms and crumbs to the brains along with softened butter, chopped parsley and shallots, salt and pepper. Stir in egg yolks. To firm the mixture, refrigerate it for one hour.

3 **Wrapping the croquettes.** Soak caul *(page 37)*, pat it dry, and cut it into pieces about 8 inches [20 cm.] square. Spread the caul out on a work surface. To shape each croquette, put about ½ cup [125 ml.] of the brain mixture in the center of a piece of caul, flatten the mixture slightly and wrap the caul around it.

3 **Moistening the feet.** Put the crumb-coated feet on a large plate. Melt butter in a skillet. Spoon the butter over the feet, making sure their upper surfaces are thoroughly moistened.

4 **Grilling the feet.** Place the feet buttered side down on the rack of a preheated grill. After 10 to 12 minutes, spoon more melted butter over the feet, then turn them over—using tongs or a pair of wooden spoons to avoid piercing the mustard-and-crumb coating.

5 **Serving the feet.** Cook the feet for another 10 to 12 minutes. When they are golden brown all over, transfer them to a warmed platter; add a garnish of sour gherkin fans, if you like. To make each fan, slice a gherkin lengthwise a few times, inserting the knife about ¼ inch [6 mm.] from the stem end; spread the slices out into a fan.

4 **Coating with bread crumbs.** In a shallow bowl, beat together eggs and olive oil. Pile fresh bread crumbs on a work surface. Dip each croquette in the egg mixture, then place it on the pile of crumbs and sprinkle additional crumbs over it in order to coat the croquette completely. Set the croquettes side by side on a baking sheet.

5 **Spooning on butter.** Put the coated croquettes in the refrigerator. When they have firmed—after about 30 minutes—generously spoon melted butter over them and place them under a preheated broiler, about 4 to 6 inches [10 to 15 cm.] from the heat.

6 **Serving the croquettes.** After four to five minutes, turn the croquettes over and spoon more melted butter over them. Cook them for another four to five minutes, or until they are golden brown. Serve the croquettes at once— here, they are garnished with watercress sprigs and accompanied by tomato sauce (recipe, page 166).

Juicy Roasts from Large Cuts

Because an oven surrounds meat with uniform heat, baking turns thick slabs of liver or whole hearts into succulent roasts. To color the surfaces without drying them, the meats are seared briefly at high heat; then the heat is reduced to cook the meats through.

Beef, veal, pork or lamb livers and hearts are all suitable for baking whole. But since a beef liver may weigh up to 14 pounds [7 kg.], and a veal liver 5 pounds [2½ kg.], roasts also may be from slices of liver—providing these are at least 4 inches [10 cm.] thick. Liver tastes best when treated very simply; to prepare it for roasting, just rub it with oil and salt, as shown at right.

By contrast, heart has a large cavity. A stuffing will help the heart keep its shape during roasting. In the demonstration below, a beef heart is filled with a breadcrumb mixture, spiked with herbs and lemon peel and enriched with beef marrow (recipe, page 107). If the heart has been slashed—as beef and pork almost

always are—it will need to be stitched together. A wrapping of caul will then hold the stuffing in place and, as it melts, baste the surface of the meat.

Beef, veal and lamb liver and heart should be cooked medium rare so that the meat is pink and juicy. For liver, allow 10 minutes a pound [½ kg.] after the roast is seared. Heart, with its denser structure, needs about 25 minutes a pound. During roasting, meat juices will accumulate in the baking dish; if the juices are mixed with a little wine or water, they can provide a sauce for the meat.

Pork liver and heart, on the other hand, should be served well done. Bake them until a meat thermometer shows the internal temperature to be 165 to 170° F. [75° C.]—about 12 minutes a pound for liver, 30 minutes for heart.

Any roast should stand in a warm place for 15 to 20 minutes before it is carved. During this resting period, the meat will become firmer and thus it will be easier to carve.

An Easy Method for Liver

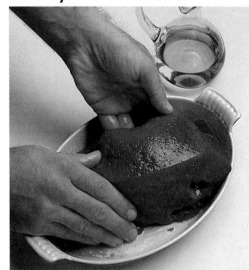

1 **Rubbing with oil.** Remove the surface membrane and any blood vessels from the liver (page 8)—here, a thick slice of veal liver weighing about 2 pounds [1 kg.]. Set the liver in a shallow baking dish just large enough to contain it. Season the liver with a little salt, and rub it all over with olive oil.

A Rich Herb Stuffing for Heart

1 **Preparing the stuffing.** Combine sliced scallions with finely chopped fresh parsley and marjoram, grated lemon peel and nutmeg, salt, pepper and fresh bread crumbs. Pry the marrow out of marrowbones with a small knife. Chop the marrow fine and add it to the other ingredients, along with egg yolks. Mix well with your hands.

2 **Stuffing the heart.** Lay a trimmed beef heart (page 9) on a work surface, with the exposed chambers facing up. Pack them with as much stuffing as they will hold, then fold the heart into its natural shape and pat it together. Fill the cavity at the upper end with stuffing.

3 **Trussing the heart.** With a trussing needle and string, sew the heart securely closed—pulling the string fairly tight after each stitch. Prepare a piece of caul (page 37) big enough to surround the heart completely. Wrap the caul around the heart and place it in a shallow, flameproof baking dish, here enameled cast iron.

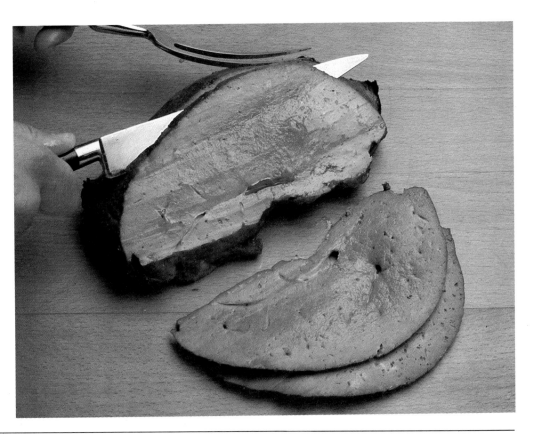

2 **Basting the liver.** Sear the liver in a preheated 450° F. [230° C.] oven for five minutes. Reduce the heat to 300° F. [150° C.] and roast the liver for another 15 minutes. Baste the liver several times as it cooks with the juices that collect in the baking pan.

3 **Carving the liver.** Remove the liver from the oven and leave it in a warm place to rest for 15 minutes. Then transfer it to a cutting board and carve the liver into thin slices. Serve at once.

4 **Roasting the heart.** Sear the heart in a preheated 450° F. [230° C.] oven for five minutes. Reduce the heat to 375° F. [190° C.] and roast the heart for about 45 minutes. Then moisten the heart with dry red wine and continue to roast it for 10 to 15 minutes more, basting it once or twice. Transfer it to a plate and let it rest for 15 minutes.

5 **Deglazing.** Set the baking dish over medium heat and add a little more wine. With a wooden spatula, loosen the small bits stuck to the bottom of the dish. Simmer the sauce for about five minutes, then strain it through a fine sieve into a warmed sauceboat.

6 **Serving the heart.** Place the heart on a cutting board and carve it crosswise into slices ½ inch [1 cm.] thick. Discard the bits of trussing string. Arrange the slices attractively on a warmed platter and serve the heart at once, accompanied by the sauce.

An Elegant Presentation of Pig's Ears

Pig's ears—a kind of variety meat that most cooks pass by as too unappealing to trouble with—can be transformed into a delectable main course. The ears form natural cases for stuffings and, once they are filled, as demonstrated at right, can be gratinéed with a coating of beaten egg and bread crumbs that gives them a crisp, golden brown crust.

Before they are stuffed, the ears must be both parboiled and poached. The parboiling draws out as scum the protein and mineral particles that might otherwise discolor the ears, but the process also tends to distort them. To mold the ears back into shape, they should be rolled up and wrapped tightly in muslin or cheesecloth. Three or four hours of poaching will then tenderize the ears. At this stage, however, they will be soft and require chilling to firm them enough so that they will be easy to stuff.

The stuffing can vary from a piquant anchovy mixture to a creamy blend of chopped ham and mushrooms (recipes, pages 141 and 143). Here the ears are filled with cooked diced sweetbreads and chicken together with flour and stock and enriched with egg yolks and cream (recipe, page 142). Any stuffing should be chilled briefly to firm it: If it is still warm and soft, it will not hold its shape when it is packed into the ears.

To prepare them for coating with egg and crumbs, the stuffed ears are floured on the underside. Flour gives the smooth skin a slightly rough surface to which the egg can adhere; the surface of the stuffing, on the other hand, is irregular enough for the egg to stick to it readily. After the ears have been rolled in egg and bread crumbs, they can be moistened with melted butter and cooked immediately. Or, for an even thicker crust, they can be chilled for one to two hours more and given a second coating of egg and bread crumbs before being baked.

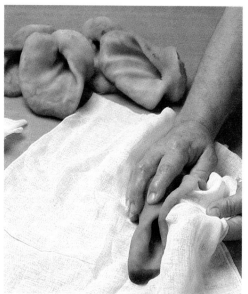

1 **Wrapping the ears.** Parboil cleaned pig's ears (page 13). Trim the bases of the ears and reserve the trimmings. For each ear, cut a rectangle of muslin or cheesecloth and fold it in half to make a square. Put the ear on the cloth square, draw the edges of the ear together to make a cone, and roll it up tightly in the cloth.

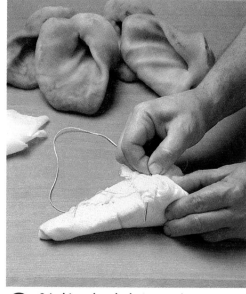

2 **Stitching the cloth.** Loop white kitchen string around the package to secure it. Then thread the string into a small trussing needle and stitch the edges of the cloth together. Repeat the wrapping and stitching process until all of the ears are enclosed in cloth.

6 **Enriching with eggs.** Stir the diced meats until they are lightly browned. Add some of the reserved braising liquid and cook for a few minutes, until the liquid thickens. Take the pan off the heat and let it cool. Beat egg yolks and cream together and add to the skillet. Stir the mixture and season it with salt, pepper and nutmeg.

7 **Stuffing the ears.** Chop the reserved ear trimmings and add them to the chicken-and-sweetbread mixture. Refrigerate the stuffing until firm—about two hours. Spoon some of the stuffing into each pig's ear, packing the mixture down with the back of a spoon.

3 **Poaching the ears.** Put the wrapped ears and trimmings in a pot just large enough to hold them in a single layer. Pour in enough veal stock *(page 16)* and white wine to cover the ears; if you like, add aromatic vegetables and herbs. Cover the pot partially; bring the liquid to a boil, then reduce the heat and simmer for about three hours.

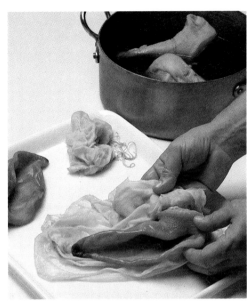

4 **Unwrapping the ears.** Take the pot off the heat and leave the ears in the cooking liquid until they are cool enough to handle. Reserve the trimmings and unwrap the ears. Put the ears on a tray, cover them with a damp cloth towel and refrigerate them until chilled— approximately one hour.

5 **Preparing the stuffing.** Braise veal sweetbreads in stock *(pages 60-61)*. Drain them; reserve the braising liquid. Sauté a boned chicken breast in butter until firm and opaque—three to five minutes on each side. Cut the chicken and sweetbreads into dice, put them into the skillet and sprinkle with flour.

8 **Coating the ears.** In a bowl, beat eggs with a little oil and water. To coat each ear, pat flour onto the skin on the underside, then dip the underside in the egg mixture and spoon egg over the top so that both the skin and stuffing are moistened. Coat the ear with fresh bread crumbs, patting them on evenly.

9 **Moistening with butter.** Transfer the ears to a buttered baking dish and refrigerate them for an hour to set the coating. If desired, repeat the coating and chilling process. Just before baking, spoon melted butter over the ears. Put the dish in a preheated 450° F. [230° C.] oven; after five minutes, reduce the temperature to 350° F. [180° C.].

10 **Serving the ears.** Bake the ears for about one hour, basting them from time to time with the pan juices. When their bread-crumb coatings have browned evenly, remove the ears from the oven and put them on warm dinner plates. Serve the ears with tomato sauce *(recipe, page 166)*.

3
Poaching
The Judicious Use of Moist Heat

Fine-tuning the timing makes it possible to cook almost every variety meat to perfection by the method known as poaching—simmering food gently in enough liquid to cover it completely. Brief poaching firms the flesh of delicate cuts, such as brains, without damaging their texture. Lengthy poaching softens the connective tissue of tougher meats while keeping them succulent and moist: The animal's head, ears, tongue, stomach, feet and tail particularly benefit from long poaching.

The liquid most appropriate for poaching depends partly on the type of meat and partly on personal taste: Water, stock and court bouillons *(page 16)* all are suitable. White meats that discolor easily, as do heads, ears and feet, will remain relatively pale if poached in a court bouillon that contains lemon juice and flour *(opposite)*. Hearty, rustic dishes such as the stuffed lamb's and pig's stomachs on pages 48-49 are usually poached in water—flavored, perhaps, with aromatic vegetables and a bouquet garni. The very mild taste of brains is enhanced by the acidity of a wine or vinegar court bouillon *(page 16)*.

Whatever the liquid, the essence of poaching is to keep it at a bare simmer. If you judge by eye, the surface of the liquid should barely tremble. If you suspend a deep-frying thermometer in the pot, the temperature it shows should remain at about 175° F. [80° C.]. Letting the liquid boil would make the meat fibers and membranes suddenly constrict, thus toughening them. Partially covering the pot with a lid will minimize evaporation of the liquid, but a small gap is needed to prevent a build-up of steam, which could raise the temperature within the pot.

The simplest way of presenting poached meat is straight from the pot. However, not the least of the virtues of poaching is that the liquid can provide a diversity of embellishments. Mixed with the uncooked flour paste called *beurre manié* or with roux, the liquid forms a sauce, which may be a simple smooth coating for the meats *(pages 50-51)* or a creamy, egg-enriched blend *(pages 52-53)*. When the poaching liquid is water, gelatinous meats—such as feet and ears—transform it into an aspic for spectacular cold presentations *(pages 54-55)*. Paradoxically, even meats that yield little gelatin of their own can be swathed in aspic made from stock, a technique demonstrated on pages 56-57, where tongue is adorned with a star burst of vegetable strips.

Blanched and boned calf's feet, neatly tied to preserve their shape, are dropped into a white court bouillon flavored with vegetables and herbs. After poaching, some of the liquid will serve as a basis for the sauce—enriched with eggs and flavored with lemon and chopped parsley—that accompanies the feet *(pages 52-53)*.

An Array of Meats Simply Poached

A calf's or pig's head offers a cornucopia of different meats—cheeks, snout, skin, ears, brains and tongue—each delicious in its own right. All can be cooked individually or, for a lavish presentation, they can be cooked simultaneously and served together as shown here with two boned calf's heads *(recipe, page 138)*.

To ensure even cooking and simplify serving, the heads are cut into portion-sized pieces before poaching. Both the pieces of head and the tongues, which are left whole, are then parboiled to draw out scum that might otherwise cloud the cooking liquid. The skin of a calf's or pig's head inevitably darkens during cooking, but can be kept from discoloring and looking blotchy by poaching the pieces —with the tongues, in this case—in a white court bouillon *(page 16)*.

After one to one and a half hours, depending on their size, the tongues will be tender and can be removed from the pot. When they have cooled a little, the tongues are peeled and set aside, ready to be returned to the pot at the last minute to warm through. The thick, gelatinous skin of the heads may need up to four hours of cooking to become succulent.

The delicate brains, on the other hand, require only brief poaching—25 minutes is usually sufficient. Put them on to cook about half an hour before you expect the head pieces to be done. To prevent them from becoming tangled with the other meats, poach them separately—here, in a vinegar court bouillon for extra flavor.

When all the elements are ready, serve them quickly while they are still very hot: The pieces of head in particular must not be allowed to cool lest they become sticky. Leave them in the pot while you slice the tongue and brains, in that order.

Traditionally, all the meats are presented on a large platter that has been covered with a napkin. If you choose to omit the napkin, be sure to warm the platter well before arranging the meats on it. The vinaigrette accompaniment shown here supplies a touch of sharpness that contrasts with the mildness of the meats. If you prefer, you can substitute a tomato sauce *(page 18)*.

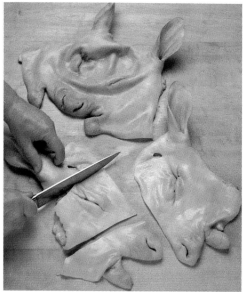

1 **Preparing the heads.** Soak two boned calf's heads *(pages 14-15)* in acidulated water—and the tongues in plain cold water—for several hours. In both cases, change the water frequently until it remains clear. Trim off any ragged edges of skin from the heads, and cut each one into six pieces.

2 **Parboiling the meats.** Put the head pieces and whole tongues into a pot of cold water. Bring the water to a boil, then reduce the heat at once, simmer for about 10 minutes, and drain the meats. Immerse them in cold water to cleanse them; remove any clinging scum by gently rubbing the meats with a towel.

6 **Poaching the brains.** Soak the brains and peel them *(page 11)*. In the meantime, prepare a court bouillon with red wine vinegar in a nonreactive pan. Put the brains in the simmering court bouillon and poach them for 25 minutes, or until they are firm to the touch. Remove the brains from the pot and drain them.

7 **Slicing the meats.** Remove the tongues from the poaching liquid and cut them into slices ¾ inch [2 cm.] thick. Arrange an opened cloth napkin on a platter and place the slices on it. Slice the brains and add them to the platter.

3 **Poaching the meats.** Put a rack in the bottom of a large pot to keep the meats from sticking, and make a white court bouillon in the pot. Add the blanched pieces of head and the tongues.

4 **Covering with paper.** To keep the meats submerged, put a piece of parchment paper on top of the court bouillon. Bring the liquid slowly to a boil; reduce the heat, partially cover the pot with a lid and simmer for about one hour, or until a skewer easily pierces the tip of each tongue.

5 **Removing the tongues.** Lift out the tongues with a skimmer. Replace the paper and cook the head pieces for another two hours or so. Peel the tongues *(page 12)* as soon as they are cool enough to handle. When the head pieces are cooked, a skewer will pierce them easily. Turn off the heat; return the tongues to the pot to reheat them.

8 **Presenting the meats.** Take the pieces of head out of the pot and place them on the platter with the sliced tongues and brains. Garnish the meats with parsley sprigs and serve them immediately, accompanied by vinegar and oil, chopped hard-boiled eggs, capers, finely chopped onion and chopped fresh parsley.

Capacious Pouches for Savory Stuffing

One of the most celebrated of variety-meat concoctions is Scotland's haggis—a lamb's stomach stuffed with ground innards and oatmeal, and poached until fork-tender, as demonstrated here (recipe, page 153). And in Germany, where pork is the staple meat, pig's stomach is treated in much the same way except that the stuffing is usually made with potatoes rather than with oatmeal (below; recipe, page 137).

Both dishes are food for feasting. A lamb's stomach makes a meal for about 12 people; a pig's stomach tends to be smaller, but two can be sewn together. When poached, the stomach shrinks and the moisture in the stuffing turns to steam so that it expands, resulting in a neat roll that can be sliced.

Both lamb's and pig's stomachs are sold slit open and scalded. Before a stomach is stuffed, it must be sewn back into its natural pouch shape, with a section left open for inserting the stuffing. If you wish, you can turn the stomach inside out so that its smooth inner surface is on the outside of the pouch. In any case, use small, firm overstitches so that there are no gaps through which filling can escape.

The texture of the stuffing can be varied by grinding the meats or chopping them. Besides potatoes or oatmeal—the Scots version is coarsely ground instead of being rolled into flakes as American oatmeal is—the stuffing can be given body with white or brown rice, cracked wheat or bread. Vegetables such as onions and mushrooms will contribute flavor, and the mixture can be enriched with butter and moistened with milk, stock, spirits or water. Adding eggs helps to bind the ingredients together.

To prevent the stomach from splitting when the stuffing expands, pack it fairly loosely and prick it all over with a needle to let air escape during cooking. To prevent the stomach itself from toughening, start the poaching process in warm water and bring it to a simmer slowly.

After poaching, the stomach can be served straight from the pot. Or, as is shown here with the pig's stomachs, the surface can be rubbed with oil and lightly browned in a hot oven. Basted with white wine and juices from the pan, the surface acquires a rich brown glaze.

Assembling a Haggis

1 Making the stuffing. Prepare lamb heart and liver (page 8). Poach them with boneless lamb shoulder for one hour. Drain the meats; then strain and reserve the poaching liquid. Cut up the meats and put them through a food grinder. Spread oatmeal in a pan, and toast it in a 350° F. [180° C.] oven for 25 minutes.

2 Adding oatmeal. In a large bowl combine the ground meats with chopped beef marrow (page 40) or suet and finely chopped onions. Add flavorings—here, mixed dried herbs, parsley, cayenne pepper, mace, nutmeg, salt and pepper. Add the oatmeal and a little poaching liquid. Blend well.

Glazed Pig's Stomachs Encasing Meat and Potatoes

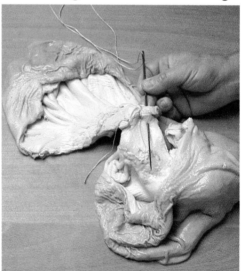

1 Sewing the stomachs. Put two cleaned pig's stomachs (page 10) on a work surface with their openings toward each other. Use a trussing needle and string to sew their edges together, turning the stomachs inside out as you stitch them. Leave a gap for inserting the stuffing, and leave the needle and string attached to the stomachs.

2 Mixing the stuffing. Sauté chopped onions and shallots in butter. Add diced, blanched waxy potatoes, and cook for five minutes. Trim and dice pork tenderloin; grind boneless pork blade. Put the meats in a bowl with eggs and herbs—here, savory, parsley and chervil. Add the potato mixture and combine all the ingredients.

3 **Stuffing the stomach.** Using a trussing needle and string, sew up any holes in a lamb's stomach, leaving one end open. Loosely fill the stomach—here, turned inside out—with the stuffing. Gather the edges of the opening together and tie them with string. Prick the stomach with the needle.

4 **Poaching the haggis.** Place the haggis on a rack in a large pan—in this case, a fish poacher. Cover the haggis with warm water or stock. Partially cover the pan with a lid and bring to a simmer. When the haggis is cooked—after about six hours—lift it out of the kettle (above).

5 **Serving the haggis.** Holding the haggis steady with a carving fork, cut it into slices about ½ inch [1 cm.] thick. Or slash the haggis lengthwise and spoon out the filling. Serve with seasoned mashed potatoes and turnips, or a combination of both.

3 **Adding the stuffing.** Fill the stomachs loosely with the stuffing. Sew up the opening and prick the roll all over with the needle. Place it on a rack in a large pot. Cover with warm water, add carrots, an onion studded with two cloves, a bouquet garni and coarse salt. Partially cover with a lid, and simmer gently for four hours.

4 **Glazing the roll.** Transfer the roll to a shallow baking dish. Strain the poaching liquid and set it aside. Rub oil over the roll, and brown it in a preheated 425° F. [220° C.] oven for 30 minutes. Drain off excess oil, add white wine and return the roll to the oven for 20 minutes, basting occasionally with the pan juices.

5 **Slicing the roll.** Make a poulette sauce (page 17) with some of the reserved poaching liquid, egg yolks, lemon and parsley. Remove the glazed roll from the oven, and cut it into ½-inch [1-cm.] slices. Serve them immediately, accompanied by the poulette sauce.

Enrichments for Mild-flavored Brains

Of all variety meats, none are so fragile as brains. They need brief, gentle cooking to become firm without losing their creamy texture, and poaching is an ideal means to this end.

Wine, vinegar or lemon court bouillons are equally appropriate as the poaching liquid. In the demonstration at right *(recipe, page 121)*, strained red-wine court bouillon turns the exterior of brains a deep brownish red—an attractive contrast to the pale meat inside. The liquid is then reduced and thickened with a flour-and-butter paste to make a smooth sauce.

A simpler strategy, shown below, is to poach the brains in a vinegar court bouillon that preserves their creamy color and to complement their delicate flavor with a dressing of *beurre noisette*—browned butter, capers and parsley.

Beef, veal, pork or lamb brains all can be poached by either method. Beef brains will take about 30 minutes to firm properly, veal 25 minutes, pork 20 minutes and lamb 15 minutes. Lamb and pork brains, being small, are usually served whole; veal and beef brains are sliced.

An Integral Red Wine Sauce

1 **Poaching.** Soak and peel brains— in this case, veal *(page 11)*. Prepare a red-wine court bouillon *(page 16)* and strain it into a nonreactive pan, pressing the solids to extract all the juices. Bring the court bouillon to a simmer, add the brains, partially cover the pan and simmer them for 25 minutes, or until the brains are firm to the touch.

2 **Draining.** Using a perforated spoon or skimmer, transfer the brains to a tray lined with a cloth that has been dampened so it will not stick to the brains. Cover the brains with the cloth and set them aside in a warm place. Increase the heat under the poaching liquid and boil it until it is reduced by half.

A Dressing of Browned Butter

1 **Poaching.** Prepare a white-wine or vinegar court bouillon. Soak and peel veal brains, poach them in the court bouillon *(Step 1, above)* and drain them. Slice the brains and arrange them on a warmed platter—adding, if you like, vegetables from the court bouillon.

2 **Making browned butter.** In a small heavy skillet, melt butter over low heat—using about 8 tablespoons [120 ml.] of butter for each 1½ pounds [¾ kg.] of brains. When the butter begins to bubble and turn brown, add a generous amount of capers and chopped fresh parsley.

3 **Serving.** Swirl the parsley and capers in the butter for a minute or so to heat them through. Immediately pour the browned butter over the sliced brains. Serve at once.

3 **Preparing garnishes.** Cut bacon strips, blanch them and sauté them in oil until crisp *(page 19)*, then drain them in a strainer. In the fat remaining in the skillet, sauté boiling onions; drain them with the bacon. Sauté mushrooms in butter and add them to the strainer. Make croutons, toss them with *persillade (recipe, page 166)* and set them aside.

4 **Finishing the sauce.** With a fork, blend equal amounts of butter and flour. Whisk this *beurre manié* into the reduced poaching liquid, and continue whisking until the mixture is thick and smooth—about three minutes. Add the bacon, onions and mushrooms and leave the pan over low heat.

5 **Slicing the brains.** Transfer the poached brains to a cutting board. Cut them into slices about 1 inch [2½ cm.] thick and arrange the slices attractively on a warmed serving platter.

6 **Serving.** Pour the sauce over the sliced brains. Scatter some of the croutons over the brains, and present the rest in a separate dish.

Velvety Sauces for Gelatinous Meats

Poaching liquid from gelatinous meats such as heads and feet provides a rich base for sauces to accompany them. The liquid need only be strained, then thickened with roux and simmered to make a velouté *(page 17)*. The sauce can be enriched with egg yolks or cream and flavored with spices—mustard, paprika or cayenne pepper, for example—or with puréed vegetables such as spinach or garlic. Lemon juice will lend a touch of sharpness; so will tomatoes.

In the demonstration at right, calf's feet are served in a lemony velouté that has been enriched with egg yolks *(recipe, page 150)*; below, a boned calf's head is accompanied by a tomato-flavored velouté *(recipe, page 138)*.

To make the feet more presentable, they are partially boned before poaching; the remaining bones are removed later. The calf's head is sewn to form a pouch, and stuffed with a meat-and-mushroom mixture *(recipe, page 138)*. The ears are wrapped to keep them intact before the whole head is enclosed in cloth.

Tying Calf's Feet to Preserve Their Shape

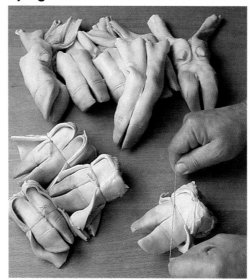

1 **Preparing calf's feet.** Remove the large bone from each foot *(page 11)*. To shape each foot into a neat package, tie back the flaps of loose skin with string. Put the feet in a pot, cover them with cold water and bring to a boil. Simmer for two to three minutes, then drain and rinse in cold water.

2 **Poaching the feet.** Make a white court bouillon *(page 16)* in a large pot. Add the feet and simmer them for four hours, or until a skewer penetrates the meat easily. Remove them from the pot. Using a bulb baster to reach under the surface fat, draw off 2 cups [½ liter] of poaching liquid for the sauce.

Forming a Head into a Compact Roll

1 **Stuffing the head.** Bone a calf's head *(pages 14-15)*; reserve the brains and the tongue for another use. With a trussing needle and string, tack together the eyelids from the inside. Fold the head in half lengthwise, sew up the back and stuff the head through the open mouth. The filling here is ground pork, veal, mushrooms, herbs and egg.

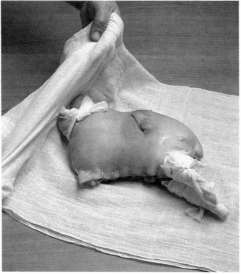

2 **Wrapping in cloth.** Rub the head with lemon juice. Using strips of muslin or cheesecloth, tie the muzzle and lower lip together to keep in the stuffing. Wind a strip of cloth around each ear. Wrap the head in a large double layer of cloth.

3 **Cooking the head.** To keep the wrapping secure, fasten it with more strips of cloth—string would mark the flesh. Place the head in a heavy pot and cover it with cold water. Add salt, carrots, an onion stuck with cloves and a bouquet garni. Bring to a boil, skim, then partially cover with a lid and simmer the head for about five hours.

3 **Removing small bones.** Cut away the strings and slice each foot in half lengthwise. The toe bones should fall out; if not, remove them with your fingers. Put the boned meat in a clean pan and set it aside.

4 **Making the sauce.** Simmer button mushrooms with a little water, salt, lemon juice and butter for two to three minutes (page 19). Add the mushrooms to the meat. Pour the mushroom liquid into the reserved poaching liquid and prepare a poulette sauce (page 17). Ladle it over the meat and mushrooms.

5 **Serving the feet.** Set the pan containing the sauced feet over low heat. Do not let the sauce boil or it will curdle. Stirring gently, allow the feet to warm through for about five minutes. Transfer them to a warmed platter, sprinkle them with fresh parsley and serve them immediately.

4 **Slicing the stuffed head.** Lift the head out of the poaching liquid. Discard the bouquet garni and vegetables, strain the liquid and reserve it. Unwrap the head, cut off the ears and cut the head into ½-inch [1-cm.] slices. Put the ears and slices on a warmed platter.

5 **Preparing the sauce.** Cook flour and butter to make a roux; add a dash of brandy and whisk in the poaching liquid. Cook for 10 minutes; add tomato paste. Place the pan half off the heat and simmer, skimming often. After 30 minutes, add julienned prosciutto and pitted olives (inset). Ladle the sauce over the head (above).

53

Pig's Feet in a Shimmering Aspic

Poached in water, rather than in court bouillon, pig's feet yield a clear gelatinous stock. Once chilled and degreased, the stock sets to a shimmering aspic in which the cooked meat may be served. In the demonstration at right, poached pig's feet are boned, and then garnished with slivers of sweet red peppers, carrots and sour gherkins before the stock is added. The vegetables add color to the mold and provide a crisp contrast to the soft, tender meat and delicate aspic.

Calf's feet, pig's ears, and boned and cut-up calf's or pig's head can be prepared in the same way. Although these meats, like pig's feet, are usually parboiled to draw out scum *(pages 52-53)*, this step is omitted when they are to be served in aspic: Parboiling would distort their shape and mar the final presentation. To protect the meats from discoloring, keep them out of contact with air. Place them in a bowl of water acidulated with a few tablespoonfuls of lemon juice or vinegar; and before poaching, roll them in lemon juice and wrap them tightly in muslin or cheesecloth. The cloth also helps to keep them neatly shaped as they cook.

The pig's feet here are poached in water flavored with aromatic vegetables and herbs. As the water heats, scum will rise to the surface and must be scrupulously skimmed off. The scum itself is not only harmless but nutritious, being composed mainly of proteins and minerals. But left alone, it eventually disperses through the stock to make it cloudy.

To ensure that they release sufficient gelatin to set the stock, pig's and calf's feet should be poached for at least four hours. After six hours, they will become meltingly tender, and their bones will almost fall from the flesh.

Pig's ears and boned heads will be tender after about three hours, and may not release enough gelatin to form an aspic. Test the setting ability of their stock by spooning a little onto a cold plate and refrigerating it. If the sample does not set within a few minutes, reduce the remaining stock to about half its original volume to concentrate its gelatin content. If the stock still does not set, add some gelatinous veal stock *(page 16)* or stir in a little powdered, unflavored gelatin that has been softened in cold water.

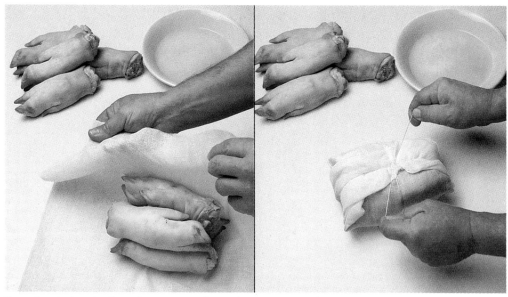

1 Preparing the feet. Remove any hairs that remain on the pig's feet *(page 11)*; put each cleaned foot into a bowl of acidulated water. When all the feet are prepared, remove them from the bowl and dry them with a towel. Squeeze lemon juice into a wide bowl. Cut a double piece of muslin or cheesecloth large enough to hold four feet in two layers. Roll four feet in the lemon juice, wrap them in the cloth *(above, left)* and secure the package with string *(right)*. Repeat with the remaining feet.

5 Peeling peppers. Roast sweet red peppers about 2 inches [5 cm.] from the heat of a preheated broiler for seven to eight minutes until they are blistered evenly on all sides. Wrap the peppers in a damp cloth and let them cool. Peel off and discard their skins. Cut each pepper in half lengthwise, and pull out and discard the stem and seeds.

6 Preparing the garnish. Cut carrots and sour gherkins into matchstick-sized strips, or julienne. Blanch the carrots in boiling water for three minutes in order to soften them; then pour them into a strainer to drain. Cut the peeled and seeded peppers into julienne.

2 **Poaching the feet.** Put the feet in a pot and cover them with cold water. Add a bouquet garni, an onion stuck with cloves, a garlic bulb, coarse salt and sliced carrots. Bring the water to a boil and skim. Partially cover the pot and simmer the feet for four to six hours. To keep the feet submerged, add boiling water as necessary.

3 **Straining the liquid.** Remove the feet from the pot and put them to one side. Line a strainer with dampened muslin or cheesecloth, and place it over a bowl. Discard the bouquet garni, onion and garlic, then strain the cooking liquid. Pour about 2 cups [½ liter] of this strained stock into another bowl, and refrigerate the rest of the stock.

4 **Boning the feet.** Cut the strings and remove the cloth from the feet. Let the feet cool until they are easy to handle. With a sharp knife, slit them in half lengthwise. Remove the bones from each foot with your fingers; place the boned feet in the bowl of lukewarm stock to inhibit discoloration.

7 **Serving the feet.** Skim the fat from the surface of the chilled stock. Then transfer the stock to a pan and melt it over low heat until it is just pourable. Drain the boned feet and arrange them in a shallow serving dish. Add the garnish, and ladle in the stock *(above)*. Cover the dish and chill overnight before serving *(right)*.

A Decorative Molding for Tongue

When tongue is poached for peeling *(page 12)*, it is ready to eat. The tongue can be sliced immediately and served hot, accompanied by mustard, grated horseradish or a piquant tomato sauce *(recipe, page 166)*. However, the robust flavor and firm texture of tongue also make it ideal as a cold meat. In this guise, it is most spectacular when used for the centerpiece of a glistening molded aspic as shown here; because tongues yield little, if any, gelatin, the aspic needs to be made from a separately prepared gelatinous stock *(page 16)*.

The mold can be any bowl, round casserole or soufflé dish that is wide and deep enough to contain the tongue easily—and flat-bottomed so that the aspic will sheathe it evenly. Before the tongue is added, the mold can be lined with stock, cooled until it is syrupy, and fancified with decoratively cut vegetables as on these pages, whole fresh chervil or parsley leaves, slices of ripe or green olives or strips of sour gherkins.

1 Lining the mold. Cut carrots and green beans into decorative shapes; blanch them for three minutes and drain them on a towel. Melt jellied stock, stir in a little Madeira and cool the stock until it is syrupy. Cover the bottom of a mold with a thin layer of stock; refrigerate until it sets. Dip the vegetables in stock and arrange them on the aspic.

2 Coating the sides. Spoon a thin layer of stock over the vegetables; refrigerate until the stock sets. Pour in a little more stock, and slowly rotate the mold in a pan of crushed ice until the sides are evenly coated and the aspic begins to set. Chill briefly to firm the aspic; add more stock and coat the mold again. Return the mold to the refrigerator.

6 Trimming the aspic. Refrigerate the weighted mold overnight, or until the stock is firmly set. Remove the weights, dish and foil. With a knife, trim excess aspic from the top and sides of the mold. Melt the trimmings over low heat, and pour the liquid over the tongue to give the top of the mold an even surface. Chill until this final layer of aspic sets.

7 Warming the mold. Insert a knife about ¼ inch [6 mm.] deep along the side of the mold, and run it around the edge of the aspic to loosen it. Dip the mold almost to its rim in a bowl of hot water for a few seconds, then lift it out of the water and wipe it dry.

8 Unmolding the tongue. Invert a flat serving plate over the mold. Holding the plate against the mold, turn the mold upside down, then lift it off. If the mold does not lift up easily, cover it for a few seconds with a cloth dipped in very hot water and wrung dry, then lift the mold off the tongue.

3 **Decorating the sides.** Cut carrots and zucchini lengthwise into strips the height of the mold. Blanch the carrots for three minutes and the zucchini for one minute; drain them. Place the mold in a large bowl filled with crushed ice. Dip the vegetables in stock, arrange them on the sides of the mold and coat them with stock. Chill until set.

4 **Adding the tongue.** Curl a poached and peeled tongue—in this case, a corned beef tongue—into a crescent and fit it into the mold. Pour in enough stock to cover the tongue. Chill the mold in the refrigerator until the stock has just begun to set.

5 **Weighting the tongue.** To catch any stock that overflows when the tongue is weighted, set the mold on a plate. Cover the mold with foil and put a dish that fits neatly inside the mold on top of the foil. Then place weights—here, about 5 pounds [2½ kg.]—on the dish, distributing them evenly.

9 **Serving the tongue.** Cut the aspic-coated tongue into thick slices, dipping the knife blade frequently in hot water so that it will pass through the aspic easily. Serve the slices of tongue accompanied—if you like—by a tangy cold sauce such as tartar or *gribiche* (recipes, page 167).

4
Braising
The Art of Concentrating Flavors

The varied roles of vegetables
Techniques suited to delicate meats
Softening tough cuts
Browning oxtail and tongue
Reducing cooking liquid to a glaze

Like poaching, braising is a method of cooking food in gently simmering liquid. However, for a braise, the food is combined with vegetables and herbs and only enough liquid to cover the ingredients—and the pot is tightly sealed. The aim is to imbue the food with flavor as it cooks and to produce a concentrated liquid that will form a rich sauce to accompany it. Any variety meat can be braised successfully, with the exception of brains, which are best poached to protect their fragile structure.

A braise should begin with one or more of the classic trio of aromatic vegetables—carrots, onions and celery—either whole or cut in pieces. The smaller the pieces, the faster they will release their flavors—as was discovered in the 18th Century by a chef to the Duke of Mirepoix, whose name lives on in the term "mirepoix," which signifies vegetables that have been finely diced and sweated in butter or oil *(pages 60-61)*.

The meats also may be cooked in fat as a preliminary step: The savory deposits left in the pan after browning the meat will give the braise extra flavor and color, and can be combined with flour to make a thicker sauce. Robust meats such as oxtail *(pages 66-67)* are better suited to browning than delicate varieties—fries, for instance—which dry out easily.

Although water may be used as a braising medium, stock, wine or beer will produce a sauce with more character. Meats such as liver, kidney and sweetbreads, which do not yield gelatin of their own, require a gelatinous stock if the braising liquid is to become a thick sauce.

Braising may be done on top of the stove or in the oven. Either way the liquid must simmer slowly lest the meat toughen. The cooking time varies with the type of meat. Tender veal kidney, for example, is braised for only half an hour to preserve its delicacy and keep it pink inside. Muscular and gelatinous meats—tails, feet and ears among them— need several hours' braising to tenderize them. Tripe can be braised for just an hour or two to give it a pleasant chewiness, or for up to 20 hours to make it soft enough to melt in the mouth *(pages 62-63)*.

The flavor and appearance of any braise is improved by cleansing the braising liquid of fatty impurities at the end of cooking. The cleansing process also thickens the liquid, resulting in a smooth, glossy sauce that can be served apart, or poured back into the braise, or used to baste the meat, giving it a rich brown glaze *(page 64)*.

Garnished with slices of truffles, a pan of braised sweetbreads is sealed with aluminum foil and a lid before being returned to the oven for a further brief cooking *(pages 60-61)*. In the tightly closed pan, the heat will draw out the truffles' delicious perfume, which will permeate the sweetbreads.

Preserving Form and Texture

A Truffle Garnish for Sweetbreads

Braising delicate variety meats for a short period in veal stock will preserve the structure of the flesh and keep it moist as it absorbs flavor. Enriched by the meat's juices and aromatic flavorings, the braising liquid will provide a savory sauce. Sweetbreads, fries, large slabs of veal liver and whole veal kidneys all profit from brief braising. Veal sweetbreads require about 40 minutes; lamb sweetbreads need only 15 to 20 minutes of cooking. Beef fries require about 45 minutes, veal or pork, 30 minutes and lamb, 20 minutes. Veal liver and kidney should be eaten while pink inside and are braised for no more than 30 minutes.

To coax the vegetables for the braise into releasing their flavor quickly, they should be finely diced or thinly sliced and softened in butter or oil before the meat is added to the pan. In the demonstration at right, veal sweetbreads are braised on a bed of diced carrots, onions and celery —a classic mirepoix. The veal kidneys shown on the opposite page *(recipe, page 97)* are wrapped in spinach and lettuce leaves to protect their tender surfaces, then braised with sliced aromatic vegetables and a bouquet garni.

Veal stock, with its fine taste, is an invaluable braising liquid. For extra flavor, a little wine—even a fortified wine such as Madeira or sherry—may be added. In any case, the liquid should just barely cover the meat. To ensure that the top of the meat does not dry out, buttered parchment paper can be laid over it before the pan is sealed.

The simplest way to finish the sauce for the meat is to strain the braising liquid, then cleanse it and reduce it until thick *(Step 5, right)*. After the liquid has been reduced, the braising vegetables can be pressed through a sieve and incorporated into it. Or, to achieve a richer result, sieved farmer cheese and puréed cooked mushrooms can be whisked in *(Step 3, opposite, below)*.

Croutons, sautéed strips of bacon and glazed small vegetables *(page 19)* all make appetizing garnishes. Truffles are a luxurious accompaniment; here, the braised sweetbreads are briefly baked with sliced truffles, which perfume the meat with their fragrance.

1 **Preparing mirepoix.** Finely dice onions, carrots and celery. Over low heat, melt butter in a heavy pan that is large enough to hold the sweetbreads in one layer. Add the vegetables, salt and mixed dried herbs. Stirring occasionally, cook gently for 15 minutes, or until the vegetables soften; do not let them brown.

2 **Assembling the braise.** Soak, parboil, peel and compact veal sweetbreads *(page 12)*. Arrange them in a single layer on the mirepoix. Add just enough gelatinous veal stock *(page 16)* to cover the sweetbreads.

6 **Finishing the braise.** Baste the sweetbreads with some of the sauce or, as here, arrange thinly sliced truffles on the sweetbreads and spoon the sauce over them. To seal in the truffles' aroma, cover the pan with foil and a lid. Bake the sweetbreads in a preheated 450° F. [230° C.] oven for 10 minutes. Serve them directly from the pan.

3 **Cooking the sweetbreads.** To keep the sweetbreads moist, butter a piece of parchment paper on one side and put it, buttered side down, on top of the meat. Cover the pan and simmer the sweetbreads gently for 40 minutes.

4 **Straining the liquid.** Discard the paper and transfer the sweetbreads to a plate. Strain the braising liquid through a sieve set over a saucepan. Return the sweetbreads to the braising pan, cover the pan and set it aside in a warm place.

5 **Cleansing the liquid.** Put the saucepan of braising liquid over low heat, half off the burner. Fatty particles will form a skin on the cooler side; remove it as it thickens. Skimming occasionally, simmer until no more skin forms and the liquid has reduced to half its original volume and become a syrupy sauce—20 minutes or so.

Leafy Envelopes for Kidneys

1 **Wrapping.** Blanch spinach and lettuce leaves for one minute, drain the leaves and lay them flat between towels. Remove the fat and membrane from veal kidneys (page 8); season the kidneys and, if you like, smear them with butter for extra flavor. Wrap each kidney first in spinach leaves, then in lettuce.

2 **Braising.** Heat oil in a pan; add sliced leeks, onions and carrots and sauté them for five to 10 minutes. Add the kidneys, a bouquet garni and enough stock to submerge them. Cover the pan and place it in a preheated 350° F. [180° C.] oven for 30 minutes. Remove the kidneys and bouquet garni; strain most of the liquid into a saucepan.

3 **Serving.** Return the kidneys to the braising pan; cover and set it aside. Cleanse and reduce the strained liquid (Step 5, above). Off the heat, whisk farmer cheese, Dijon mustard and puréed mushrooms into the liquid to form a sauce. Slice the kidneys and put them on serving plates. Pour a little sauce around each portion.

The Versatility of Tripe

Because of its sturdy structure, tripe can be braised for just about any length of time from one hour up to 20—depending on the effect desired. After an hour or two, the tripe will be tender if somewhat chewy and will be imbued with the flavors of the vegetables and herbs with which it was braised (*opposite, below; recipe, page 127*). Additional cooking further softens and flavors the tripe until, after about 20 hours, it is satiny and saturated with tastes from the braise.

Tripe has no natural gelatin so, for a long braise, the liquid is usually enriched by the addition of gelatinous meats—feet, for example, or pork rinds. In this demonstration, blanched pork rinds are used to line the casserole because they also render fat and thus prevent the tripe and a boned calf's foot from sticking to the pot (*recipe, page 132*).

To minimize evaporation, the braising vessel must be tightly sealed. Choose a heavy casserole or ovenproof pot that has a well-fitting lid. Then cover the braise with foil before setting the lid in place or, using a time-honored cookery trick, seal the lid in place on the casserole with flour paste (*Step 3*). After the tripe is done, the hard crust of paste can be easily removed.

In a short braise, feet and rinds would have no time to render their gelatin. Indeed, rather than being covered with liquid, the tripe is braised in a moist vegetable mixture. At the end of the cooking, the tripe can be put into a shallow baking dish, sprinkled liberally with Parmesan cheese and dotted with butter, then broiled for a few minutes to give the top a lightly browned gratin finish.

Long Cooking for Maximum Succulence

1 **Assembling the braise.** Line the bottom of a large, broad casserole with blanched pork rinds. Add whole carrots, an onion stuck with two cloves, a bouquet garni and a boned, split calf's foot *(page 11)*. Rinse tripe *(page 10)* and cut it in 2-inch [5-cm.] squares.

2 **Layering the tripe.** Place a layer of tripe squares on top of the vegetables; season with salt and pepper. Strew chopped garlic and shallots over the tripe. Continue layering the tripe and flavorings until all are used up. Add half a bottle of dry white wine and just enough gelatinous veal stock *(page 16)* to cover the contents of the casserole.

6 **Serving the tripe.** Remove the calf's foot, pick out its small bones, cut the meat into pieces and return them to the casserole. Discard the onion, carrots and bouquet garni. Pour the reduced liquid back into the casserole, stir gently to coat the tripe and serve it at once from warmed soup plates.

3 **Sealing the casserole.** Make a thick paste from 2 cups [½ liter] of flour and ¾ cup [175 ml.] of water. Roll the paste into a rope, and coil it around the rim of the casserole. Set the lid in place and press it down into the paste rope. Place the casserole in a 250° F. [120° C.] oven and braise the tripe for at least 12 hours—up to 20 hours if you like.

4 **Breaking the seal.** Remove the casserole from the oven and set it on a trivet. Use the dull side of a knife blade to crack the hardened paste and the tip of the blade to chip the paste away. Brush off excess crumbs and pry off the casserole lid with a metal spatula.

5 **Degreasing the liquid.** Using a ladle, skim off the fat that has risen to the top of the braising liquid. Transfer most of the braising liquid to a small saucepan. Put the pan over low heat, setting it half off the burner, and simmer the liquid until it has reduced to half its original volume. Skim off the skin that forms on the cooler side of the pan.

A Gratin Topping for a Short Braise

1 **Flavoring the tripe.** Heat butter and oil in a heavy pot. Add finely chopped celery, carrots and onions, a whole garlic clove and a crumbled bay leaf. Cook the vegetables gently for 20 minutes; discard the garlic. Cut tripe into strips and add them to the pan. Pour in white wine and boil the mixture until the wine evaporates.

2 **Adding tomatoes.** Add chopped, peeled tomatoes (page 18) to the tripe strips. Season the mixture with salt and pepper. Pour in enough veal stock to barely submerge the tripe, then cover the pot and reduce the heat. Stirring occasionally, simmer the tripe for about two hours; pour in more stock if the mixture looks dry.

3 **Adding a gratin finish.** Stir in chopped fresh basil. Cut more basil leaves into thin strips and set them aside. Transfer the tripe to a shallow baking dish, sprinkle with grated Parmesan, dot with butter and place the dish under a broiler to brown the top lightly—one to two minutes. Garnish with the basil and serve immediately.

A Honeycomb Wrapping for an Herb-flecked Stuffing

A large piece of beef tripe can be sewed up to make a package that will hold a substantial amount of spicy meat stuffing *(recipes, pages 133 and 135)*, and braising will keep the assembly moist while its flavors develop. If possible, the tripe piece should include the honeycomb section, which can be drawn over the stuffed package, as shown here, to give its surface a unique pattern.

To form the tripe into a package, trim the edges to make the piece rectangular. Then fold the rectangle in half and sew it, keeping an opening for the stuffing and leaving the honeycomb section free until the package is full. In this case, the entire tripe piece was about 1 foot [30 cm.] wide and 3 feet [90 cm.] long and required about 10 cups [2½ liters] of stuffing.

The stuffed tripe can be braised in water or, as here, in veal stock *(page 16)* enriched with wine. A calf's foot will contribute gelatin to the liquid. After braising, the tripe is glazed to burnish its surface before serving.

1 **Sewing the tripe.** Clean beef tripe *(page 10)* and trim the edges to create a rectangle. Chop and reserve the trimmings. Fold the tripe in half lengthwise; leave the honeycomb section free. With a trussing needle and string, sew the edges of the folded tripe together, leaving an opening where the honeycomb tripe begins.

2 **Making the stuffing.** Put the chopped tripe into a bowl. Add ground lean beef, cooked rice, fresh bread crumbs and finely chopped garlic. Sauté finely chopped onion in butter and add it to the bowl. Chop fresh coriander and mint leaves and add them.

6 **Adding stock.** Clean a calf's foot, remove the large bone and split the foot *(page 11)*. Put it in a pan of cold water; bring to a boil, reduce the heat and simmer for three or four minutes to draw out the scum. Drain the foot, rinse well and put it in the pot. Add a glass of white wine and enough veal stock to almost submerge the package.

7 **Braising the tripe.** Cover the package with buttered parchment paper and a lid. Over medium heat, bring the liquid to a simmer; transfer the pot to a 250° F. [120° C.] oven. After six to eight hours, transfer the tripe to a shallow baking dish; set the foot aside for another use. Strain the liquid into a saucepan; discard the vegetables.

8 **Basting the tripe.** Position the saucepan half off the burner and reduce the liquid over low heat, skimming off the skin that forms repeatedly on the cooler side of the pan. Bake the tripe in a preheated 425° F. [220° C.] oven for 30 minutes, basting it every five minutes or so with the reduced liquid.

3 **Filling the package.** Season the stuffing mixture with ground mace, cinnamon, nutmeg, cayenne pepper, black pepper and salt. Mix the ingredients together with your hands. Put the the stuffing into the tripe pouch, packing it in fairly loosely to allow for its expansion as it cooks.

4 **Securing the package.** Pull the flap of honeycomb tripe over the package, completely enclosing it. With the trussing needle and string, stitch the loose edges of the honeycomb tripe to keep it in place.

5 **Assembling the braise.** Melt butter in a pot that is large enough to hold the stuffed tripe easily. Add coarsely chopped onions and carrots and mixed dried herbs, and cook them gently for 20 minutes. Lower the package onto the bed of vegetables.

9 **Garnishing tripe.** Transfer the tripe to a warmed platter and let it rest in a warm place for 30 minutes to make it easier to slice. Meanwhile, boil whole, peeled potatoes in salted water for 20 minutes. Drain the potatoes, return them to their pan, and toss with butter and chopped parsley. Cut peeled carrots into pieces and boil them until tender; drain them and toss them with butter. Glaze whole onions (page 19). Garnish the tripe with the vegetables, and serve the meat cut into slices.

Oxtails with a Burnished Glaze

To give them extra flavor and color, robust variety meats that benefit from long braising can be browned in fat at the start. This tactic, which could dry out delicate innards, gives hearty meat a mahogany color and leaves a concentrated residue of juices in the pan. When this residue is scraped up and dissolved in a little brandy or wine, it becomes a rich flavoring element for the braising liquid. To thicken the final sauce, the browned meat can then be sprinkled with flour before the liquid is added. In this demonstration, oxtails and aromatic vegetables are browned in butter and the pan deglazed with brandy. After the tails are lightly floured, they are braised in stock and red wine (recipe, page 150).

Oxtail is tough meat, and it needs at least four hours of braising to soften the muscle fibers and connective tissue. Ears, feet, tongues and beef cheeks require similar leisurely braising to make them succulent. Beef or pork liver and kidney also profit from long braising—not so much to make them tender as to attenuate their strong taste.

Any lean meat that is to be braised for a long time may be kept moist during cooking by larding it with strips of fatback. To flavor the meat as well as nourish it, the lardons can be rolled in a *persillade (recipe, page 166)* before being threaded through the meat.

For a sauce, the braising liquid can be strained, cleansed and reduced either at the end of cooking (*page 61*) or halfway through. If reduced at the halfway point, the liquid should be returned to the pan to cook down further during the remaining hours of braising and coat the meat with a thick, dark glaze. To prevent the meat from drying out as the sauce simmers away, baste the meat frequently with the sauce.

At whatever point the braising liquid is strained, the vegetables cooked with the meat will have released all their flavor and must be discarded. They can be replaced with a garnish that is added to the braise—such as the mushrooms and bacon shown here—or with boiled root vegetables, cooked separately and served with the meat.

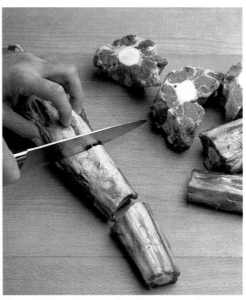

1 Slicing the oxtails. Trim excess fat from oxtails (*page 10*). Cut the tails into sections about 3 inches [8 cm.] long by slicing through them at the slight indentations in their surface where cartilage separates the vertebrae.

2 Larding with fat. To make lardons, slice fresh pork fatback ¼ inch [6 mm.] thick and cut the slices into strips about 5 inches [13 cm.] long and ¼ inch wide. Toss the lardons in a mixture of chopped parsley and garlic. With a knife, cut slits through each section of oxtail, on both sides of the bone. Push the lardons through the slits.

6 Adding a garnish. Return the meat to the braising pan. Cook whole mushrooms in butter and lemon juice; sauté blanched bacon strips in oil and drain them (*page 19*). Add the mushrooms and bacon strips to the pan (*above, left*). Skim off any fat that has collected on the surface of the cooled braising liquid. Put the liquid over low heat, half off the burner, and reduce it for 15 minutes, skimming off the skin that forms on the cooler side of the pan. Pour the cleansed, reduced liquid over the meat and garnish (*right*).

3 **Browning the oxtail.** In a large ovenproof pan, sauté chopped carrots and onions in butter until they color slightly; remove and set them aside. Add the oxtail sections to the pan and turn them frequently until they are evenly browned—about 15 minutes. Return the vegetables to the pan and add salt.

4 **Adding flour.** Pour a glass of brandy into the pan and ignite it with a match. When the flame dies, stir the contents of the pan, scraping browned deposits from the bottom. Add flour and cook over medium heat for five minutes, turning the meat to distribute the flour. Add red wine, stock, a bouquet garni and unpeeled garlic cloves.

5 **Straining the braise.** Stirring all the time, bring the liquid to a boil. Cover the pan, put it in a preheated 300° F. [150° C.] oven and let the oxtail stew gently for about two hours. Transfer the oxtail pieces to a plate. Strain the braising liquid into a saucepan and let it cool. Discard the bouquet garni and the aromatic vegetables.

7 **Serving the braise.** Cover the pan and return it to the oven. Basting the oxtail several times with the cooking juices, braise it until the meat is very tender—about two hours. Serve the oxtail straight from the pan, accompanied by mashed potatoes, boiled rice or, as here, buttered noodles.

Hearty Support for Tongues

Braising can make any tongue tender enough to cut with a fork and—if the process starts with browning—can darken the color and intensify the taste of the meat. The savory juices left in the pan used for browning can then be used as enrichment for the braising liquid if deglazed as shown in this demonstration. Here lamb's tongues are cooked with blanched pork rinds, which add body and flavor to the liquid *(recipe, page 114)*.

All tongues need lengthy braising to soften their compact, muscular flesh, but the cooking times vary with the type and size of the tongue. Beef tongues need four or five hours of braising to tenderize them. Veal tongues require three hours, pork tongues two and one half hours; lamb tongues will become tender in two hours. After braising, the tongues can be baked briefly in a hot oven and basted with their cooking liquid: The tongues will become mahogany brown, and the liquid will thicken still further to coat them with a shiny glaze.

1 Browning tongues. Soak, poach, peel and trim lamb's tongues *(pages 12-13)*. Melt fatback in a skillet, add sliced onions and carrots, and sauté for 15 minutes. Put the vegetables in a braising pan. Over medium heat, brown the tongues in the skillet, turning them often for even coloring. Add the tongues to the braising pan.

2 Deglazing. Pour any excess fat out of the skillet; set it over high heat and add white wine. With a wooden spoon, scrape up the crusty deposits from the bottom of the skillet, stirring continuously until the wine comes to a boil. Boil the wine until it has reduced to one third of its original volume.

A Smooth Purée of Lentils

1 Cooking lentils. Rinse lentils and soak them for one hour. Drain them and put them in a large pan. Cover with cold water. Add a clove-studded onion, a carrot, a bulb of garlic, blanched salt pork and a bouquet garni. Bring the water slowly to a boil, then simmer the lentils, uncovered, for about two hours.

2 Puréeing the lentils. Discard the aromatic vegetables and bouquet garni. Slice the salt pork and set it aside. Drain the lentils in a strainer over a bowl; reserve the liquid. Press the lentils through the medium disk of a food mill. With a plastic scraper, force the lentil purée through a fine-meshed drum sieve to eliminate the skins.

3 Finishing the purée. In a pan set over high heat, reheat the purée, stirring constantly to prevent it from sticking. If the purée is very stiff, add some reserved cooking liquid or some of the braising liquid from the tongues. Season to taste with salt and pepper. Off the heat, beat cubes of butter into the purée.

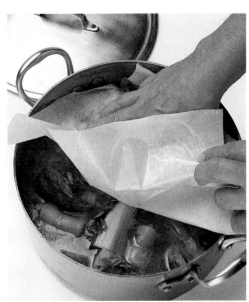

3 **Adding the wine.** Cut pork rinds into strips about 2 by 3 inches [5 by 7 ½ cm.]. Roll the strips into scrolls and tie them with string. Blanch the scrolls for two to three minutes, drain and rinse under cold water. Add the scrolls and a bouquet garni to the braising pan. Pour the reduced wine over the meats.

4 **Cooking the braise.** Add just enough veal stock *(page 16)* to cover the tongues. Butter parchment paper on one side and place it, buttered side down, over the tongues. Cover the pan and put it in a preheated 300° F. [150° C.] oven. When the tongues are tender, after about two hours, remove the pan from the oven.

5 **Basting the tongues.** Strain most of the braising liquid into a saucepan; place the pan half off the heat, and skim the liquid occasionally as it reduces. Raise the temperature of the oven to 400° F. [200° C.]. Return the uncovered braising pan to the oven for about 20 minutes, basting the tongues often with the simmering strained liquid.

6 **Serving the braise.** Prepare a lentil purée *(box, opposite)*. Sauté the reserved sliced salt pork in oil until lightly browned. Spoon the purée onto a warmed platter, and place the sautéed pork slices at one end. Cut the strings from the scrolls of rind, and place the scrolls at the other end of the platter. Arrange the tongues around the purée and garnish with parsley sprigs. Serve the remaining braising liquid separately in a sauceboat.

Stew: A Blend of Contrasting Elements

Stews start with small meat pieces, but the cooking method is the same as for a braise: Meat is barely covered by liquid, then simmered gently with vegetables and herbs until tender. Because most variety meats can be cut small—and many are naturally that size—stewing is an ideal way to cook a mixture such as the turkey giblets and trimmings shown in this demonstration. When the meats are stewed together, their flavors mingle— each one enhancing the other—and their differing textures produce an intriguing combination in the finished dish.

Any variety meat suitable for braising *(chart, page 7)* can be used in a stew. Even such delicate parts as parboiled sweetbreads or raw poultry livers can be included, so long as they are added to the pot toward the end of the stewing to keep them from overcooking. About the only restriction is that the meats should come from poultry or from a single type of animal, since each type has a unique flavor.

All the tougher meats should be cut into pieces of similar size so that they will cook in the same amount of time; tender meats need not be cut up until after they are stewed. The meats can be browned or not, as you wish. Here, all the turkey pieces, except the tender liver, are browned in oil. For a deeper color, a little sugar can be added to the pan and cooked until it caramelizes; for a thicker sauce, flour can be sprinkled over the browned meats before the braising liquid is added.

After the sauce is cleansed *(Step 5, right)*, the stew can be served immediately or combined with a garnish and cooked for 15 minutes or so to allow the flavors to mingle. Glazed onions, stewed mushrooms or sautéed bacon strips *(page 19)* are all suitable; so are parboiled and sautéed root vegetables, as shown here.

1 **Preparing the meats.** Assemble the giblets, wings, feet and neck of a turkey; add a few extra gizzards and hearts—either turkey or chicken. Peel and trim the feet and pare the flesh off the gizzards *(page 10)*. Trim the hearts and liver. Cut each wing apart at its joint. Cut the feet into halves and the neck into three or four pieces.

2 **Browning the meats.** Heat olive oil in a sauté pan with a well-fitting lid. Add the pieces of feet and neck, the gizzard flesh, and the hearts and wings. Turning them frequently with a spatula, sauté the meats over medium heat until they are well browned on all sides—about 20 minutes.

6 **Preparing the vegetables.** Cut peeled turnips into pieces and cook them in butter, in a covered skillet over medium heat for 10 minutes; uncover them and cook them for a further 20 minutes. Meanwhile, parboil peeled small potatoes in salted water for 10 minutes. Drain the turnips and potatoes, and add them to the meats.

7 **Covering with sauce.** Pour the cleansed sauce over the ingredients in the sauté pan. Turn all of the ingredients gently to ensure that they are evenly coated. Cover the pan and put it over low heat.

3 **Adding flour.** Add coarsely chopped onions to the pan and cook for five minutes. Add 1 teaspoon [5 ml.] of sugar and cook for a few minutes, turning the meat over. Add 2 tablespoons [30 ml.] of flour and mix it in well. Pour in a splash of white wine and scrape up any residue from the bottom of the pan.

4 **Cooking the stew.** Stirring constantly, pour in just enough boiling water to cover the meats. Add a bouquet garni, cover the pan and reduce the heat to low. Simmer the stew for about one and one half hours on a heat-diffusing pad or in a preheated 300° F. [150° C.] oven.

5 **Straining the sauce.** Transfer the meats to a tray. Discard the bouquet garni. Pour the braising liquid through a strainer set over a saucepan; press the onions through the strainer. Return the meats to the sauté pan. Put the strained liquid over low heat; set it half off the burner and simmer for 15 or 20 minutes, skimming off any skin that forms.

8 **Adding the liver.** After 15 minutes, add the turkey liver. With a wooden spoon or a spatula, turn the liver over gently in the sauce so that it is covered by liquid. Cover the pan and simmer the stew gently for about 10 minutes, turning the liver two or three times.

9 **Serving the stew.** Transfer the liver to a cutting board. Carve the liver into thin slices and scatter the slices over the stew. Serve the stew straight from the pan onto warmed plates, making sure each portion includes a variety of meats and vegetables.

Sausage Making
A Profusion of Methods and Materials

The term sausage covers everything from Pennsylvania Dutch scrapple made with pig's head and cornmeal *(pages 74-75)* to a chitterling concoction known in France as *andouillettes (pages 82-83)*. The common denominators are that the meat is boneless and that it is molded by being packed into a loaf, shaped into a cake or stuffed into a casing. Usually the meat is precooked, then cut up or ground, and in most cases the sausage itself is cooked twice—after it is assembled and before it is served.

Whether alone or in combination with other cuts, variety meats of every kind can play a part in sausage making. The selection depends on how bland or strong-flavored you want the sausage to be; the handling depends on the character of the meat and the finished texture you desire. Liver, for example, gives sausage an assertive taste; because it is tender, it can be added raw—ground, chopped or cut into small pieces. By comparison, fragile brains and fries contribute a delicate flavor, but first should be firmed by a brief parboiling, then chopped or diced. And the equally mild-tasting heads or cheeks require lengthy poaching before they can be easily chopped to bite size or minced in a food grinder.

When casings are wanted, chitterlings are suitable. But the specially prepared natural sausage casings available at specialty butchers are more convenient to use and flexible enough to form link sausages *(pages 78-79)*. The casings themselves qualify as innards: They are intestines that have been stripped of their fat, salted and dried. The casings are sold by the yard [meter] and vary in diameter from ¾ inch [2 cm.] for lamb casing to 1½ inches [4 cm.] for hog to 4 inches [10 cm.] for beef. Lamb and hog casings are fragile as well as small and are therefore best suited to a fairly soft filling that does not need lengthy cooking, such as the liver mixture on pages 78-79. The more robust beef casings will accommodate a firm stuffing—even a whole beef tongue *(opposite; pages 80-81)*.

The cooking method you choose when you are ready to serve the sausage will depend to some extent on the casing—or absence of one. Scrapple is best kept in shape by frying or baking the slices. Caul-wrapped sausages require the dry heat of grilling, broiling or baking to melt the fatty membrane. Sausages stuffed in casings or chitterlings can be poached, but grilling, broiling or sautéing will crisp them and give them a brown finish.

A whole beef tongue, flavored with spices and truffles and enclosed in sausage casing, is lifted out of its cooking vessel—here, a fish poacher—after being braised in a rich gelatinous stock. The calf's foot cooked with the tongue will be boned and cut into pieces to provide a garnish.

A Spicy Loaf Bound with Cornmeal

Cornmeal not only sets scrapple apart from other variety-meat sausages, but also identifies it as American. Cooked into a thick porridge, cornmeal serves as a matrix for bits of seasoned poached pork. When the mixture is packed into a mold and chilled, it becomes firm enough to hold its shape without a casing and to be neatly sliced for frying.

Traditionally scrapple is made from a pig's head, as in this demonstration *(recipe, page 163)*, but other pork variety meats such as liver or heart may be added or substituted. As the head poaches, it releases gelatin. The poaching liquid then is used to cook the cornmeal porridge, lending it flavor and helping it set into a solid loaf. Once molded, scrapple can be kept in the refrigerator for one week or frozen for three months.

Before frying, flour the slices so that they will crisp slightly or dip them in flour, in beaten egg and finally in fresh bread crumbs to give them a crunchy coating. Scrapple may be fried in butter, oil, rendered bacon fat or, as here, in lard.

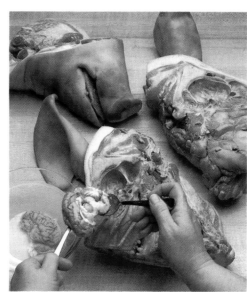

1 **Removing the brains.** Ask the butcher to cut a pig's head into three pieces. Rinse them well. Scoop out the brains with two small spoons, drop them into cold water and reserve them for another use. Then soak the pieces of head in several changes of cold acidulated water for several hours, or until the water remains clear.

2 **Cooking the meat.** Parboil the pieces of head for 10 minutes to remove the scum. Rinse the pieces, then put them into a large pot of cold water with carrots, onions and a bouquet garni. Bring the water to a boil, reduce the heat, and simmer partially covered for two to three hours, or until the meat begins to fall away from the bone.

6 **Adding the meat.** Whisking from time to time, cook the cornmeal porridge for about 30 minutes. When the porridge is very thick and a spoon drawn across the surface leaves a sharp impression, turn off the heat. Gently stir the seasoned meat into the cornmeal porridge with a wooden spoon.

7 **Preparing the loaves.** Spoon the warm scrapple mixture into lightly oiled metal or glass loaf molds; pack the mixture down firmly with the back of the wooden spoon to eliminate any air pockets. Cover the molds with plastic wrap and refrigerate them overnight to firm the loaves.

8 **Slicing the scrapple.** To unmold a loaf, run a knife around its edges, then turn the mold upside down on a cutting board; the scrapple should slide out easily when you lift the mold. Use a sharp knife to cut the loaf into slices about ½ inch [1 cm.] thick. Dip the scrapple slices in flour to coat both sides and lay the slices on a tray.

3 **Boning the meat.** Transfer the pieces of head to a work surface. Strain the poaching liquid into a bowl to cool. Pull the meat away from the large head bones with your fingers. Cut off large chunks of fat, small bones and bits of gristle, and discard them.

4 **Chopping the meat.** In a small bowl, combine coarsely chopped onion with seasonings—in this instance, nutmeg, sage, cayenne pepper and salt are used. With a large knife, chop the meat coarse, put it in a large bowl and blend in the seasonings.

5 **Cooking the cornmeal.** Measure cornmeal into a sifter. Skim the fat from the poaching liquid, pour it into a heavy pot and bring it to a boil over high heat. Whisking constantly, sift in the cornmeal. Continue to whisk the cornmeal until craters appear on its surface. Then reduce the heat.

9 **Frying the scrapple.** Melt lard in a heavy skillet. When it is hot but not smoking, add the scrapple slices and fry them until their undersides are golden brown—about four minutes. Turn them over carefully with a large metal spatula, and brown the other side. Drain the slices on paper towels.

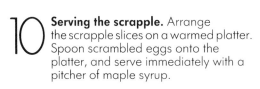

10 **Serving the scrapple.** Arrange the scrapple slices on a warmed platter. Spoon scrambled eggs onto the platter, and serve immediately with a pitcher of maple syrup.

Hand-molded Meats Enclosed in Caul

Filmy sheets of fat-veined caul are the most adaptable of sausage casings. They can be cut into any size or shape and then simply wrapped around a filling. The caul adheres to itself and requires no stitching or tying. When the sausage is broiled or baked, the caul's fat melts to moisten the meat inside, and the lacy membrane crisps and browns to give the sausage an appetizing finish.

In this demonstration, caul is used as a wrapping for strips of precooked feet that are sandwiched between ground pork, shaped to form sausages that resemble the original pig's feet (recipe, page 164). Tripe, pig's ears or calf's feet could be substituted for the pig's feet.

To soften and flavor them, the pig's feet are poached in veal stock enriched with Madeira before they are cut into strips. Their gelatinous cooking liquid is then reduced to make a sauce for the sausages.

In order to produce a soft, fine-textured ground pork that will complement the firm strips of foot meat, equal parts of lean pork and fresh pork fat are ground twice—first through the coarse disk of a food grinder, then through the fine disk. Here the ground meat is flavored with chopped fresh herbs, mixed spices, brandy, fresh truffles and a bit of garlic. Suitable herbs include sage, thyme, parsley and savory; wine can take the place of the brandy, and canned truffles substitute for fresh ones.

If truffles are used, garlic should be added sparingly; a little garlic enhances the flavor of truffles, but an excess would overwhelm their delicate perfume. The ground pork is moistened with some of the liquid in which the feet cooked, and this, too, should be added with restraint, for if there is too much liquid, the ground pork will not hold its shape.

Once the ground pork mixture and pig's-feet meat are assembled and the caul is drawn around them, the sausages are ready for cooking. Instead of being broiled, as shown here, they can be baked in a 425° F. [220° C.] oven for 25 minutes. And, for a crisper surface, you can coat the sausages with butter and bread crumbs before placing them in the oven.

1 **Poaching the feet.** Clean pig's feet (page 11). To draw out scum, parboil the feet for five minutes, then rinse them in cold water. Put them in a shallow pan, add Madeira and pour in enough stock to cover them. Cover the pan and poach the feet, turning them occasionally, until tender—about four hours.

2 **Boning the feet.** Transfer the feet to a rack to drain and cool. Strain the poaching liquid into a saucepan; set the pan half off the heat and simmer the liquid, skimming off any skin. Split the feet, remove the bones with your fingers, and cut the meat into finger-shaped pieces. Chop any trimmings fine and reserve them separately.

6 **Assembling the sausages.** Prepare caul (page 37). With a knife, cut it into 10 pieces each about 6 by 10 inches [15 by 25 cm.]. To make each sausage, put some of the meat mixture in the center of a piece of caul, and pat it into the shape of a triangle ½ inch [1 cm.] thick. Cover the ground meat with pieces of feet (above, left); put another layer of ground meat on top, shaping it in the same manner as before. Put a truffle slice on top of the sausage and fold the caul over it (right).

3 **Grinding the meat.** Cut lean pork and fresh fatback into chunks, and pass them through a food grinder fitted with a coarse disk. Replace the coarse disk with a fine one, and grind the meat and fat again. Clean the grinder of the pork scraps that cling to it by grinding a slice of bread; add the bread to the ground meat.

4 **Adding flavorings.** Slice truffles thin; reserve 10 slices to top the sausages and chop the remaining slices coarse. Put the meat in a bowl with the chopped truffles and a little garlic. Add salt, spices, herbs and brandy. Use your hands to mix the ingredients together well.

5 **Moistening the mixture.** Add the reserved meat trimmings to the ground meat. Moisten the mixture with a few ladlefuls of the reduced poaching liquid, and thoroughly blend the ingredients.

7 **Broiling the sausages.** Brush the rack of a preheated broiler pan with oil and put the sausages on it. Place the pan under the broiler so that the sausages are about 3 inches [8 cm.] from the heat. After about 10 minutes, when one side is brown, turn the sausages, and cook them for 10 more minutes to brown the other side.

8 **Serving the sausages.** Reheat the reduced braising liquid and pour it into a warmed sauceboat. Transfer the sausages from the broiler-pan rack to a warm serving plate and garnish them, if you like, with watercress. Serve them with the braising liquid.

Forming Perfect Links

Natural sausage casings are easy to prepare *(box, below)* and fill with ground or chopped meat. Here, hog casing is packed with a blend of pork liver, hearts and cheeks to yield links with robust flavor.

The liver can go into the casing raw. But the hearts and cheeks must be parboiled so that when the sausages are assembled, all the meats will cook through in the same time. Including fatback will keep the filling moist and bread crumbs or rice will add body *(recipe, page 163)*.

The simplest way to fill casing is to use a food grinder and sausage-stuffing funnel as shown here. The casing is slipped onto the funnel and the filling fed in through the mouth of the grinder. Filling can also be pressed into casing through a pastry bag fitted with a plain tip, or casing can be gathered onto a sausage funnel and filling pushed in with a pestle.

After the sausages are poached to cook the meats and tenderize the casing, they are refrigerated overnight to firm them and intensify their flavor. They then can be broiled, grilled, baked or sautéed.

1 **Precooking the meats.** Trim pork hearts *(page 9)*. Put the hearts together with pork cheeks in a pot of cold water and bring to a boil. Boil for five minutes, drain and rinse the meats. Put them in fresh salted water, bring to a simmer and cook for one hour. Remove the meats from the pot and drain them on a towel.

2 **Slicing liver.** When the hearts and cheeks are cool enough to handle, cut them in chunks. Remove the membrane and blood vessels from pork liver *(page 8)*. Cut the liver into thick slices, then cut them into rough cubes.

Cleaning Casing

Preparing the casing. Soak sausage casing in tepid acidulated water until it becomes soft and elastic — about 30 minutes. To rinse the casing, fit a wide-mouthed funnel into one end and pour cold water through the casing, or attach the casing to a faucet and run cold water through it.

6 **Forming links.** When the casing is almost full, detach it from the funnel and knot the end. Twist a 5-inch [13-cm.] section through one complete turn to form a link. Twist sections in alternate directions to keep the links from unwinding. Tie two pieces of string around each twist. Cut between strings to divide the chain into sets of four.

7 **Poaching the sausages.** Prick the sausages and add them to a pan of simmering salted water. Cover and simmer for 30 minutes. Drain the sausages on a rack that is covered with a damp towel to prevent them from being marked. Wrap them in plastic and chill for eight to 12 hours.

3 **Grinding the meats.** Using a coarse disk, grind the parboiled meats and the raw liver, a handful at a time. To help force the meats through the grinder, push them down with your fingers held flat or use a wooden pestle.

4 **Adding rice.** Cook long-grain rice for 15 minutes in boiling water; drain the rice. Sauté finely chopped onion in fat until soft. Finely chop fatback. Put the onion, rice and fatback into a large bowl with the ground meats. Add salt, pepper, dried herbs and paprika. With your hands, mix all the ingredients together thoroughly.

5 **Filling the casing.** Soak and rinse hog casing; secure a sausage-stuffing funnel to a food grinder. Tie a knot about 3 inches [8 cm.] from one end of the casing and ease the other end onto the funnel. Gather the casing on the funnel, leaving a few inches free. Crank the grinder to press the sausage mixture into the casing.

8 **Sautéing the sausages.** Cut between the links to separate them; prick each one. Heat olive oil and butter in a sauté pan. Add the sausages and fry them over low to medium heat, using wooden spatulas (above) or tongs to turn them. When they are evenly browned, serve them with mashed potatoes or, as shown at right, blanched cabbage that has been sautéed in butter.

A Truffled Tongue Transformed into Sausage

When cooked in a casing, a whole tongue becomes meltingly tender and yields a smooth-textured sausage that is equally good eaten hot or cold. Veal, lamb, pork or beef tongue, as shown in this demonstration, all can be prepared this way, providing the diameter of the tongue is matched to that of the casing.

For extra succulence, the tongue can be larded with fatback and spiked with strips of truffle *(recipe, page 162)*. Ham could be used as a substitute for fatback; and brined green peppercorns or blanched, peeled and slivered pistachios or almonds could replace the truffles. Marinating the assembled sausage in spiced salt *(recipe, page 167)* both tenderizes and flavors it. The salt draws out the tongue's juices and mingles with them to form a brine that penetrates the meat.

The sausage can be poached in water or meat stock. Adding a calf's foot enriches the liquid and, once the sausage is done, provides a garnish for it.

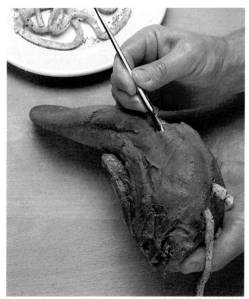

1 Larding the tongue. Parboil a tongue—in this case, fresh beef tongue—then cook and peel it *(page 12)*. Cut pork fatback into lardons ¼ inch [6 mm.] wide; toss them in spiced salt. With a larding needle, insert the lardons in the tongue, making stitches ½ inch [1 cm.] deep along its length.

2 Flavoring with truffles. Cut truffles into strips. Make incisions about ¾ inch [2 cm.] deep in the tongue and insert a piece of truffle in each cut. Distribute the pieces in even rows over the top and sides of the tongue.

6 Rinsing off excess salt. Remove the sausage from the dish and discard the marinade. Wash the sausage in a bowl of water or under cold running water, and rub it well with your fingers to remove any traces of the salt.

7 Cooking the sausage. Split a boned calf's foot *(page 11)* and blanch it for three minutes to remove scum. Drain and rinse the foot. Set a rack in a pan long enough to hold the sausage easily—here, a fish poacher—and put into the pan the sausage, foot, carrots and onions. Cover with meat stock and simmer with the lid ajar for five hours.

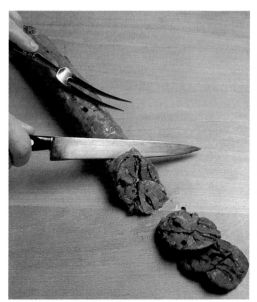

8 Slicing the sausage. Take the calf's foot out of the pan; remove the small bones and cut the meat into even-sized pieces. Put the pieces in a bowl with a little of the hot poaching liquid, and cover to keep them warm. Cut the sausage diagonally into slices ½ inch [1 cm.] thick. Keep the slices warm with the pieces of foot.

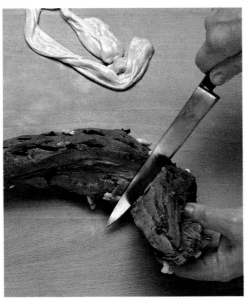

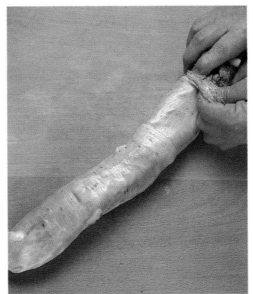

3 **Shaping the tongue.** Soak and clean beef casing *(box, page 11)*. To give the tongue an even shape, make a cut—parallel with the top surface— starting at the point where the tongue begins to thicken and stopping just short of the tongue's base. Bend the loose flap of tongue backward over the base.

4 **Encasing the tongue.** Tie a knot 3 inches [8 cm.] from an end of the casing. Insert both thumbs into the other end and use your fingers to gather the casing. Ease the tip of the tongue into the casing. Gradually release the casing, smoothing it over the tongue. Tie the open end of the casing with string.

5 **Salting.** With a trussing needle or skewer, prick the sausage all over and put it in a dish. Sprinkle it liberally with spiced salt, rubbing in the salt. Cover the dish and refrigerate the sausage for two to three days, turning it occasionally and spooning the briny juices over it.

9 **Serving the sausage.** Strain about 4 cups [1 liter] of the poaching liquid into a pan. With the pan half off the heat, simmer the liquid until it is reduced to half its original volume, skimming off any skin that forms. Parboil spinach, drain it and sauté it in butter. Put the spinach on a warmed platter with the foot and the sliced sausage. Serve the poaching liquid separately.

Filling and Casing from a Single Source

Chitterlings provide a delicious filling for sausages, while the last couple of yards from the wider end provide the casings. The chitterling filling may be either chopped or—for an interestingly firm texture—wound into coils to create the French dish known as *andouillettes*.

The chitterlings must be purchased whole to provide casings. In all likelihood, you will need to order them in advance from a specialty butcher. (If whole chitterlings are not obtainable, you can use presplit chitterlings—fresh or frozen—for the filling and enclose them in large sausage casings.) To clean the portion of whole chitterlings that will be used for the filling, first split them open and then soak them to dissipate their strong odor. After removing the excess fat, slice them lengthwise into thin strips to make them easier to coil.

Here, the chitterlings are tossed in a spiced salt mixture and marinated overnight in wine with aromatic vegetables and herbs *(recipe, page 161)*. After the chitterlings are wound into coils *(Step 5)*, strips of *persillade*-coated fatback are intertwined with them to add flavor and help keep them moist during cooking.

The chitterlings that will be used for casings are left intact; soaking is enough to clean them. Like the filling, the casings are seasoned with spiced salt and marinated before they are used.

Attaching a piece of string to each coil makes it possible to draw it easily into the casing *(Step 9),* and tucking in the flaps of excess casing encloses the filling securely *(page 84, Step 10)*. If you are using chopped chitterlings as a filling, it can be pressed into the casings through a sausage funnel and secured by knotting the casing at both ends.

The sausages must be poached for four hours to become tender. They can then be served immediately—hot or cold—or wrapped in plastic wrap and stored; they will keep in a refrigerator for up to one week or in a freezer for three months. To color and crisp them, grill, broil or sauté the sausages and serve them hot.

1 **Preparing the filling.** Set aside several yards of the wider end of each chitterling for the casing. Cut the remaining chitterlings into 3-foot [90-cm.] lengths and slit them open. Soak them for two hours in several changes of acidulated water; drain and pat them dry. Pull off fat and cut the chitterlings into strips 1 inch [2½ cm.] wide.

2 **Adding seasonings.** Soak the casing pieces in several changes of acidulated water for about one hour. Then turn them inside out and soak them for another hour. Put the filling and casing on separate trays and sprinkle with spiced salt *(recipe, page 167)*. Toss both sets of chitterlings to coat them thoroughly with the salt.

6 **Adding pork fat.** Cut thinly sliced pork fatback into strips about 12 inches [30 cm.] long and ¼ inch [6 mm.] wide. Prepare a *persillade (recipe, page 166)* and add finely chopped shallots. Toss the fatback in the *persillade* and put two or three strips on top of each chitterling loop, arranging them between the strands of chitterlings.

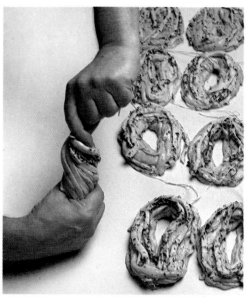

7 **Twisting the loops.** Thread a 10-inch [25-cm.] length of string through the center of each chitterling loop; leave the string untied at the top of each loop. Lift each loop by raising the string ends and, with your free hand, give the loop one complete turn.

3 **Marinating the chitterlings.** In a bowl, arrange alternate layers of the seasoned filling and sliced carrots and onions, dribbling a little olive oil over each layer. Add thyme sprigs, a bay leaf and a garlic clove. Pour white wine over the mixture, cover with plastic wrap and marinate overnight. Marinate the casing in the same way.

4 **Draining the filling.** Place the filling in a colander set over a bowl and let it drain for 15 minutes or so. With your fingers, lift the chitterlings onto a tray. Discard the bay leaf and thyme. Return the sliced vegetables to the marinade and reserve it.

5 **Winding into loops.** Form each strip of drained chitterling into a loop by holding one end between your thumb and forefinger and loosely winding the strand around your hand several times to make a loop about 6 inches [15 cm.] long. Lay the loops on a work surface.

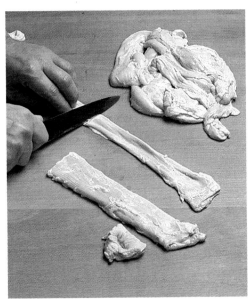

8 **Preparing the casing.** Drain the casing in a colander set over the bowl that contains the marinade from the filling. Discard the bay leaf and thyme, and return the vegetables to the marinade. Pat the casing dry. Trim off any thick, fatty ends. Cut the casing into lengths that are 4 inches [10 cm.] longer than the chitterling loops.

9 **Filling the casing.** Gather a piece of casing—fatty side out—over your forefinger and thumb (above, left) and, with the same finger and thumb, grasp the string attached to a chitterling loop (center). Holding the string and the bottom end of the casing, use your free hand to pull the casing over the loop, turning it right side out as you pull (right). Remove the string. ▶

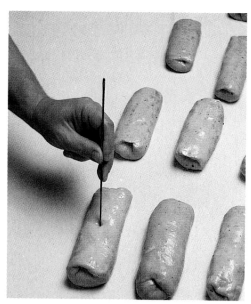

10 **Securing the filling.** Fold over the excess casing at one end of each sausage and use the handle of a teaspoon to tuck the flap between the filling and the inside of the casing. Repeat the process at the other end.

11 **Pricking the sausages.** Prick the casing of each sausage in several places with a trussing needle, as here, or with a skewer so that steam can escape and the sausages will not split open while they are cooking. Then turn the sausages over and prick the undersides.

12 **Poaching.** Put the sausages in a pan that will hold them in one layer. Add the reserved marinade and vegetables and a bouquet garni. Add enough veal stock (page 16) to submerge the sausages. Cover them with parchment paper and set a lid on the pan. Poach over low heat until tender—about four hours.

13 **Cooling.** Transfer the sausages from the pan to a deep dish. Strain the poaching liquid and pour it over them. Discard the vegetables. Cover the sausages with parchment paper and refrigerate them overnight. The next day, peel off the paper, lift out the sausages and pat them dry.

14 **Scoring the sausages.** Rub the sausages with oil. Make three or four shallow cuts across the top and underside of each sausage. Cook the sausages over an open grill or under a broiler until golden brown— about 10 minutes; turn them over and brown the other side.

15 **Serving the sausages.** Transfer the sausages to warmed plates and serve them at once. Here, they are accompanied by mustard and a purée of potatoes and rutabagas that has been flavored with onions and garlic and enriched with butter.

Anthology
of Recipes

Drawing upon the cooking literature of more than 20 countries, the editors and consultants for this volume have selected 204 recipes for the Anthology that follows. These selections comprise simple dishes such as liver and onions as well as elegant ones—for example, sliced sweetbreads and ham sandwiched around spinach purée, coated with Madeira sauce and baked in paper cases.

Many of the recipes were written by world-renowned exponents of the culinary art, but the Anthology also includes selections from rare and out-of-print books and from works that have never been published in English. Whatever the sources, the emphasis is on fresh ingredients that blend harmoniously and on techniques that are practical for home cooks.

Since many early recipe writers did not specify amounts of ingredients, sizes of pans or even cooking times and temperatures, the missing information has been judiciously added. In some cases, clarifying introductory notes have also been supplied; they are printed in italics. Modern recipe terms have been substituted for archaic language and some instructions have been expanded; but to preserve the character of the original recipes and to create a true anthology, the authors' texts have been changed as little as possible.

For ease of use, the Anthology is organized chiefly according to types of meat with sausage recipes grouped separately. All of the mixed variety meat recipes call for more than one meat type. However, a recipe that includes a calf's or pig's foot merely to enrich the cooking liquid—as some tripe braises do—appears in the category in which the main ingredient belongs. Standard preparations—stock, sauces and court bouillons among them—appear at the end of the Anthology. Uncommon ingredients are explained in the combined General Index and Glossary.

Apart from the primary components, all ingredients are listed within each recipe in order of use, with the customary U.S. measurements and the metric measurements provided in separate columns. All quantities reflect the American practice of measuring such solid ingredients as flour by volume rather than by weight, as is done in Europe.

To make the quantities simpler to measure, many of the figures have been rounded off to correspond to the gradations on U.S. metric spoons and cups. (One cup, for example, equals 237 milliliters; however, wherever practicable in these recipes, the metric equivalent of 1 cup appears as a more readily measured 250 milliliters—¼ liter.) Similarly, the weight, temperature and linear metric equivalents have been rounded off slightly. Thus the American and metric figures do not exactly match, but using one set or the other will produce the same good results.

Liver, Kidney, Heart and Spleen

Liver Dumplings as Rothschild Ate Them

Leberklösse wie sie Rothschild Ass

The consistency of the dumpling mixture can be tested by dropping one dumpling into the pan of boiling water. If the dumpling disintegrates during cooking, stir another tablespoon [15 ml.] of flour into the mixture. If the interior appears to be too dry when the dumpling is cooked and sliced open, stir in a tablespoon of melted butter.

To serve 4

1 lb.	veal liver, membrane removed, finely chopped	½ kg.
6 oz.	suet, chopped	175 g.
10	hard rolls, crusts removed, soaked in milk and squeezed dry	10
4 or 5	eggs	4 or 5
3 tbsp.	flour	45 ml.
	salt and pepper	
	freshly grated nutmeg	
	dried marjoram	
7 tbsp.	butter	105 ml.
¾ cup	dry bread crumbs or chopped onion	175 ml.

In a mixing bowl, mix the chopped liver, suet, squeezed rolls, eggs and flour. Season with salt and pepper and a large pinch each of grated nutmeg and dried marjoram. Refrigerate the mixture for at least one hour.

Bring a large pan of salted water to a boil. Use a soup spoon to shape the mixture into small balls. Drop a few of the dumplings into the pan and cook them, uncovered, for 15 minutes from the time they rise to the surface. Remove them with a skimmer and keep them warm on a serving dish while you poach the remaining dumplings in small batches.

In a frying pan, melt the butter and lightly brown the bread crumbs or onions over high heat. Then sprinkle them over the dumplings.

FRED METZLER AND KLAUS OSTER
KOCHBUCH AAL BLAU UND ERRÖTHETES MÄDCHEN

Liver with Sage

Fegato alla Salvia

Another way to flavor the liver with garlic and sage is demonstrated on pages 22-23.

To serve 4

1½ lb.	veal liver, membrane removed, cut into 8 slices	¾ kg.
	flour	
	salt	
⅓ cup	vegetable oil	75 ml.
2	garlic cloves, crushed	2
8	fresh sage leaves	8

Dip the slices of veal liver in the flour, brush off the excess flour and season each slice with a pinch of salt. Heat the oil in a large skillet and add the garlic and sage leaves. Place the slices of liver on top and fry them for only a few minutes on each side so that they are still rare when served.

GIOVANNI RIGHI PARENTI
LA GRANDE CUCINA TOSCANA

Masala Liver

To serve 3

½ lb.	veal liver, membrane removed, thinly sliced	¼ kg.
2 tbsp.	vegetable oil or *ghee*	30 ml.
2	onions, 1 thinly sliced, 1 chopped	2
4	garlic cloves	4
½-inch	piece fresh ginger, peeled and chopped	1-cm.
½ tsp.	cumin seeds	2 ml.
2	fresh green hot chilies, stemmed, seeded and chopped	2
3 tbsp.	coarsely chopped fresh coriander	45 ml.
⅓ cup	water	75 ml.
¾ tsp.	salt	4 ml.

Heat the oil or *ghee* over low heat and in it fry the sliced onion until it is brown—about 15 minutes.

In a large mortar, pound the garlic, ginger, cumin seeds, chopped onion, green chilies and coriander to make a *masala* paste. Add the paste and 2 tablespoons [30 ml.] of the water to the fried onion and cook for five minutes. Add the liver slices and cook, stirring frequently, for two minutes. Add the remaining water and the salt and cook until the liver is firm—about five minutes.

JEROO MEHTA
101 PARSI RECIPES

Liver Baked in Wine

Gebratene Leber in Wein

To serve 4

1 lb.	veal liver, membrane removed	½ kg.
	salt and pepper	
1 oz.	pork fat, cut into lardons	30 g.
2	onions, chopped	2
1 cup	finely chopped, mixed root vegetables: carrot, turnip, rutabaga, kohlrabi	¼ liter
½ cup	dry white wine	125 ml.
4 tbsp.	butter, melted	60 ml.
½ cup	heavy cream	125 ml.
3 tbsp.	flour	45 ml.

Salt and pepper the lardons. Cut slits in the liver and insert the lardons. Simmer the onions and root vegetables in the wine for 15 minutes. Pour the melted butter into a casserole and add the liver. Strain the wine and pour it over the liver. Cover the casserole and bake the liver in a preheated 350° F. [180° C.] oven, basting it every 10 minutes, until it is firm—25 to 30 minutes.

Remove the liver from the casserole and keep it warm. Mix the cream and flour, stir them into the cooking juices and simmer the mixture for five minutes. Strain this sauce over the liver and serve it at once with rice or dumplings.

JOZA BŘÍZOVÁ AND MARYNA KLIMENTOVÁ
TSCHECHISCHE KÜCHE

—◆—

Liver Julienne

To serve 4

1 lb.	veal liver, membrane removed, thinly sliced and cut into short strips about ½ inch [1 cm.] wide	½ kg.
¼ cup	flour, seasoned with salt, pepper and 2 tsp. [10 ml.] paprika	50 ml.
2 tbsp.	olive oil	30 ml.
2 tbsp.	butter	30 ml.
1	garlic clove, chopped	1
½ cup	dry white wine	125 ml.
2 tbsp.	chopped fresh parsley	30 ml.
¾ cup	sour cream	175 ml.
	salt and pepper	

Dredge the liver strips with the seasoned flour. Heat the olive oil and butter in a large skillet. Sauté the garlic over high heat and add the liver strips. Cook very quickly, turn-ing them with a spatula so that all the strips become uniformly browned. This should take about two minutes.

Remove the liver to a hot platter and add the white wine and parsley to the pan. Shake the pan well so that the wine rinses the pan thoroughly. Add the sour cream, stir into the pan juices and heat thoroughly. Do not let the sauce boil. Taste the mixture and rectify the seasoning.

Remove the pan from the heat, return the liver strips to the pan and mix them well with the sauce. Serve with buttered noodles or boiled rice.

JAMES A. BEARD
THE FIRESIDE COOK BOOK

Braised Liver

Gedämpfte Leber

To serve 6 to 8

one 4 lb.	veal liver, membrane removed	one 2 kg.
½ lb.	pork fat, cut into lardons	¼ kg.
1 tsp. each	pepper, salt and ground allspice	5 ml. each
4 tbsp.	butter	60 ml.
about 2 cups	boiling water	about ½ liter
2	onions, finely chopped	2
2	bay leaves	2
1 cup	fresh bread crumbs	¼ liter
1 tbsp.	cooked puréed pear, applesauce or sugar	15 ml.
2 tbsp.	vinegar	30 ml.
½ cup	red wine (optional)	125 ml.

Sprinkle the lardons with the pepper, half of the salt and half of the allspice. With a sharp knife, make cuts in the liver and press the lardons into them. Melt 3 tablespoons [45 ml.] of the butter in a pan, add the liver, cover the pan and cook over low heat for 15 minutes. Then pour in enough boiling water to half-cover the liver. Add the onions, bay leaves, the rest of the salt and allspice, and the remaining butter. Cover and cook over low heat until firm to the touch but pink inside—about 12 minutes. Add the bread crumbs with the puréed pear, applesauce or sugar, the vinegar and the wine, if using. Simmer for three more minutes. The sauce should be thick and plentiful. Serve with boiled potatoes.

HENRIETTE DAVIDIS
PRAKTISCHES KOCHBUCH

Marinated Liver
Foie M'chermel en Sauce

To pickle lemons, first quarter each of them, cutting down to but not through the base. Open the quarters, cover them with a layer of coarse salt and close them up to return each lemon to its original shape. Place a handful of coarse salt in the bottom of a canning jar. Pack in the lemons and press them down to release their juice. Cover them with another handful of salt, a few coriander seeds, some peppercorns and a bay leaf. If the juice does not cover the lemons, add lemon juice. Seal the jar and let it stand for at least one month, inverting it occasionally. Before using a lemon, rinse it; discard the pulp if you wish.

	To serve 4	
1½ lb.	veal liver, membrane removed, thinly sliced	¾ kg.
	flour	
about 1 cup	vegetable oil	about ¼ liter
2 tbsp.	fresh lemon juice	30 ml.
1½ cups	water	375 ml.
12	green olives, pitted	12
1	pickled lemon, cut into pieces	1
	Spiced marinade	
1 cup	fresh coriander leaves	¼ liter
	salt	
2 tbsp.	paprika	30 ml.
2 tsp.	cumin seeds	10 ml.
3 tbsp.	white wine vinegar	45 ml.
1 cup	water	¼ liter

To make the marinade, pound the coriander and salt to a paste in a mortar. Add the paprika, cumin seeds, vinegar and water. In a shallow dish, combine the liver with the marinade, turning the slices to coat them evenly. Cover and marinate the liver in the refrigerator for four or five hours.

Drain and dry the liver, reserving the marinade. Lightly coat the liver with the flour. Heat about half of the oil in a skillet over high heat and fry the liver, a few slices at a time, until it is browned on both sides—about five minutes. Add more of the oil to the pan as necessary. Dice the liver and set it aside. Strain the oil remaining in the skillet.

Pour the marinade into a saucepan. Add the strained oil, the lemon juice and water. Bring the liquid to a boil, then add the olives, pickled lemon and diced liver. Let the mixture simmer for two to three minutes.

Pour the contents of the pan into a warmed serving dish. Remove the pickled lemon and olives from the mixture and use them to decorate the dish.

AHMED LAASRI
240 RECETTES DE LA CUISINE MAROCAINE

Aunt Lilja's Liver Pancakes
Maksaplättyjä

Serve the pancakes with a tart cranberry sauce or currant jelly and melted butter to pour over them.

	To serve 4	
1 lb.	veal liver with the membrane removed, coarsely ground or finely chopped	½ kg.
½ cup	fresh bread crumbs	125 ml.
¼ cup	heavy cream	50 ml.
1	egg, lightly beaten	1
1	medium-sized onion, finely chopped	1
1 tsp.	salt	5 ml.
¼ tsp.	pepper	1 ml.
2 tbsp.	butter	30 ml.

Combine the liver with the bread crumbs, cream, beaten egg, onion, salt and pepper; beat well. Heat the butter in a frying pan, and spoon the liver mixture into the pan—using about 2 tablespoonfuls [30 ml.] for each pancake. Brown the pancakes for two minutes on each side. Repeat with the remaining mixture until it is used up. Serve the pancakes hot.

BEATRICE A. OJAKANGAS
THE FINNISH COOKBOOK

Liver and Onions
Fegato alla Veneziana

Any leftovers from this dish can be ground, mixed with an equal weight of butter, wrapped in wax paper and refrigerated to make a perfect pâté.

	To serve 4	
14 oz.	veal liver, membrane removed, thinly sliced	400 g.
5 tbsp.	olive oil	75 ml.
2 tbsp.	butter	30 ml.
4	medium-sized onions, thinly sliced	4
	salt and pepper	
2 tbsp.	chopped fresh parsley (optional)	30 ml.

Heat the oil and butter together and gently fry the onions until they are transparent—about 30 minutes. Season them with salt and pepper. A few minutes before serving, add the liver and cook it over high heat. Season it with a little salt, sprinkle it with the parsley, if using, and serve at once.

STELLA DONATI
LA GRANDE CUCINA RÉGIONALE

Veal Liver with Bacon, Onions and Apples

Kalfslever met Bacon, Ui en Appel

To serve 4

four 3½ oz.	slices veal liver, membrane removed	four 100 g.
2 tbsp.	butter	30 ml.
8	slices bacon	8
	salt and pepper	
2 tbsp.	Calvados (optional)	30 ml.
2	large onions, sliced and separated into rings	2
4	small cooking apples, cored, peeled and cut into slices ½ inch [1 cm.] thick	4

Heat half of the butter in a skillet and fry the bacon over medium heat until it is crisp and pale brown. Remove the bacon from the pan and drain it on paper towels. Season the liver slices with salt and pepper, and fry them in the bacon fat for a few minutes on each side—five to seven minutes in all. Transfer them to a warmed platter and sprinkle them with the Calvados, if using. Cover the platter loosely with foil to keep the liver slices hot.

Add the remaining butter to the skillet and fry the onion rings and apple slices over medium heat until the onions are transparent and lightly browned—about 10 minutes. Spoon the onion-and-apple mixture over the liver and garnish it with the bacon.

BERTHE MEIJER
NRC HANDELSBLAD MENUBOEK

Braised Liver with Sour Cream

To serve 4

1 lb.	sliced veal or lamb liver, membrane removed, cut into thin strips	½ kg.
½ cup	flour, seasoned with salt and pepper	125 ml.
2 tbsp.	butter	30 ml.
1	onion, chopped	1
1	garlic clove, crushed to a paste	1
1 cup	meat stock (recipe, page 165)	¼ liter
½ cup	milk	125 ml.
½ cup	sour cream	125 ml.
	salt and pepper	

Roll the liver strips in the seasoned flour. In a skillet, melt the butter over medium heat and sauté the onion until it is soft but not brown. Add the liver strips and sauté them over medium-high heat to brown all sides. Add the garlic. Stir in the stock, milk and sour cream, and correct the seasoning. Cover the skillet and cook gently for half an hour.

BERYL GOULD-MARKS
EATING THE RUSSIAN WAY

Liver Wrapped in Caul

Geklöpfte Leber im Netz Gebraten

To serve 8 to 12

4 lb.	veal liver, membrane removed, chopped and puréed in a processor	2 kg.
5	slices bacon, finely chopped	5
⅔ cup	dried currants	150 ml.
6	eggs, the yolks separated from the whites, the whites stiffly beaten	6
⅓ cup	dry bread crumbs	75 ml.
½ tsp.	ground allspice	2 ml.
	salt and pepper	
¼ lb.	caul, soaked and drained	125 g.
3 tbsp.	butter	45 ml.
Red wine sauce		
½ cup	red wine	125 ml.
2 tbsp.	butter	30 ml.
1 tbsp.	flour	15 ml.
1	onion, finely chopped	1
½ cup	meat stock (recipe, page 165)	125 ml.
	grated nutmeg and ground allspice	
	salt and pepper	
1 tsp.	sugar (optional)	5 ml.
4	thin lemon slices, halved	4

Mix the liver with the bacon, currants, egg yolks and bread crumbs. Season with the allspice, salt and pepper, then gently fold in the egg whites. Spread out the caul, mound the liver mixture in the center and wrap the caul around it.

Melt the butter in a saucepan and put in the liver package, folds downward. Cook over low heat for 15 minutes. Then turn the package over and cook it until the juices run clear when a skewer is inserted deeply—about 30 minutes.

For the sauce, melt the butter and add the flour and chopped onion. When the onion is lightly browned, season the stock with a pinch each of nutmeg and allspice, salt, pepper and the sugar, if using. Add the stock with the wine and lemon. Simmer the sauce gently for 15 minutes, or until thickened slightly. To serve, pour the sauce over the liver.

HENRIETTE DAVIDIS
PRAKTISCHES KOCHBUCH

Stewed Liver with Almond Sauce

Higado à la Asturiana

To serve 4

2 lb.	veal or lamb liver with the membrane removed, cut into small pieces	1 kg.
4 tbsp.	butter	60 ml.
2 oz.	lean salt pork with the rind removed, coarsely chopped	60 g.
4	onions, finely chopped	4
4	tomatoes, peeled, seeded and chopped	4
1 cup	dry white wine	¼ liter
	salt and pepper	
12	almonds, blanched, peeled and chopped	12
1	garlic clove, chopped	1
1 cup	water	¼ liter

In a large skillet melt the butter over low heat, then add the salt pork and fry it until lightly browned. Add the liver and chopped onions. Cook them for two to three minutes, then add the tomatoes and wine. Season with salt and pepper, cover the skillet and stew the contents for 30 minutes.

Pound the almonds and garlic to a paste in a mortar, gradually adding the water. Add the mixture to the stew and cook it for 30 minutes. To serve, pour the stew into a warmed serving dish and garnish it with triangles of toasted bread.

ELIZABETH CASS
SPANISH COOKING

Bacon-wrapped Liver Rolls

To serve 4

½ lb.	veal liver, membrane removed	¼ kg.
8	bacon slices	8
	salt and freshly ground black pepper	
2 tbsp.	fresh lemon juice	30 ml.
	fresh marjoram or thyme	
2 tbsp.	butter	30 ml.
2 tsp.	flour	10 ml.
⅓ cup	port or Marsala	75 ml.
4	tomatoes, peeled, seeded and finely chopped, or ½ cup [125 ml.] tomato sauce *(recipe, page 166)*	4
1 cup	chicken or meat stock *(recipe, page 165)*	¼ liter

Cut the liver into very thin slices, a little smaller than the bacon slices. On each bacon slice lay a slice of liver, season with a very little salt, ground black pepper and lemon juice; add three or four leaves of marjoram or thyme. Roll up the liver in the bacon and secure the rolls with little skewers.

Heat the butter, sauté the rolls in it, and sprinkle them sparingly with the flour; stir and add the port or Marsala; let it bubble, then add the tomatoes or tomato sauce, then the stock. Cover the pan and cook over low heat for about 10 minutes. Remove the skewers and serve the rolls at once.

ELIZABETH DAVID
SUMMER COOKING

Beef Liver, Venetian-Style

To serve 4

1 lb.	sliced beef or veal liver, membrane removed, cut into short strips ¼ inch [6 mm.] wide	½ kg.
4 tbsp.	butter	60 ml.
2 tbsp.	vegetable oil	30 ml.
2	medium-sized onions, thinly sliced	2
¼ tsp.	rubbed sage	1 ml.
	salt and pepper	
½ cup	flour	125 ml.
3 tbsp.	fresh lemon juice	45 ml.
1 cup	dry white wine	¼ liter
2 tbsp.	chopped fresh parsley	30 ml.

Heat one half of the butter and oil in a heavy skillet and add the onions. Sprinkle on the sage, stir, cover and simmer very slowly for 10 to 15 minutes, or until the onions begin turning golden. Scrape the onions out of the skillet into a small bowl.

Put the strips of liver on a plate, sprinkle them with salt, pepper and flour, and toss them with both hands until all of the strips are coated with flour. Shake off the excess flour.

Using the same skillet, heat the remaining butter and oil until very hot. Add the liver strips to the skillet. Keep the heat high while turning the meat to sear it all over—a minute or two. Scrape in the cooked onions, add the lemon juice and wine, cover and simmer for two minutes. Taste for salt and pepper and correct if necessary. Add the parsley and mix. Spoon the liver and onions into the center of a warm platter. Make a border of neat mounds of mashed potatoes or a ring of noodles. Serve at once.

CAROL CUTLER
THE SIX-MINUTE SOUFFLÉ AND OTHER CULINARY DELIGHTS

Liver and Oatmeal Pudding

The oatmeal called for in this recipe is ground oat kernels—not the familiar rolled oats. Oatmeal is obtainable at health-food stores. To ensure that the pudding cooks through evenly, the wrapped pudding basin should be set on a trivet or rack in a pot containing enough boiling water to reach at least three quarters of the way up the sides of the basin—and the water should be kept at this level throughout the cooking time.

	To serve 4	
½ lb.	pork or lamb liver, membrane removed	¼ kg.
¼ lb.	suet, finely chopped	125 g.
2	onions, sliced	2
1⅓ cups	medium oatmeal	325 ml.
	salt and pepper	
about ¾ cup	meat stock (recipe, page 165)	about 175 ml.

Melt the suet and fry the liver in it until it is lightly browned—about seven minutes. Remove the liver from the pan and chop it fine. Put the onions into the pan, fry them until they are soft—about 10 minutes—and remove them from the pan. Fry the oatmeal in the pan for four minutes, or until it is golden, stirring it to prevent burning.

Mix the liver, onions and oatmeal together, and season with salt and pepper. Add enough of the stock to give a firm but moist texture. Butter a 5-cup [1¼-liter] pudding basin and put the pudding into it. Cover the pudding with parchment paper or foil tied on securely, and steam it in a pan of simmering water for two hours. Serve the pudding with a variety of vegetables and good gravy.

JOAN POULSON
OLD THAMES VALLEY RECIPES

———— ❦ ————

Stuffed Roast Liver

Foie de Veau Farci

	To serve 4	
1 lb.	pork or veal liver, in 1 piece, membrane removed	½ kg.
2	eggs, hard-boiled	2
¾ cup	fresh bread crumbs, soaked in 2 to 3 tbsp. [30 to 45 ml.] meat stock (recipe, page 165)	175 ml.
1 tbsp.	chopped fresh parsley	15 ml.
1	garlic clove, finely chopped	1
	salt and pepper	
¼ lb.	caul, soaked and drained	125 g.

Mash the eggs with the soaked bread crumbs and mix with the parsley, garlic, and salt and pepper to make a stuffing.

In the liver, make deep cuts close together and pack them with the stuffing. Wrap the liver in a piece of caul large

enough to enclose it and set it in an oiled gratin dish. Bake in a preheated 550° F. [275° C.] oven for five minutes. Reduce the heat to 300° F. [150° C.] and cook for another 15 minutes. Remove the dish from the oven and let the liver rest in a warm place for 15 minutes before slicing and serving it.

GOMBERVAUX (EDITOR)
LA BONNE CUISINE POUR TOUS

Baked Pork Liver with Truffles

Gratin de Foie aux Truffes de Périgord

The author recommends serving the dish with a Madeira-flavored sauce. A simple way to make such a sauce is to stir ¼ cup [50 ml.] of Madeira into 2 cups [½ liter] of velouté sauce (recipe, page 166).

	To serve 4	
1 lb.	pork liver, membrane removed, cut into small pieces	½ kg.
3	onions, chopped and crushed	3
2	garlic cloves, chopped and crushed	2
10	slices bacon, finely chopped	10
4	slices firm-textured white bread with the crusts removed, soaked in milk and squeezed	4
	salt and pepper	
¼ tsp.	grated nutmeg or *quatre épices*	1 ml.
1 tsp.	dried thyme	5 ml.
1	bay leaf, crumbled	1
3	eggs, beaten	3
2 oz.	truffle peelings (about ½ cup [125 ml.])	60 g.
4 tbsp.	butter, cut into small pieces	60 ml.

In a skillet, fry the onion and garlic with the bacon over medium heat for five minutes. Add the liver and brown it lightly. Remove the skillet from the heat. Stir the squeezed bread into the mixture in the skillet and season it with salt and pepper, the nutmeg or *quatre épices*, thyme and bay leaf. Mix well, taste for seasoning and add the eggs and truffle peelings. Turn the mixture into a well-buttered gratin dish, sprinkle the butter pieces over the top and bake in a preheated 300° F. [150° C.] oven for at least 45 minutes, or until the mixture has set to a custard consistency.

ODETTE REIGE
LES GRATINS

Homemade Liver Faggots

Faggots are savory meat cakes whose cylindrical shape resembles a bundle of sticks—once known in Great Britain as a faggot. To keep them moist, the faggots can be wrapped in pieces of caul before baking.

To serve 4

½ lb.	pork liver, membrane removed, ground	¼ kg.
6 oz.	pork belly, ground	175 g.
1	medium-sized onion, finely chopped	1
2	sprigs thyme, finely chopped	2
2	sprigs parsley, finely chopped	2
1 cup	fresh bread crumbs	¼ liter
1	egg, beaten	1
	salt and pepper	

Mix the liver, pork belly and onion in a bowl. Add the thyme, parsley, bread crumbs, egg, and salt and pepper to taste.

Butter a small, shallow ovenproof dish. Shape the mixture into four equal-sized, cylindrical cakes, or faggots. Put each faggot against the edge of the dish; do not let them touch one another. Cover the dish with buttered parchment paper or foil and bake the faggots in a preheated 375° F. [190° C.] oven for one hour. Remove the paper or foil and bake the faggots for a further 15 minutes to brown them.

WHAT'S COOKING IN DORSET

Faggots

To serve 4

1½ lb.	pork liver, membrane removed	¾ kg.
3	onions, sliced	3
¼ lb.	fresh pork fat, cut into small pieces	125 g.
	salt and pepper	
1 tsp.	chopped fresh sage leaves	5 ml.
½ lb.	caul, soaked, drained and cut into eight 6-inch [15-cm.] squares	¼ kg.

Blanch the liver in boiling water for a few minutes and then slice it. Grind the liver, onions and pork fat through the coarse disk of a food grinder and put them into a large bowl. Mix the ingredients well and season them with salt, pepper and the sage. Divide the mixture into eight portions and shape them into cylindrical cakes, or faggots. Wrap a square of caul around each faggot. Place the faggots in rows in a buttered roasting pan, making sure that they do not touch one another. Bake the faggots in a preheated 350° F. [180° C.] oven for one hour, or until they are firm and browned.

S. MINWEL TIBBOTT
WELSH FARE

Pork Liver, Florentine-Style

Fegatelli alla Fiorentina

To serve 6

1½ lb.	pork liver, membrane removed, cut into 12 pieces	750 g.
¾ cup	fresh bread crumbs	175 ml.
3 tbsp.	fennel seeds	45 ml.
	salt and freshly ground pepper	
½ lb.	caul, soaked, drained and cut into twelve 6-inch [15-cm.] squares	¼ kg.
6	bay leaves, cut into halves	6
⅓ cup	olive oil	75 ml.
½ cup	red wine	125 ml.

Combine the bread crumbs, fennel seeds, salt and pepper in a large bowl and mix them well with a wooden spoon. Add the pieces of liver and coat them with the bread-crumb mixture. Spread out the caul on a board. Then place each piece of liver on top of a square of caul. Place half a bay leaf on each piece of liver and enclose the liver in the caul. Fasten the top folds of the caul to the liver with a wooden pick.

In a large skillet, heat the olive oil over medium heat and add all of the caul-wrapped liver pieces. Fry them gently for 10 minutes, turning them once or twice, then sprinkle them with salt and pepper. Add the wine, cover the skillet and simmer for 20 minutes, turning the pieces after 10 minutes.

Transfer the liver pieces to a warmed platter, sprinkle them with one or two spoonfuls of the cooking liquid and serve them immediately.

GIULIANO BUGIALLI
THE FINE ART OF ITALIAN COOKING

Liver and Spinach Gratin

Gratin de Foie

To serve 6

2 lb.	chicken or game-bird livers, trimmed, chopped and pounded to a paste	1 kg.
2 lb.	spinach, stems removed, blanched in salted water for 1 minute, drained, squeezed dry and chopped	1 kg.
1 cup	milk	¼ liter
⅔ cup	freshly grated Parmesan cheese	150 ml.

Mix the livers and spinach together; moisten with the milk. Pour the mixture into a large buttered gratin dish. Sprinkle with the grated cheese. Bake in a preheated 350° F. [180° C.] oven for 45 minutes, or until the cheese is melted and golden and the liver mixture is firm.

LA CUISINE LYONNAISE

Duck Liver with Grapes

Foie de Canard aux Raisins

Chicken livers can be substituted very well. They won't give off much fat, but will stiffen and, when done, the liquid should be poured off. Chicken livers need not be sliced; they are already small enough so just dab the Armagnac on them.

This dish does not suffer from having the grapes unpeeled. However, they do have to be seeded, unless you use seedless grapes.

To serve 5 or 6		
1¼ to 1½ lb.	duck livers, trimmed	⅔ to ¾ kg.
	salt and pepper	
1 cup	grapes, any kind, peeled and seeded	¼ liter
½ cup	Armagnac	125 ml.

Put the livers into an earthenware casserole or a small iron one. Add salt and pepper. Over very low heat, cook the livers until they "sweat," that is until they become stiffened and heated through and give off their fat. This should take about 20 minutes. Meanwhile, put the grapes into a small saucepan and heat them gently.

Pour the rendered fat off the livers and cut the livers into slices about ½ inch [1 cm.] thick. Dab both faces of each piece with Armagnac. Return the livers to the casserole with the heated grapes and cook until everything is just reheated through. Serve on hot plates with slices of toast.

MADELEINE PETER (EDITOR)
FAVORITE RECIPES OF THE GREAT WOMEN CHEFS OF FRANCE

Goose Liver with Apples

Gänseleber mit Äpfeln

If goose livers are not obtainable, eight duck livers or 1 pound [½ kg.] of chicken livers may be substituted. In that case, use an extra 2 tablespoons [30 ml.] of butter to sauté the liver.

To serve 4		
four ¼ lb.	goose livers, trimmed	four 125 g.
1 tbsp.	butter	15 ml.
2	cooking apples, cored, peeled and cut into rings ½ inch [1 cm.] thick	2
2 tsp.	superfine sugar	10 ml.
2 tbsp.	fresh lemon juice (optional)	30 ml.

Melt the butter and in it sauté the goose livers until lightly browned. Drain the butter, which will now be mixed with fat from the livers, into a small baking dish. Add the apple rings. Lay the livers on top of the apple rings and sprinkle them with the sugar and the lemon juice, if using. Cover the dish and set it in a pan partly filled with hot water. Bake the livers in a preheated 350° F. [180° C.] oven for 30 minutes, or until firm. To serve, spoon the hot liver and apple over slices of hot white bread.

DOROTHEE V. HELLERMANN
DAS KOCHBUCH AUS HAMBURG

Chicken Livers with Cucumbers

Les Foies de Volaille aux Concombres

The original version of this recipe calls for the pale-colored livers from chickens raised in the Bresse region of France. Ordinary chicken livers, soaked in milk, are a suitable substitute. A few pieces of butter can be stirred into the livers and cucumbers before serving to enrich the sauce.

To serve 4		
½ lb.	chicken livers, trimmed, cut into halves, soaked in milk for 2 to 3 hours and drained	¼ kg.
2 tbsp.	butter	30 ml.
2	cucumbers, peeled, sliced, parboiled in salted water for 1 minute, drained and patted dry	2
3 tbsp.	clarified butter	45 ml.
3	shallots, finely chopped	3
	salt and pepper	
¼ cup	Armagnac	50 ml.
1 tbsp.	chopped fresh chervil	15 ml.
1 tbsp.	chopped fresh parsley	15 ml.

In a skillet, melt the butter and sauté the cucumber slices until they are translucent—about two minutes on each side. Remove them from the pan and keep them warm.

In a clean skillet, melt the clarified butter over high heat but do not let it darken. Add the chicken livers and shallots. Sprinkle them with salt and pepper, and sauté, stirring constantly to prevent sticking, for about three minutes on one side, or until the livers are lightly browned; then turn them over. Add the Armagnac and set it aflame. When the flame has died down, add a few of the cucumbers to the skillet and cook for a further two minutes.

Arrange the livers on a serving platter and cover them with the cucumber slices. Sprinkle the cucumber with the chervil and parsley.

RAYMOND THUILIER AND MICHEL LEMONNIER
LES RECETTES DE BAUMANIÈRE

Curried Chicken Livers

Foies de Poulet au Curry

To serve 4

14 oz.	chicken livers, trimmed, or a mixture of chicken livers, trimmed, and chicken hearts, trimmed and cut into halves	400 g.
1 tbsp.	cornstarch	15 ml.
1 tsp.	brown sugar	5 ml.
1 tsp.	curry powder	5 ml.
1 cup	meat stock *(recipe, page 165)*	¼ liter
2 cups	vegetable oil	½ liter
1	medium-sized onion, sliced	1
1 cup	sliced fresh mushrooms	¼ liter
2-inch	piece ginger root, peeled, finely chopped and lightly crushed (optional)	5-cm.
2	garlic cloves, lightly crushed and finely chopped	2
Soy sauce and sherry marinade		
2 tbsp.	soy sauce	30 ml.
2 tbsp.	dry sherry or dry white wine	30 ml.
1 tbsp.	cornstarch	15 ml.
1 tbsp.	vegetable oil	15 ml.

Mix the marinade ingredients in a bowl and add the livers, or livers and hearts. In another bowl, dissolve the cornstarch, brown sugar and curry powder in the stock and set the mixture aside.

Marinate the livers, or hearts and livers, for 20 minutes. Then drain them and pat them dry. In a deep fryer, heat all except 1 tablespoon [15 ml.] of the oil until it reaches 320° F. [160° C.] on a deep-frying thermometer. Deep fry the livers, or livers and hearts, for two to three minutes. Remove them with a skimmer and drain them on paper towels. Arrange them on a serving dish and keep them warm.

Heat the remaining tablespoon of oil in a skillet. Add the onion, mushrooms, ginger, if using, and the garlic. Stirring constantly, sauté the vegetables for two minutes. Add the flavored stock and slightly reduce the heat. Cook for a few minutes, stirring gently. When this sauce thickens, pour it over the livers, or livers and hearts, and serve immediately.

NGUYEN NGOC RAO
LA CUISINE CHINOISE À L'USAGE DES FRANÇAIS

Sautéed Chicken Livers

Foies de Volaille Sautés

To serve 2

½ lb.	chicken livers, trimmed and cut into halves	¼ kg.
	salt and pepper	
	flour	
2 tbsp.	butter, melted	30 ml.
3 oz.	ham, cut into julienne (about 1 cup [¼ liter])	90 g.
⅓ cup	port, Madeira or Marsala	75 ml.
¾ cup	chicken or veal stock *(recipe, page 165)*	175 ml.
2 tbsp.	chopped fresh parsley	30 ml.

Season the chicken livers and dust them with the flour. In the melted butter, sauté the ham for one minute. Add the livers. After two minutes, pour in the port, Madeira or Marsala. Let the mixture bubble for a few seconds, then add the stock. Cook gently for five minutes, stirring frequently. Stir in the parsley, and serve with fried croutons or boiled rice.

ELIZABETH DAVID
SUMMER COOKING

Beef Kidney and Salt Pork Casserole

Rognon de Boeuf à la Mode

To serve 6 to 8

two 1½ lb.	beef kidneys, outer fat and membrane removed, halved, cored and thinly sliced	two ¾ kg.
½ lb.	fresh fatback, thinly sliced	¼ kg.
	salt and pepper	
3 or 4	scallions, chopped	3 or 4
2	shallots, chopped	2
1	garlic clove, chopped	1
2 tbsp.	chopped fresh parsley	30 ml.
1 lb.	lean salt pork with the rind removed, cut into thin slices, blanched for 3 minutes and drained	½ kg.
2 tbsp.	*eau-de-vie* or other brandy	30 ml.

Line the bottom of the casserole with the fatback. Arrange a layer of sliced kidney on top. Season with salt and pepper. Mix the scallions, shallots, garlic and parsley, and sprinkle some of the mixture over the kidney. Add a layer of the sliced salt pork and sprinkle it with the scallion mixture. Continue to add the kidney, salt pork and scallion mixture until all the ingredients are used up, ending with a layer of salt pork. Cover the casserole and bake in a preheated 300° F. [150° C.] oven for three hours, adding the *eau-de-vie* or brandy 10 minutes before the end of the cooking time. Serve straight from the casserole, hot or cold.

MENON
LES SOUPERS DE LA COUR

Stewed Kidney with Juniper Berries

To serve 4

1 lb.	beef kidney, outer fat and membrane removed, halved, cored and cut into small pieces	½ kg.
	salt and pepper	
4 tbsp.	butter, 2 tbsp. [30 ml.] cut into pieces	60 ml.
1 cup	white wine	¼ liter
16	juniper berries, crushed to a powder	16

Season the kidney pieces with salt and pepper. Heat 2 tablespoons [30 ml.] of the butter in a pan and brown the kidney all over. Add the juniper berries, wine and butter pieces. Cover and cook very gently until the kidney is tender—about 30 to 40 minutes. If necessary, add a little more wine so that the kidney is kept submerged by liquid.

BERYL GOULD-MARKS
EATING THE RUSSIAN WAY

Veal Kidneys with Cider and Calvados

Rognons de Veau à la Normande

To serve 4

1½ lb.	veal kidneys, outer fat and membrane removed, halved, cored and cut into strips ¼ inch [6 mm.] thick	350 g.
7 tbsp.	butter	105 ml.
5 oz.	lean bacon, diced	150 g.
24	small boiling onions, peeled	24
	salt and pepper	
1 tbsp.	flour	15 ml.
1	garlic clove, crushed to a paste	1
⅔ cup	dry cider	150 ml.
⅓ cup	Calvados	75 ml.

Heat half of the butter in a skillet, add the bacon and onions, and cook them over low heat until they are lightly browned—15 minutes. In another skillet, heat the remaining butter. Add the kidneys and season with salt and pepper. Sauté the kidneys for seven to eight minutes, or until golden brown. Add the bacon and onions, sprinkle the flour over the mixture, stir, then add the garlic, cider and Calvados. Reduce the heat, cover the skillet and simmer the kidneys for 20 minutes, or until cooked through.

MARIE BISSON
LA CUISINE NORMANDE

Veal Kidney Risotto

Risotto z Nerek Cielęcych

To serve 4

1 lb.	veal kidney, outer fat and membrane removed, halved, cored, soaked in cold water for 1 hour and cubed	½ kg.
2 tbsp.	butter	30 ml.
½	medium-sized onion, sliced	½
½ cup	water	125 ml.
¼ lb.	fresh mushrooms, sliced (about 1¼ cups [300 ml.])	125 g.
	salt	
½ cup	raw white rice, boiled in salted water for 15 minutes and drained	125 ml.
	pepper	
½ cup	sour cream	125 ml.
1	egg yolk, beaten	1
½ cup	freshly grated Parmesan cheese	125 ml.

Melt the butter in a saucepan and fry the onion until it is lightly browned. Add the kidneys and the water. Cover the pan and simmer for about 10 minutes. Add the mushrooms and cook for another 10 minutes. Season with salt and cook for five minutes.

Mix the rice with the kidneys and mushrooms; add salt and pepper. Put this risotto into a buttered baking dish.

Season the sour cream with salt and stir in the egg yolk. Pour the mixture over the risotto and sprinkle it with the grated cheese. Bake in a preheated 375° F. [190° C.] oven for 20 to 30 minutes, or until the cheese has browned.

HELENA HAWLICZKOWA
KUCHNIA POLSKA

Beef Kidney Stewed in Wine with Mushrooms

Rognons de Boeuf à la Charentaise

Cooked in this way, the toughest beef kidney will become tender and have a most excellent flavor. One way of making the sauce for this dish less expensive is to cook it when you have some rich gravy left over from a meat stew made with wine. The wine can then be omitted, for the gravy is already flavored with it.

To serve 2 or 3

½ lb.	beef kidney, all fat and membrane removed, soaked in water for 2 hours, and cut into ½-inch [1-cm.] slices	¼ kg.
2 tbsp.	butter	30 ml.
	salt and pepper	
½ cup	chopped fresh mushrooms	125 ml.
2 tbsp.	brandy, warmed	30 ml.
⅓ cup	dry white wine	75 ml.
⅓ cup	meat stock (recipe, page 165)	75 ml.
¼ cup	heavy cream	50 ml.

Heat the butter in a skillet and turn the kidneys over and over in this, over high heat, for a minute or so. Add salt and pepper and the mushrooms. Pour in the brandy, set light to it and shake the skillet until the flames go out. Pour the wine into the skillet, let it bubble, then add the stock. Turn the kidneys and their juice into a small earthenware casserole, cover it, and put it into a preheated 300° F. [150° C.] oven for 30 to 40 minutes.

Boil the cream in a small, wide pan; pour in the sauce from the kidneys. Stir, and cook quickly over high heat until the sauce is thick, about one minute. Pour the mixture over the kidneys; serve with croutons of fried bread.

ELIZABETH DAVID
FRENCH PROVINCIAL COOKING

Veal Kidney with Tomatoes and Cepes

Le Rognon de Veau à la Bordelaise

The veal kidney called for in this recipe is cooked whole, protected by a layer of its outer fat. You may need to order it in advance to ensure that the butcher will leave this layer intact. The cepes called for in this recipe are edible wild mushrooms. The author specifies fresh cepes, which are not sold commercially in the United States; dried cepes—obtainable where fine foods are sold—make a suitable substitute. For additional flavor, a chopped garlic clove and a dash of lemon juice can
be added to the cepe mixture; remove the garlic before serving. The cooked kidney can be sliced and returned to the sauté pan for a few minutes just before serving.*

To serve 4

one 1 lb.	veal kidney, outer fat trimmed to a ¼-inch [6-mm.] layer	one ½ kg.
6 tbsp.	butter	90 ml.
	salt and pepper	
2	medium-sized tomatoes, peeled, halved and seeded	2
½ lb.	lean salt pork with the rind removed, cut into narrow strips 1 inch [2½ cm.] long, blanched for 2 to 3 minutes and drained	200 g.
¼ cup	oil	50 ml.
2 oz.	dried cepes, soaked in warm water for 30 minutes and drained	60 g.
1 tbsp.	bread crumbs	15 ml.
1 tbsp.	chopped fresh parsley	15 ml.
1 tbsp.	chopped shallot	15 ml.

Melt 2 tablespoons [30 ml.] of the butter in a heavy sauté pan set over low heat. When the butter has melted, add the whole kidney and season it to taste with salt and pepper. Cover the pan and cook the kidney, turning it occasionally, for 30 to 35 minutes.

Meanwhile, in a skillet, sauté the tomato halves in 2 tablespoons [30 ml.] of the butter for five to 10 minutes, depending on the ripeness of the tomatoes. They must stay in shape. Remove them from the skillet. Season them with salt and pepper, and reserve them.

Melt the rest of the butter in the skillet and sauté the salt-pork strips until they are quite crisp, about 10 minutes. Drain the pork on paper towels.

In a clean skillet, heat the oil. Add the cepes and, stirring occasionally, cook them over medium heat for one or two minutes. Then add the bread crumbs, parsley and shallots. Cook the mixture for another two to three minutes.

Add the tomatoes, the pork strips and the cepe mixture to the kidney. Cover the pan again and cook the mixture over low heat for 10 minutes. Serve straight from the pan.

ÉDOUARD NIGNON
LES PLAISIRS DE LA TABLE

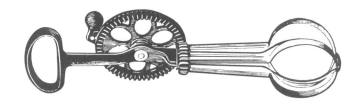

Veal Kidney Braised in Spinach and Lettuce Leaves

Rognon de Veau "en Habit Vert"

To make the mushroom purée called for in this recipe, cook one or two fresh button mushrooms in milk—seasoned with salt, pepper and grated nutmeg—over medium heat for 20 minutes. Drain the mushrooms and purée them in a blender or processor, adding a few drops of the cooking liquid.

Fromage blanc is a French skim-milk cheese with the consistency of lightly whipped cream. If it is not available, substitute farmer cheese.

	To serve 2	
one 6 to 8 oz.	veal kidney, outer fat and membrane removed	one 175 to 250 g.
	salt and pepper	
4 to 6	large spinach leaves, stems removed, blanched in salted water for 1 minute	4 to 6
4 to 6	large lettuce leaves, blanched in salted water for 1 minute	4 to 6
1 tsp.	olive oil	5 ml.
1	carrot, sliced	1
1	leek, white part only, sliced	1
1	small onion, sliced	1
¾ cup	veal stock (recipe, page 165)	175 ml.
1	small bouquet garni	1
1 tsp.	mushroom purée	5 ml.
½ tsp.	*fromage blanc*	2 ml.
½ tsp.	Dijon mustard	2 ml.

Season the veal kidney with salt and pepper and wrap it in the spinach and lettuce leaves. Heat the olive oil in an enameled cast-iron casserole, and in it cook the carrot, leek, and onion until they soften and give off some of their liquid. Add the wrapped kidney, veal stock and bouquet garni. Cover and braise the kidney over low heat for 25 to 30 minutes, basting frequently with the juices in the casserole. (Do not overcook the kidney; when it is done, it should still be pink in the center.)

Remove the kidney and pour the braising liquid through a fine-meshed strainer. Put the braising liquid in a blender, add the mushroom purée, *fromage blanc* and mustard, and blend. Pour this sauce into a small saucepan and reheat it, but do not allow it to boil.

Unwrap the veal kidney and slice it thin. Pour a ribbon of the sauce inside the edges of two heated dinner plates; arrange the spinach and lettuce leaves in the center, and the slices of kidney on top of them.

MICHEL GUÉRARD
MICHEL GUÉRARD'S CUISINE MINCEUR

Veal Kidneys in Mustard Sauce

Rognons de Veau du Moulin

Stock and either white wine or Madeira can be added to the cooking juices instead of the Calvados.

	To serve 2	
two 1 lb.	veal kidneys, outer fat and membrane removed, halved, cored and sliced ¼ inch [6 mm.] thick	two ½ kg.
	salt and pepper	
2 tbsp.	butter	30 ml.
2 tbsp.	chopped shallots	30 ml.
3 tbsp.	Calvados	45 ml.
⅓ cup	heavy cream	75 ml.
1 tbsp.	Dijon mustard	15 ml.
2 tbsp.	coarsely chopped fresh chervil or parsley	30 ml.

Lay the kidney slices on a plate and season them well with salt and pepper.

Over medium to high heat, melt 1 tablespoon [15 ml.] of the butter in a heavy skillet about 10 inches [25 cm.] in diameter. When the butter sizzles, add half of the kidney slices. Brown them well on one side, then turn them and brown the other side. This will take about four or five minutes. Drain the cooked kidneys in a sieve, placed over a bowl to catch the juices. Cook the rest of the kidney slices the same way, using the remaining tablespoon of butter. Then drain them in the sieve with the first batch.

Do not clean the skillet. Over very low heat, add the shallot with the Calvados. Stir with a wooden spoon, detaching all particles sticking to the bottom and sides of the skillet. Be careful to keep the heat low so that the alcohol does not ignite; in this instance, this is not your goal.

When all the residue from the kidneys has dissolved, pour in the heavy cream and simmer two minutes, while stirring with a wire whisk. Then pass the sauce through a fine sieve into a clean skillet. Press down hard so that all the sauce passes through the sieve.

Whisk in the mustard and, when it is well blended, stir the drained kidney slices into the sauce. Bring the sauce just to a simmer. Season to taste and add the chopped chervil or parsley. Serve at once on hot plates.

ROGER VERGÉ
ROGER VERGÉ'S CUISINE OF THE SOUTH OF FRANCE

Veal Kidney Sauté

Riñones Salteados

To serve 4 to 6

2 lb.	veal kidneys, outer fat and membrane removed, halved, cored and cubed	1 kg.
3 tbsp.	rendered bacon fat	45 ml.
1	small onion, chopped	1
1	garlic clove, chopped	1
1 tbsp.	flour	15 ml.
2	whole cloves	2
¼ tsp.	crushed thyme leaves	1 ml.
2 tbsp.	chopped fresh parsley	30 ml.
	paprika	
	salt and pepper	
½ to ¾ cup	red wine	125 to 175 ml.
½ to ¾ cup	water	125 to 175 ml.

Sauté the kidneys in 2 tablespoons [30 ml.] of the bacon fat over low heat and if any juice accumulates, drain it. Add the remaining bacon fat and the onion and garlic to the meat. Stir and fry until the vegetables are golden. Stir in the flour and allow it to brown. Now add the cloves, thyme, parsley and a little paprika. Season to taste with salt and pepper, and pour in equal parts of wine and water to just cover the meat. Cover the pot and simmer slowly for one hour.

ANN ROGERS
A BASQUE STORY COOK BOOK

Water Chestnuts with Pork Kidneys

To serve 4

¾ lb.	pork kidneys, fat and membrane removed, soaked and cubed	350 g.
1 tsp.	cornstarch	5 ml.
2 tbsp.	soy sauce	30 ml.
1 tbsp.	dry sherry	15 ml.
1½ tbsp.	fresh lemon juice	22½ ml.
1 tsp.	brown sugar	5 ml.
¼ cup	peanut oil	50 ml.
1	onion, thinly sliced	1
6 to 8	water chestnuts, thinly sliced	6 to 8

Moisten the cornstarch with the soy sauce, sherry and lemon juice, and stir in the sugar. Pour this sauce over the kidneys and let them marinate for half an hour. Drain the kidneys, reserving the sauce.

Heat the oil in a heavy skillet. Stirring constantly, lightly fry the onion and water chestnuts for a minute or so. Move them to one side of the skillet and fry the kidneys—stirring all the while—for five minutes, or until they change color completely. Now add the sauce; stir and cook for a few minutes, until the gravy thickens. Serve at once.

MARIA KOZSLIK DONOVAN
THE FAR EASTERN EPICURE

Stir-fried Kidneys with Cauliflower

Rognons Sautés au Chou-fleur

The kidneys called for in this recipe can be replaced by an equal weight of pork heart or liver. Any julienne of flavorful root vegetables, such as celeriac, parsnips, turnips or the carrots shown on pages 22-23, can be substituted for the cauliflower. The volatile oils in the hot chilies may make your skin sting and your eyes burn; after handling chilies, avoid touching your face and wash your hands promptly.

To serve 4

1 lb.	pork kidneys, fat and membrane removed, each halved lengthwise and cut crosswise into ½-inch [1-cm.] strips	½ kg.
1 tbsp.	cornstarch	15 ml.
¾ cup	chicken stock *(recipe, page 165)*	175 ml.
2 tbsp.	vegetable oil	30 ml.
1	garlic clove, finely chopped	1
1 lb.	cauliflower, cored, separated into florets, cut lengthwise into julienne	½ kg.
1	onion, sliced	1
1	fresh hot red chili, stemmed, seeded and cut into julienne (optional)	1
2-inch	piece fresh ginger, peeled and cut into julienne	5-cm.
2 tsp.	sesame-seed oil (optional)	10 ml.

Sweetened soy sauce marinade

1 tbsp.	vegetable oil	15 ml.
1 tbsp.	cornstarch	15 ml.
2 tbsp.	soy sauce	30 ml.
1 tbsp.	dry sherry or brandy	15 ml.
	pepper	
1 tsp.	sugar	5 ml.

To make the marinade, mix the oil, cornstarch, soy sauce, dry sherry or brandy, 3 pinches of pepper and the sugar in a bowl. Add the kidney and marinate it for 15 minutes.

Dissolve the cornstarch in the stock. Heat a skillet over high heat and add 1 tablespoon [15 ml.] of the oil. When the oil is very hot, add the garlic and fry for 30 seconds. Discard the garlic and add the kidneys. Cook them, stirring occasionally, for three minutes. Remove the kidneys and reserve them. Add the rest of the oil to the skillet and, when it is very hot, add the cauliflower. Stirring constantly, cook it for two minutes. Stir in the onion, the chili, if using, and the ginger. Cook for three minutes, then add the kidney and the dissolved cornstarch. Slightly reduce the heat. Cook for another two minutes, stirring constantly. Add the sesame-seed oil, if using, then remove the mixture from the heat. Serve hot.

NGUYEN NGOC RAO
LA CUISINE CHINOISE A L'USAGE DES FRANÇAIS

Skirts and Kidneys

Skirts is the term used in County Cork, Ireland, for the fluted trimmings cut away from pork steaks. Boneless pork shoulder is a suitable substitute.

Traditionally, this dish is eaten with potatoes boiled in their jackets. Sometimes 1 pound [½ kg.] of corned spareribs is added to the stew at the beginning of cooking. Then the parsnips and salt are left out.

To serve 6

two 6 oz.	pork kidneys, fat and membrane removed, halved, cored and chopped into small pieces	two 150 g.
2 lb.	boneless pork shoulder, cut into strips	1 kg.
1½ tbsp.	flour, seasoned with salt and pepper	22½ ml.
1½ tbsp.	rendered bacon fat	22½ ml.
3	onions, sliced	3
1 cup	water	¼ liter
	mixed dried herbs	
	salt and pepper	
2	parsnips, sliced	2

Toss the kidneys and pork with the seasoned flour. Melt the fat and fry the kidneys and pork over medium heat until they are browned—about five minutes. Put the onions in the bottom of a heavy pot with the meats on top. Add the water and a pinch of mixed dried herbs, season to taste and bring to a boil over high heat. Reduce the heat, cover and simmer for 30 minutes. Add the parsnips and continue cooking until all is tender—about 20 minutes.

MONICA SHERIDAN
THE ART OF IRISH COOKING

Shrimp and Kidney

To serve 4

1 lb.	pork kidneys, fat and membrane removed, halved and cored	½ kg.
3 tsp.	salt	15 ml.
2	slices fresh ginger, 1 by 1½ inches [2½ by 4 cm.]	2
¼ cup	dry sherry	50 ml.
½ lb.	shrimp, peeled, deveined and washed	¼ kg.
⅓ cup	vegetable oil	75 ml.
1	garlic clove, crushed	1
½ tsp.	sugar	2 ml.
1 tbsp.	dark soy sauce	15 ml.
¼ cup	sliced Smithfield ham	50 ml.
¼ cup	sliced bamboo shoots	50 ml.
1	scallion, cut into 2-inch [5-cm.] pieces	1
1 tbsp.	cornstarch, dissolved in 2 tbsp. [30 ml.] cold water	15 ml.

Score each kidney half, then cut it into ½-by-1-inch [1-by-2½-cm.] pieces. Rinse the kidneys several times in cold water. Drain, add 1 teaspoon [5 ml.] of salt and one ginger slice, and let stand 10 minutes. Rinse and drain. Add 2 tablespoons [30 ml.] of sherry and let stand 10 minutes. Drain again. Add cold water to cover and soak the kidneys in the refrigerator overnight, or for at least 10 to 12 hours.

Add 1 teaspoon of salt to a bowl of water and add the shrimp. Stir or whip with chopsticks for about two minutes, then rinse the shrimp and dry them on paper towels. Heat 2 tablespoons of the oil in a wok or skillet and stir fry the shrimp for just a minute. Add 1 tablespoon [15 ml.] of the sherry and the remaining teaspoon of salt. Stir, then remove the shrimp from the pan and set them aside. Discard the oil.

Add the remaining oil to the wok or skillet and let the garlic sizzle for a few seconds in the oil. Drain the kidney pieces, pat them dry and add them to the pan. Stir quickly for just 30 seconds. Add the remaining sherry, soy sauce and sugar, and stir, then add the ham, bamboo shoots, remaining ginger slice and scallion. Stir, then add the reserved shrimp and stir again. Thicken with the dissolved cornstarch (stirred again to make sure the water and cornstarch are thoroughly mixed) and serve immediately.

GRACE ZIA CHU
MADAME CHU'S CHINESE COOKING SCHOOL

Fried Chopped Pork Kidneys with Snow Peas and Bamboo Shoots

Chao Yao-hua

Wood ears or cloud ears (auricularia polytricha) are fungi that are sold dried at Chinese groceries.

This recipe calls for the kidneys to be scored, which aids cooking by creating more surface area. As they cook, the kidney pieces open slightly and are said to resemble flowers. Thus the word *hua*, or "flower," in the Chinese name.

To serve 2

two 6 oz.	pork kidneys, fat and membrane removed, cut open, cored, washed, scored ½ inch [1 cm.] deep at ½-inch intervals, in a crosshatch pattern, then cut into 1-inch [2½-cm.] pieces	two 175 g.
2 tsp.	cornstarch, dissolved in 3 tbsp. [45 ml.] cold water	10 ml.
2 tsp.	rice wine or sherry	10 ml.
1 tbsp.	soy sauce	15 ml.
1 tsp.	salt	5 ml.
½ tsp.	sugar	2 ml.
1 tsp.	vinegar	5 ml.
2 tsp.	sesame-seed oil	10 ml.
¼ cup	vegetable oil	50 ml.
2	scallions, finely chopped	2
1 tbsp.	finely chopped garlic	15 ml.
1 tbsp.	finely chopped fresh ginger	15 ml.
¼ lb.	fresh snow peas, ends trimmed and strings removed, blanched in boiling water for one minute and drained	125 g.
¼ cup	bamboo shoots, cut into ¼-inch [6-mm.] slices	50 ml.
5 to 8	wood ears, soaked in warm water for 4 hours or until soft, rinsed, drained, tough parts cut away, cut into shreds (optional)	5 to 8

Mix the diluted cornstarch, the rice wine or sherry, soy sauce, salt, sugar, vinegar and sesame-seed oil, and set the mixture aside. Bring 4 cups [1 quart] of water to a boil. Add the kidney pieces and simmer over low heat until the pieces have turned white—about seven minutes. Drain the pieces, discarding the water.

Heat the vegetable oil in a wok or large skillet over medium heat. Add the scallions, garlic and ginger, and toss them until you can smell the garlic—about 30 seconds. Then add the snow peas and bamboo shoots, and the wood ears, if you are using them, and toss the vegetables until they are well heated and coated with oil. Add the kidneys and toss them quickly until they are covered with oil and slightly heated.

Stir the cornstarch mixture and add it to the pan; continue to toss the contents over medium heat for a few more moments until everything is mixed and heated. Transfer the mixture to a warmed serving platter and serve hot.

ROBERT A. DELFS
THE GOOD FOOD OF SZECHWAN

Sautéed Pork Kidneys

Masak Jotjio

To serve 4

1 lb.	pork kidneys, fat and membrane removed, rubbed with coarse salt and cut into halves, scored in a crisscross pattern, rinsed several times and cut into 1-inch [2½-cm.] slices	½ kg.
¼ lb.	pork liver, membrane removed, cut into slivers	125 g.
½ cup	dry sherry	125 ml.
2 tbsp.	vegetable oil	30 ml.
1	medium-sized onion, sliced	1
3	garlic cloves, sliced	3
¼ inch	slice fresh ginger, peeled and cut into julienne	6 mm.
¼ lb.	boneless lean pork, cut into slivers	125 g.
2 tbsp.	soy sauce	30 ml.
1	celery rib, cut into julienne	1

Soak the kidneys in the sherry for 30 minutes. Heat the oil and brown the onion and garlic in it. Then add the ginger, liver, pork and kidneys with the sherry and soy sauce. Stir and simmer gently for 30 minutes. One minute before serving, add the celery. Serve hot.

LIE SEK-HIANG
INDONESIAN COOKERY

Roast Lamb Kidneys

Grillstegte Lammenyrer

To serve 4

1 to 1½ lb.	lamb kidneys, outer fat left on and trimmed to a ½-inch [1-cm.] layer	250 to 375 g.

Place the kidneys on a rack in a roasting pan and roast them in a preheated 400° to 450° F. [200° to 230° C.] oven for 30 to 40 minutes, until the fat is brown and cooked through. Serve the kidneys smoking hot with rye bread and coarse salt. When the fat is removed, the kidneys will be found to be pink and tender inside.

GRETE GRUMME
DANISH FOOD

Grilled Lamb Kidneys

Rognons de Mouton Grillés

To serve 2

four ¼ lb.	lamb kidneys, fat and membrane removed, split open	four 125 g.
	salt and pepper	
3 tbsp.	vegetable oil	45 ml.
	Herb butter	
7 tbsp.	unsalted butter, softened	105 ml.
1 tbsp.	chopped fresh chervil	15 ml.
1 tsp.	chopped fresh parsley	5 ml.
2 tbsp.	fresh lemon juice	30 ml.
	salt and pepper	

To make the herb butter, mix the butter with the chervil, parsley, lemon juice, salt and pepper. Divide the butter into four portions and chill them.

Thread the kidneys onto two skewers. Season the kidneys with salt and pepper and brush them on both sides with the oil. Broil them about 3 inches [8 cm.] from the heat source under a preheated broiler for about three minutes on each side. Place them on a serving dish and top each kidney with a piece of the herb butter.

LÉON ISNARD
LA CUISINE FRANÇAISE ET AFRICAINE

Kidneys in Sour Sauce

Saure Nieren

Serve the kidneys with boiled potatoes or noodles.

To serve 2

two ½ lb.	lamb kidneys, fat and membrane removed, thinly sliced	two ¼ kg.
2 tbsp.	butter	30 ml.
1	onion, finely chopped	1
1 tbsp.	flour	15 ml.
½ cup	water or meat stock (recipe, page 165)	125 ml.
1 tbsp.	white wine vinegar	15 ml.
¼ cup	dry white wine	50 ml.
2 tbsp.	fresh lemon juice	30 ml.
¼ cup	meat stock	50 ml.
	salt and pepper	

In a saucepan, melt the butter and sauté the onion over medium heat until it is lightly browned—about 10 minutes. Add the kidneys and, turning them frequently, sauté them until they are pinkish brown—about five minutes. Remove them from the pan and keep them warm.

Sprinkle the flour into the saucepan, stir it until it is lightly browned, then stir in the ½ cup [125 ml.] of water or stock. Add the vinegar, wine, lemon juice, ¼ cup [50 ml.] of stock and a pinch of pepper. Cook, stirring constantly, until the liquid boils, then reduce the heat and simmer, stirring occasionally, until the sauce is well reduced—about 20 minutes. Add the kidneys and cook them for five minutes to heat them through. Just before serving, add a pinch of salt.

ELIZABETH SCHULER
MEIN KOCHBUCH

Kidneys in Wine Sauce

Nefra me Saltsa

To serve 4

1 lb.	lamb kidneys, fat and membrane removed, cut into quarters	½ kg.
5 tbsp.	butter	75 ml.
1 tbsp.	flour	15 ml.
½ cup	dry red wine	125 ml.
¼ cup	water or meat stock (recipe, page 165)	50 ml.
1	garlic clove, finely chopped	1
½ tsp.	ground marjoram or thyme	2 ml.
1	bay leaf	1
	salt and pepper	
1½ tbsp.	fresh lemon juice	22½ ml.
12	fresh button mushrooms	12

First make the sauce. Melt 1 tablespoon [15 ml.] of the butter in a nonreactive saucepan, add the flour and cook until light brown, stirring constantly. Pour in the wine gradually and stir in the water or stock, garlic, marjoram or thyme, bay leaf, and salt and pepper. Put over low heat and simmer for 15 minutes. Strain and return the sauce to the pan.

Sprinkle the kidneys with the lemon juice. In a skillet melt the remaining butter, and when hot sauté the kidneys and the mushrooms for about five minutes. Add them to the sauce and cook for two or three minutes, but do not allow the mixture to boil.

MARO DUNCAN
COOKING THE GREEK WAY

Kidney Dumpling

The dumpling is done when the onion feels soft if pierced with the tip of a small knife. If the pastry browns before the onion is tender, cover the dumpling with foil to prevent burning.

	To serve 2	
one ¼ lb.	lamb kidney, fat and membrane removed, quartered	one 125 g.
1	large onion, halved	1
	salt and pepper	
	Meat pudding dough	
6 oz.	suet, finely chopped	175 g.
2 cups	flour	½ liter
1 tsp.	salt	5 ml.
	water	

To make the dough, mix the suet with the flour, salt and sufficient water to make a smooth, pliant dough. Roll it out and it is ready. Take out part of the middle of the onion halves and fill the spaces with the lamb kidney quarters. Season the kidney with salt and pepper. Join the onion halves and wrap them in the dough. Bake the dumpling on a buttered baking sheet in a preheated 375° F. [190° C.] oven for about one hour, or until the pastry is golden.

MRS. ROUNDELL
MRS. ROUNDELL'S PRACTICAL COOKERY BOOK

Skewered Lamb Kidneys

Rognons de Mouton à la Brochette

	To serve 4	
eight ¼ lb.	lamb kidneys, fat and membrane removed, each split almost in half along its outer curve and pressed flat	eight 125 g.
	salt and pepper	
¼ cup	chopped fresh parsley	50 ml.
8 tbsp.	butter, softened	120 ml.
3 tbsp.	fresh lemon juice	45 ml.

Beat the parsley into the butter and divide the mixture into eight portions. Set them aside. Thread the flattened kidneys crosswise onto four skewers, opening out the halves so that the kidneys look like open shells. Sprinkle them with salt and pepper and place them cut side down on a broiling pan. Broil them under a preheated broiler for two minutes, then turn and broil them until the juices run.

Take the kidneys off the skewers. Place a portion of the parsley butter between the cut halves of each kidney, sprinkle the kidneys with the lemon juice and serve them.

A.-B. DE PÉRIGORD
LE TRÉSOR DE LA CUISINIÈRE ET DE LA MAÎTRESSE DE MAISON

Lamb Hearts with Zucchini

Corazones de Cordero con Calabaza

Either beef or veal heart is equally delicious. Lengthen the cooking time by a good 10 minutes.

	To serve 6 to 8	
2 lb.	lamb hearts, fat, tubes and fibrous tissue removed, cut into small pieces	1 kg.
1 tbsp.	olive oil	15 ml.
1	medium-sized onion, finely chopped	1
2	garlic cloves, finely chopped	2
1 tsp.	salt	5 ml.
¼ tsp.	pepper	1 ml.
½ cup	dry red wine	125 ml.
2 lb.	zucchini, rinsed, trimmed and sliced lengthwise	1 kg.

Brown the heart pieces in the oil. When the meat is well browned on both sides, add the onion and garlic. Stir and cook until the vegetables are golden. Season with salt and pepper and pour in the wine. Cover the pan and simmer the meat for 15 to 20 minutes, or until it is tender. If the mixture seems too dry, add a little water.

In the meantime, cook the zucchini in boiling salted water for seven to 10 minutes. Drain the zucchini and transfer it to a warmed platter. Pour the meat and its juices over the zucchini.

ANN ROGERS
A BASQUE STORY COOK BOOK

Stuffed Lamb Hearts with Apples

	To serve 4	
four ½ lb.	lamb hearts, fat, tubes and fibrous tissue removed	four ¼ kg.
3 tbsp.	vegetable oil	45 ml.
2 cups	fresh bread crumbs	½ liter
4 tbsp.	butter, melted	60 ml.
½ cup	finely chopped celery	125 ml.
½ cup	chopped onion	125 ml.
1½ tsp.	finely chopped fresh sage leaves	7 ml.
¼ tsp.	dried marjoram	1 ml.
	salt and pepper	
4	cooking apples, peeled and cored	4
1 cup	red wine	¼ liter

Heat the oil, add the hearts and brown them well over high heat. In a bowl, combine the bread crumbs, butter, celery, onion, sage, marjoram, salt and pepper. Stuff the mixture into the heart cavities and into the cored apples. Place the hearts in the center of a baking dish and set the apples around them. Pour the wine over all. Cover the dish and put it into a preheated 350° F. [180° C.] oven. Bake for one and one half hours, or until the hearts are tender.

JANA ALLEN AND MARGARET GIN
INNARDS AND OTHER VARIETY MEATS

French Stew of Lamb Hearts

To serve 4

1 lb.	lamb hearts, fat, tubes and fibrous tissue removed, and the flesh sliced crosswise	½ kg.
2 tbsp.	butter	30 ml.
1 tbsp.	flour	15 ml.
2	thin slices lemon	2
1	large bay leaf	1
1	bouquet garni of thyme and parsley sprigs	1
½ tsp.	salt	2 ml.
⅛ tsp.	pepper	½ ml.
about 2 cups	boiling water	about ½ liter
	chopped fresh parsley	

In a heavy pot, melt the butter over medium heat and brown the heart slices on both sides. Add the flour and let that brown also. Add the lemon, bay leaf, bouquet garni, salt and pepper. Add just enough boiling water to come level with the top of the meat. Bring to a boil, reduce the heat, partially cover the pot and simmer gently for one and one half hours. At the end of this time most of the liquid should have cooked away; the hearts should be tender and moistened with a rich lemony sauce. Correct the seasoning with more salt and pepper, if necessary. Discard the bay leaf and bouquet garni. Sprinkle the stew with the chopped parsley before serving it.

MORTON G. CLARK
FRENCH-AMERICAN COOKING

Lamb Hearts, Flemish-Style

Lamshart op Zijn Vlaams

To serve 2

two ½ lb.	lamb hearts, fat, tubes and fibrous tissue removed, diced	two ¼ kg.
6 tbsp.	butter	90 ml.
2	slices bacon, diced	2
2	onions, chopped	2
2 tbsp.	flour	30 ml.
	salt and pepper	
	chopped fresh basil	
2 cups	beer	½ liter
1 tbsp.	vinegar	15 ml.
1 tbsp.	prepared mustard	15 ml.
1 tsp.	sugar	5 ml.

In a heavy pan set over low heat, melt the butter and in it fry the bacon until its fat melts. Add the heart and onions and cook them until they are lightly browned. Sprinkle them with the flour, salt and pepper, and a pinch of basil. Pour in the beer and vinegar and stir well. Bring to a boil. Cover the pan and simmer the contents gently for one hour. Stir in the mustard and sugar and cook for a further 15 minutes.

HUGH JANS
BISTRO KOKEN

Hearts with Potatoes and Spinach

Serca Wieprzowe z Ziemnakami i Szpinakiem

To serve 4

1 lb.	pork, beef or veal heart, fat, tubes and fibrous tissue removed, and the flesh cut into ½-inch [1-cm.] cubes	½ kg.
2 cups	water	½ liter
	salt	
2	bay leaves	2
½ tsp.	ground allspice	2 ml.
2	garlic cloves, chopped	2
4	potatoes, cut into ½-inch [1-cm.] cubes	4
1 lb.	spinach, deribbed and chopped	½ kg.

Put the cubed heart into a saucepan with the water. Add salt, bring to a boil, then simmer—partially covered—for two hours. Add the bay leaves, allspice, garlic and potatoes, and cook for 20 minutes, until the heart and potato cubes are tender. Stir in the spinach and cook for three minutes.

ANNA ROŚCISZEWSKA-STOYANOW (EDITOR)
DOBRA KUCHNIA

Veal Heart, St. Gallen-Style

Kalbsherz auf St.-Gallener Art

To serve 2 or 3

one 1½ lb.	veal heart, fat, tubes and fibrous tissue removed	one ¾ kg.
	salt and pepper	
4 tbsp.	butter	60 ml.
1	onion	1
1½ cups	boiling water	375 ml.
½ lb.	fresh pork rind, cut into strips ½ inch [1 cm.] wide	¼ kg.
2 tbsp.	flour	30 ml.
½ cup	sour cream	125 ml.

Spiced white-wine marinade

1 cup	dry white wine	¼ liter
½ cup	white wine vinegar	125 ml.
½ cup	water	125 ml.
1	onion, chopped	1
1	bay leaf	1
10	peppercorns	10
3	whole cloves	3

Ground pork stuffing

¼ lb.	ground pork	125 g.
1 tbsp.	bread crumbs	15 ml.
1	egg	1
¼ cup	finely chopped ham	50 ml.
1 tbsp.	finely chopped fresh parsley	15 ml.
	grated nutmeg	
	salt (optional)	

Combine the marinade ingredients in a large nonreactive saucepan, bring the mixture to a boil and let it cool. Put in the heart, turning it to coat all sides; cover the pan and refrigerate it for two to three days.

To make the stuffing, mix together the ground pork, bread crumbs, egg, ham, parsley, a pinch of nutmeg and salt to taste. Drain the heart and season it inside. Stuff the heart with the stuffing mixture and sew it up. In a heatproof casserole with a lid, melt the butter and in it sauté the heart and the whole onion, turning them occasionally until both are evenly browned. Pour in the boiling water and cover the heart with the rind strips. Cover the casserole and set it in a preheated 350° F. [180° C.] oven. Basting the heart every 15 minutes, bake it for one to one and one half hours, or until tender. Drain the heart, reserving the cooking liquid,

and keep it warm. Pour the cooking liquid into a saucepan. Stir in the flour and the sour cream, and bring this sauce to a boil. Strain the sauce. Slice the heart into finger-thick slices; pour the sauce over the slices. Serve with dumplings or mashed potatoes.

GRETE WILLINSKY
KULINARISCHE WELTREISE

Veal Heart in Spicy Sauce

Cuore di Vitello in Salsa Piccante

To serve 4

one 1½ lb.	veal heart, fat, tubes and fibrous tissue removed, thinly sliced	one ¾ kg.
4 tbsp.	butter	60 ml.
1	garlic clove	1
	salt and pepper	
2 tbsp.	white wine vinegar	30 ml.
2	salt anchovies, filleted, soaked in water for 30 minutes, drained and crushed to a paste	2
1 tbsp.	flour	15 ml.
½ cup	meat stock *(recipe, page 165)*	125 ml.
¼ cup	chopped sour gherkins	50 ml.
1 tbsp.	chopped capers	15 ml.
1 tbsp.	finely chopped fresh parsley	15 ml.
	Worcestershire sauce	

Melt half of the butter in a skillet and sauté the garlic clove over medium heat until it is evenly browned. Discard the garlic and sauté the heart slices in the flavored butter for two minutes on each side. Season the slices with very little salt and pepper. Sprinkle them with the vinegar and cook until the vinegar has evaporated. When the slices are well browned—after about 10 minutes—remove them from the skillet and keep them warm.

To make the sauce, add the rest of the butter to the skillet. When the butter melts, mix in the anchovies and the flour. Stir well for a few minutes, then stir in the stock. Simmer for 10 minutes. Remove the skillet from the heat and add the gherkins, capers, parsley and a few drops of Worcestershire sauce. Return the heart slices to the skillet and reheat them gently for a few minutes. Arrange the slices on a warmed serving dish, pour the sauce over them and surround them with boiled new potatoes that have been tossed in butter.

SAVINA ROGGERO
COME SCEGLIERE E CUCINARE LE CARNI

Veal Heart with Pork and Herb Stuffing

Coeur de Veau Farci Braisé

Serve the heart with a heart-of-chicory salad garnished with a few cubes of bread that have been rubbed with garlic.

To serve 3

one 1 ½ lb.	veal heart, fat, tubes and fibrous tissue removed, the top half cut vertically into 6 slices of equal width	one ¾ kg.
2 oz.	piece caul (about 10 by 10 inches [25 by 25 cm.] square), soaked and drained	60 g.
3 oz.	pork rind	90 g.
1 tbsp.	lard	15 ml.
3	small onions, sliced	3
1	garlic clove, chopped	1
1	small bouquet garni	1
3	medium-sized young carrots, thickly sliced	3
2½ cups	meat stock *(recipe, page 165)*	625 ml.
2 tbsp.	*beurre manié* (optional)	30 ml.

Pork and herb stuffing

¼ lb.	ground pork	125 g.
2	shallots	2
3	sprigs parsley	3
1	sprig tarragon	1
1	small garlic clove	1
1	slice firm-textured white bread, crusts removed, soaked in milk and squeezed	1
1	egg, lightly beaten	1
	salt and pepper	

To make the stuffing, chop together the shallots, parsley and tarragon and garlic. Mash the bread with the shallot mixture, stir in the pork, then add the egg, salt and pepper. Beat the mixture into a smooth paste. Fry a little of the mixture to taste it and check the seasoning. Stuff the mixture between the slices cut in the top of the heart. When the heart is well filled, squeeze it in your hand to restore it as nearly as possible to its original shape. Spread out the caul, fold it in half and wrap the heart in it; sew the edges of the caul together.

In a heavy casserole or saucepan just large enough to hold the heart, combine the lard and pork rind, placing the rind with its fat side downward. Set over low heat and cook until the lard melts. Then add the onions, garlic, bouquet garni, carrots and the heart. Pour in enough stock to cover the heart and bring the liquid to a boil. Reduce the heat to

low, cover and simmer for three and one half to four hours, turning the heart several times.

Transfer the heart to a cutting board to rest. Remove the bouquet garni from the sauce remaining in the casserole and discard it. If the sauce is not thick and syrupy, add the *beurre manié* and, stirring with a wooden spoon, cook until the sauce thickens and comes to a boil.

Carefully cut and remove the thread from the heart, then slice it crosswise. Arrange the heart slices on a warmed platter and place the carrots and onions around them. Strain the sauce, return it to the heat and bring it to a boil, then pour it over the heart and vegetables.

RENÉE DE GROSSOUVRE
LES RECETTES D'UNE GRAND'MÈRE ET SES CONSEILS

Veal Heart Casserole

Ovenschotel van Kalfshart

To serve 4

1 lb.	veal heart, fat, tubes and fibrous tissue removed, and the flesh cut into ¼-inch [6-mm.] dice	½ kg.
6	medium-sized potatoes, cut into slices ¼ inch [6 mm.] thick	6
5 tbsp.	butter	75 ml.
1	large onion, sliced	1
	salt and pepper	
½ cup	sliced fresh mushrooms	125 ml.
3	tomatoes, peeled, seeded and sliced	3
½ tsp.	dried sage	2 ml.
2 tsp.	ground cumin	10 ml.
⅔ cup	meat stock *(recipe, page 165)*	150 ml.

Drop the potato slices into boiling salted water, boil for five minutes and drain them. Melt 2 tablespoons [30 ml.] of the butter in a skillet and fry the onion over medium heat until golden. Transfer the onion to a bowl, add the diced heart to the skillet and brown it. Salt and pepper the heart and onion.

Butter a casserole and fill it with alternate layers of heart, onion, mushrooms and tomatoes. Reserve a few slices of mushroom and tomato for garnish.

Sprinkle the contents of the casserole with the sage and cumin. Pour in the stock, then add the potato slices in a single layer. Season with salt and pepper. Melt the remaining butter and brush half of it over the potatoes. Set the uncovered casserole in a preheated 375° F. [190° C.] oven and bake for one and one half hours, or until the heart is tender and the potatoes are browned. About 10 minutes before the end of the cooking time, garnish the casserole with the reserved mushroom and tomato slices and brush them with the rest of the melted butter.

HUGH JANS
BISTRO KOKEN

Veal Heart with Veal and Ham Stuffing

Gefülltes Kalbsherz

To serve 2 or 3

one 1½ lb.	veal heart, cut open, fat, tubes and fibrous tissue removed	one ¾ kg.
1	onion, sliced	1
4 tbsp.	butter	60 ml.
3 to 4 cups	boiling water	¾ to 1 liter
	salt and pepper	
2 to 3 tbsp.	flour	30 to 45 ml.
2 to 3 tbsp.	milk	30 to 45 ml.
½ cup	sour cream	125 ml.

White wine and vinegar marinade

1½ cups	dry white wine	375 ml.
5 tbsp.	wine vinegar	75 ml.
5 tbsp.	water	75 ml.
1	bay leaf	1
1	onion, sliced	1
10	peppercorns	10
4	whole cloves	4

Veal and ham stuffing

¼ lb.	ground veal (about ½ cup [125 ml.])	125 g.
¼ cup	finely chopped ham	50 ml.
1 tbsp.	fresh bread crumbs	15 ml.
1	egg	1
1 tbsp.	chopped fresh parsley	15 ml.
1 tbsp.	chopped fresh marjoram	15 ml.
	salt and pepper	

Bring the marinade ingredients to a boil; cool to room temperature. Add the heart, cover and refrigerate for four hours.

In a large bowl, mix all the stuffing ingredients. Remove the heart from the marinade and pat it dry. Stuff the heart and sew it up with string. Strain and reserve the marinade.

In a deep saucepan, fry the heart and sliced onion in the butter over medium heat, turning the heart frequently to brown all sides. Add the reserved marinade and enough boiling water to cover the heart. Season with salt and pepper. Cover the pan and simmer for at least one hour. Then remove the heart, cut it into thick slices and keep them hot.

In a saucepan, stir the flour into the milk; whisk in the cooking liquid and sour cream. Stir the sauce over medium heat until it boils. Strain and serve over the sliced heart.

EVA MARIA BORER
TANTE HEIDI'S SWISS KITCHEN

Skewered Duck Hearts

Brochettes de Coeurs de Canards

If duck hearts are not available, 12 chicken hearts—left whole—make a suitable substitute. Similarly, the duck fat can be replaced by rendered chicken fat.

To serve 3

6	duck hearts, trimmed and cut lengthwise into halves	6
12	fresh mushrooms, stems removed	12
5 oz.	fresh pork belly, cut into 1-inch [2½-cm.] cubes	150 g.
	salt and pepper	
4 tbsp.	rendered duck fat, melted	60 ml.
¾ cup	dry bread crumbs	75 ml.
2	garlic cloves, finely chopped	2
3 tbsp.	chopped fresh parsley	45 ml.

Thread three skewers with pieces of heart alternated with mushroom caps and pork-belly cubes. Season to taste.

Dip the skewers in the melted duck fat, then roll them in the bread crumbs. Place the skewers on an ovenproof plate, sprinkle them with the garlic and parsley, and bake them in a preheated 425° F. [220° C.] oven for 15 minutes—turning and basting them every five minutes.

ÉLIANE AND JACQUETTE DE RIVOYRE
CUISINE LANDAISE

Mock Goose

To serve 8

one 4 lb.	beef heart, fat, tubes and fibrous tissue removed	one 2 kg.
4 cups	meat stock (recipe, page 165)	1 liter
	salt and pepper	
2	bay leaves	2
4	whole cloves	4
1	egg	1
4	large onions, very finely chopped	4
8 to 10	large fresh sage leaves, finely chopped	8 to 10
¼ lb.	chopped suet	125 g.
2 cups	bread crumbs	½ liter
2 to 3 tbsp.	rendered bacon fat, melted	30 to 45 ml.
1 tbsp.	cornstarch, mixed with 2 tbsp. [30 ml.] water	15 ml.

Place the heart in a saucepan with enough stock to cover. Add salt and pepper, the bay leaves and cloves. Simmer for four or five hours. Remove the meat and refrigerate it until the next day. Take off the fat from the stock, strain the stock and reserve 2 cups [½ liter] of it in the refrigerator.

Mix together with the egg, the onions, sage leaves, chopped suet and bread crumbs. Use a little of the mixture to stuff the heart, and form the rest into forcemeat balls. Put the stuffed heart in a greased baking dish with the forcemeat balls around it. Sprinkle the heart with the bacon fat. Bake in a preheated 400° F. [200° C.] oven for one half hour. Meanwhile, warm the reserved stock over low heat; stir in the cornstarch and simmer the mixture until it thickens into a good brown gravy. Serve the gravy with the heart.

BARBARA HARGREAVES (EDITOR)
FARMHOUSE FARE

To Roast a Bullock's Heart

The techniques of stuffing a beef heart and trussing it are demonstrated on pages 40-41. The suet or butter called for in this recipe may be replaced by an equal amount of chopped beef marrow. If the heart is wrapped in caul before baking, larding it is unnecessary. The authors suggest serving melted butter and currant jelly as accompaniments.

To serve 6 to 8

one 4 lb.	beef heart, fat, tubes and fibrous tissues removed	one 2 kg.
2 cups	fresh bread crumbs	½ liter
2 oz.	suet, chopped, or 4 tablespoons [60 ml.] butter, softened	60 g.
1 tbsp.	chopped fresh parsley	15 ml.
1 tsp.	chopped fresh marjoram	5 ml.
1 tsp.	grated lemon peel	5 ml.
	freshly grated nutmeg	
	salt and pepper	
1	egg yolk	1
2 oz.	fresh pork fatback with the rind removed, cut into lardons (optional)	60 g.
¾ cup	red wine	175 ml.

In a bowl, mix the bread crumbs with the suet or butter. Add the parsley, marjoram, lemon peel, a pinch of nutmeg, salt and pepper and the egg yolk. Stuff the heart with this mixture, then truss it. You may, if you wish, lard it with lardons.

Put the heart into an ovenproof dish and roast it in a preheated 450° F. [230° C.] oven for five minutes. Reduce the heat to 375° F. [190° C.] and cook it for another 45 minutes. Pour the wine into the dish and roast the heart for another 10 minutes, or until tender. Remove the string, slice the heart and lay the slices on a serving dish. Strain the cooking liquid and serve it as a gravy with the heart.

F. COLLINGWOOD AND J. WOOLAMS
THE UNIVERSAL COOK

Stuffed Spleen

Gefilte Milts

To serve 2

1	beef spleen, fat and membrane removed, slit lengthwise along one edge	1
1 tbsp.	vegetable oil	15 ml.
1	onion, chopped	1
2 cups	dry bread crumbs	½ liter
2	eggs, beaten	2
	salt and pepper	
2 tbsp.	butter, melted, or substitute vegetable oil	30 ml.

Scrape out most of the pulp of the spleen without cutting the surface. Put this pulp through the fine disk of a food grinder. Heat the oil, fry the onion until it is golden, and mix it well into the spleen pulp with the bread crumbs, beaten eggs, salt and pepper. Stuff the spleen with this mixture and sew it shut. Paint it with the melted butter—or oil, if using. Bake the spleen in a preheated 350° F. [180° C.] oven for about two hours, basting it with hot water every 20 minutes, or until it is well browned.

CALVIN W. SCHWABE
UNMENTIONABLE CUISINE

Baked Stuffed Veal Spleen

Milza Ripiena

To serve 4

1	veal spleen, fat and membrane removed	1
½ cup	chopped fresh mint	125 ml.
¼ cup	chopped fresh parsley	50 ml.
½ tsp.	crushed hot red pepper	2 ml.
1	large garlic clove, finely chopped	1
	salt	
¼ cup	olive oil	50 ml.
¼ cup	wine vinegar	50 ml.

Rinse the spleen well with cold water; dry it with a paper towel. Cut a deep pocket in the spleen and fill it with a mixture of the mint, parsley, crushed pepper, garlic and salt to taste. Close the open end of the pocket with wooden picks or skewers. In a skillet, heat the oil and sauté the spleen for 20 minutes. Cool the spleen on a chopping block. Cut the spleen into thin slices and return them to the skillet. Pour vinegar over the slices; cover and cook until the spleen is tender—about 30 minutes.

ANNA MUFFOLETTO
THE ART OF SICILIAN COOKING

Tongue

Braised Tongue, Roman-Style

Langue de Boeuf à la Romaine

Hamburg parsley root is the parsnip-shaped root of a hardy parsley. If unavailable, a small parsnip may replace the two roots called for in this recipe.

To serve 8

one 3 lb.	beef tongue, soaked, poached for 1½ hours and peeled	one 1½ kg.
	salt and pepper	
4 tbsp.	lard	60 ml.
1	carrot	1
1	large onion, quartered	1
1	bouquet garni	1
¼ cup	brandy, warmed	50 ml.
3 cups	red wine	¾ liter
1 tbsp.	cornstarch, dissolved in 3 tbsp. [45 ml.] cold water	15 ml.
½ cup	dried currants, soaked in warm water for 15 minutes and drained	125 ml.

Olive-oil marinade

½ cup	olive oil	125 ml.
2	large onions, sliced	2
1	large carrot, sliced	1
3	unpeeled garlic cloves, crushed	3
2 cups	wine vinegar	½ liter
5 cups	red wine	1½ liters
	coarse salt	
8	shallots, sliced	8
4 tsp.	crushed peppercorns	20 ml.
4	celery ribs	4
4	cloves	4
4	sprigs thyme	4
2	bay leaves	2
2	Hamburg parsley roots	2

To make the marinade, heat the oil and add to it the onions, carrot and garlic cloves. Sauté them until they are lightly colored, then pour in the vinegar and red wine. Add a pinch of coarse salt and the rest of the marinade ingredients, and boil over high heat until the liquid is reduced by half—about 45 minutes. Allow the marinade to cool, then strain it into a large bowl—pressing down on the herbs and vegetables to extract their liquid.

Put the peeled tongue into the marinade, cover and refrigerate for 48 hours.

To cook the tongue, remove it from the marinade and pat it dry. Reserve the marinade. Salt and pepper the tongue. Heat the lard in a large pot and, when it is very hot, put the tongue into the pot. Add the carrot, onion and bouquet garni. Sauté the vegetables until they are lightly colored. Pour the brandy over the tongue and set it alight. When the flame has died, pour about 1 cup [¼ liter] of the marinade liquid and all of the red wine into the pot, and season the mixture very lightly with salt. Cover the pot and simmer the tongue for three and one half hours, turning it over twice.

Remove the tongue and put it in a saucepan. Over high heat, reduce the tongue cooking liquid by about half. Then stir in the diluted cornstarch. Strain this sauce over the tongue. Season the sauce to taste, cover the pan and simmer the tongue for 15 minutes. Add the currants, then place the tongue in a deep platter and pour the sauce over it.

PAUL BOUILLARD
LA CUISINE AU COIN DU FEU

Braised Beef Tongue

Glossa Vodini Braisé

To serve 4 to 6

one 3 lb.	beef tongue, soaked, blanched for 3 minutes and rinsed	one 1½ kg.
	salt and peppercorns	
4 tbsp.	butter	60 ml.
1	onion, finely chopped	1
2	carrots, cut into small pieces	2
2	celery ribs, cut into small pieces	2
⅓ cup	dry white wine	75 ml.
3	medium-sized tomatoes, peeled, seeded and finely chopped	3
2	cinnamon sticks, 2 inches [5 cm.] long	2
3	whole cloves	3

Put the tongue in a pan with enough hot water to cover. Add salt and a few peppercorns and simmer about two hours. Remove the tongue from the stock and drop it into a basin of cold water. Reserve 2 to 3 tablespoons [30 to 45 ml.] of the stock. Peel the tongue and remove the bones at the root. Heat the butter in a nonreactive saucepan and brown the tongue all over. Transfer the tongue to a dish and add the onions, carrots and celery to the pan. Fry for five minutes, then place the tongue on the bed of vegetables. Pour in the wine and add the tomatoes and the reserved stock. Adjust the seasoning and add the cinnamon and cloves. Cover the pan and simmer gently for 35 to 40 minutes.

MARO DUNCAN
COOKING THE GREEK WAY

Beef Tongue with Almonds

Lingua di Bue alle Mandorle

To serve 4

one 3 lb.	beef tongue, soaked, blanched, rinsed, poached in salted water for 1½ hours or until tender, peeled, trimmed and sliced	one 1½ kg.
2 tbsp.	butter	30 ml.
½ cup	almonds, blanched, peeled and sliced	125 ml.
¼ cup	flour	50 ml.
¾ cup	veal stock (recipe, page 165)	175 ml.
¼ cup	port	50 ml.
1 tbsp.	tomato paste	15 ml.
1 tsp.	wine vinegar	5 ml.
	ground cinnamon	
	salt and pepper	
¼ cup	light cream	50 ml.
6	medium-sized potatoes, boiled, peeled, sliced and tossed in 2 tbsp. [30 ml.] melted butter	6
3 or 4	sprigs fresh parsley	3 or 4

Over medium heat, melt the butter in a pan, add the almonds and fry them lightly, turning them often, until they are golden brown. Add the flour, mix well for a few minutes, then add the stock and port. Stir until the sauce is creamy and thick. Mix the tomato paste with the vinegar and add them to the sauce. Still stirring, add a pinch of cinnamon, a little salt and pepper and, finally, the cream. Reduce the heat and continue stirring. Bring the sauce to a boil, but remove it from the heat when you see the first bubble.

Arrange the potato slices on a heated serving dish, covered with the slices of tongue. Pour the sauce over the tongue and garnish with the sprigs of parsley.

SAVINA ROGGERO
COME SCEGLIERE E CUCINARE LA CARNI

Beef Tongue with Liver Pâté Filling

Langue de Boeuf Lucullus

To serve 8 to 10

one 3 lb.	smoked beef tongue, soaked	one 1½ kg.
8 oz.	imported smoked goose-liver pâté	¼ kg.
2	garlic cloves	2
1	bay leaf	1
1	medium-sized onion, quartered	1
6	peppercorns	6
2 tbsp.	unflavored powdered gelatin	30 ml.
¼ cup plus 2 tbsp.	Madeira or port	80 ml.
3 cups	beef stock (recipe, page 165)	¾ liter
4 tbsp.	butter, softened	60 ml.
	salt and pepper	

Place the tongue in a heavy casserole, cover it with cold water, and add the garlic, bay leaf, onion and peppercorns. Bring the water to a boil and simmer slowly for one to one and one half hours, or until the tongue is tender. Drain the tongue, cool it, remove the skin and bones, cover tightly with plastic wrap, then refrigerate it.

Put the gelatin in a small bowl and pour ¼ cup [50 ml.] of Madeira over it. Bring the stock to the boiling point in a small pot; add the softened gelatin and stir to dissolve it. Put this aspic aside to cool.

Prepare the stuffing by creaming together the liver pâté and the butter. Add 2 tablespoons [30 ml.] of Madeira, salt and pepper, and 2 tablespoons of the cool aspic, and mix well. Put aside ½ cup [125 ml.] of the pâté stuffing.

Cut the tongue into slices ¼ inch [6 mm.] thick. Leave a piece about 2 inches [5 cm.] thick at the larger end. Place this piece at one end of a rectangular platter. Coat a slice of tongue with the stuffing and place it—stuffing outward—against the piece on the platter. Coat each of the remaining slices similarly and arrange them side by side to re-form the tongue in its original shape. Spread the reserved stuffing over the entire surface of the tongue. Refrigerate the tongue for two hours and chill it well.

With a pastry brush, paint on a coating of the aspic. Chill the tongue; repeat the painting and chilling processes one or two more times. Refrigerate the remaining aspic.

Remove the tongue from the refrigerator at least one hour before serving. Chop the leftover aspic into small pieces and scatter them along the top and sides of the tongue.

CAROL CUTLER
THE SIX-MINUTE SOUFFLÉ AND OTHER CULINARY DELIGHTS

Jellied Beef Tongue
Langue de Boeuf à la Ferry

To serve 10 to 12

one 3 lb.	beef tongue, soaked	one 1½ kg.
½	calf's foot, cleaned and rinsed	½
7 cups	beef stock *(recipe, page 165)*	1¾ liters
1½ cups	dry white wine	350 ml.
¼ lb.	pork rind	125 g.
2	sprigs thyme	2
2	sprigs parsley	2
1	bay leaf	1
2	garlic cloves	2
1	onion	1

Combine all the ingredients in a heavy pan. Bring the mixture to a boil, cover partially and simmer the tongue over very low heat for a minimum of six hours. Remove the tongue and strain the cooking liquid through a fine-meshed sieve; discard the contents of the sieve. Peel the tongue and trim it. Place it in the strained liquid and refrigerate it. Serve the following day, when the liquid will have jelled.

GASTON DERYS
LES PLATS AU VIN

Sweet-and-Sour Tongue

To serve 8

one 3 lb.	smoked or corned beef tongue, soaked, poached for 1½ hours, peeled, trimmed and sliced	one 1½ kg.
4 tbsp.	butter	60 ml.
1	medium-sized onion, thinly sliced	1
2 tsp.	flour	10 ml.
about ¼ cup	fresh lemon juice	about 50 ml.
1½ cups	beef stock *(recipe, page 165)*	375 ml.
¼ cup	red wine vinegar	50 ml.
4 tsp.	sugar	20 ml.
	freshly ground black pepper	
½ cup	golden raisins, soaked in warm water for 15 minutes and drained	125 ml.

To prepare the sauce, melt the butter in a heavy saucepan, add the onion and cook over very low heat until it is golden. Add the flour, stirring with a wooden spoon. Then add ¼ cup [50 ml.] of lemon juice and the stock, stirring until smooth. Cover the pan and simmer the sauce over very low heat.

In a small saucepan, heat the vinegar. Stir in the sugar

and, stirring constantly, cook over high heat for five to six minutes or until the mixture is slightly syrupy. Gradually add the syrup to the sauce, stirring to combine the flavors. Add pepper to taste. If the sauce is not quite tart enough for your taste, add additional lemon juice. Stir in the raisins and simmer the sauce for a few minutes longer.

If you are using the sauce over just-cooked tongue, place the tongue slices on a warmed platter and spoon the sauce on top. If the slices are cold, place them in a pan, pour the sauce over them and heat them gently for five to 10 minutes.

DORIS TOBIAS AND MARY MERRIS
THE GOLDEN LEMON

Beef Tongue in Gray Sauce

Hamburg parsley root is the parsnip-shaped root of a hardy parsley. If unavailable, a small parsnip may be substituted.

This is one of the traditional old Polish dishes and is considered a national delicacy. Serve it with either mashed potatoes or boiled noodles. The sauce should be mildly sour, spicy with a slight note of barely discernible sweetness.

To serve 8

one 3 lb.	corned beef tongue, soaked	one 1½ kg.
1	celeriac, peeled and cut into quarters	1
1	Hamburg parsley root	1
2	carrots, cut into halves	2
2	leeks, white parts only, sliced into halves	2
1	onion, stuck with a whole clove	1
5	peppercorns	5
3	whole allspice	3
1	small bay leaf	1
Gray sauce		
4 tbsp.	butter	60 ml.
¼ cup	flour	50 ml.
½ cup	red wine	125 ml.
1 tbsp.	fresh lemon juice plus 1 strip lemon peel	15 ml.
½ cup	almonds, blanched, peeled and slivered	125 ml.
1 tbsp.	sugar cubes	15 ml.

Put the tongue into a deep pan. Pour in boiling water to cover it and add the celeriac, parsley root, carrots, leeks, onion, peppercorns, allspice and bay leaf. Simmer the tongue for two to three hours, or until tender. Let it cool in the cooking liquid before peeling it. Strain and reserve 1½ cups [375 ml.] of the cooking liquid. Carve the tongue diagonally into thin slices.

To make the gray sauce, melt the butter in a saucepan and add the flour. Stirring constantly, cook until the mixture is lightly browned. Add the reserved cooking liquid, red wine, lemon juice and peel, and the almonds.

In a skillet, melt the sugar with a few drops of water over high heat. When the syrup turns a caramel color, stir it gradually into the sauce. Simmer for another five minutes, put in the sliced tongue and bring the sauce to a boil.

Arrange the tongue on a warmed platter and pour some sauce over it. Serve the remaining sauce in a sauceboat.

MARIA LEMNIS AND HENRYK VITRY
OLD POLISH TRADITIONS IN THE KITCHEN AND AT TABLE

Tongue and Mushroom Crumble

To serve 6

one 3 lb.	corned beef tongue, soaked overnight	one 1½ kg.
1	medium-sized carrot, chopped	1
2	medium-sized onions, 1 coarsely chopped, 1 finely chopped	2
1	bouquet garni	1
1¼ cups	hard cider	300 ml.
¼ lb.	fresh mushrooms, sliced (about 1¼ cups [300 ml.])	125 g.
	salt and pepper	
8 tbsp.	butter	120 ml.
1 tbsp.	flour	15 ml.
⅓ cup	dry white wine	75 ml.
¾ cup	fresh white bread crumbs	175 ml.

Put the tongue into a large pan with the carrot and coarsely chopped onion. Add the bouquet garni, the cider and enough water to cover the tongue by about ½ inch [1 cm.]. Bring the liquid slowly to a boil, skim it and cover the pan. Let the tongue simmer until it is cooked—approximately one and a half to two hours. Remove the tongue to a dish, peel off the skin and cut out any tiny bones. Let it cool. Strain the cooking liquid into a bowl.

To assemble the dish, slice the tongue and place it in a buttered shallow ovenproof dish. Cook the mushrooms in 2 tablespoons [30 ml.] of the butter, season them with salt and pepper and distribute them evenly over the tongue slices. In a small, heavy pan, cook the finely chopped onion in 4 tablespoons [60 ml.] of the remaining butter until soft; cover the pan so that the onion does not brown. Stir in the flour, cook for two minutes, then add the white wine and enough strained cooking liquid to make a thin sauce, about 1¼ cups

[300 ml.]. Let this mixture cook uncovered until it forms a well-flavored, moderately thick sauce, then tip it over the tongue slices. Add enough sauce so that the slices are well moistened, but not swimming about. Melt the remaining butter, mix in the bread crumbs and spread this mixture on top of the tongue. Bake in a preheated 400° F. [200° C.] oven until everything is well heated through and bubbling, and the top is nicely browned.

JANE GRIGSON
ENGLISH FOOD

Braised Veal Tongues

To serve 6

6	small veal tongues, soaked	6
1	onion, sliced	1
1	carrot, sliced	1
2 tbsp.	butter	30 ml.
	salt and pepper	
⅔ cup	Madeira	150 ml.
2 cups	veal stock *(recipe, page 165)*	½ liter
1	bouquet garni	1
3	whole cloves	3
⅓ cup	heavy cream, mixed with 1 tsp. [5 ml.] arrowroot	75 ml.
1 tbsp.	finely cut chives	15 ml.

Sauté the onion and carrot in the butter. Set the tongues on the vegetables and sprinkle with salt and pepper. Cover the pot and keep it over very low heat until the tongues look steamed, 25 to 30 minutes. Add one third of the Madeira and reduce it over high heat until 1 teaspoon [5 ml.] of the liquid is left. Repeat the same operation twice with the remaining Madeira. Add the stock, bouquet garni and cloves; bring to a boil. Cover with foil and the pot lid and bake in a 325° F. [160° C.] oven for one and one half to two hours.

Strain and degrease the cooking juices. Peel the tongues and cut them lengthwise into halves. Place on a serving platter. Bring the juices to a boil and thicken them with the cream mixture. Add the chives and immediately spoon this sauce over the tongues.

MADELEINE KAMMAN
THE MAKING OF A COOK

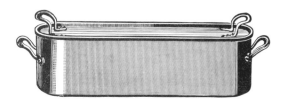

Tongue in Spicy Sauce
Langue de Veau en Sauce

The volatile oils in hot chilies may make your skin sting and your eyes burn; after handling chilies, avoid touching your face and wash your hands promptly.

To serve 4

one 1½ lb.	veal tongue, soaked, poached in salted water for 45 minutes, peeled and cut into cubes	one 375 g.
1	fresh hot red chili, stemmed, seeded, chopped and crushed to a paste	1
2 tsp.	paprika	10 ml.
2	onions, chopped	2
10 tbsp.	butter	150 ml.
1 tsp.	cumin seeds	5 ml.
1 tsp.	coriander seeds, crushed	5 ml.
about 5 tbsp.	wine vinegar	about 75 ml.

Put the tongue into a saucepan and add the crushed chili, paprika, onions and butter. Pour in water to cover. Cover the saucepan with a lid and simmer the mixture over low heat for three hours. Prick the tongue with a skewer. If the meat is tender and the juices run clear, it is cooked.

Add the cumin seeds, coriander and vinegar to taste. Boil the sauce until it is smooth and slightly thickened. Serve the tongue in the sauce in a warmed serving dish.

AHMED LAASRI
240 RECETTES DE LA CUISINE MAROCAINE

Veal Tongue in Red Sauce
Langue de Veau en Sauce Rouge

To serve 4

one 1½ lb.	veal tongue, soaked, poached for 45 minutes, peeled and cut into 1½-inch [3-cm.] cubes	one ¾ kg.
½ cup	olive oil	125 ml.
4	garlic cloves, crushed to a paste	4
1 tsp. each	ground coriander, cumin and paprika	5 ml. each
½ tsp.	cayenne pepper (optional)	2 ml.
	salt	
4 cups	water	1 liter
1 tbsp.	white wine vinegar	15 ml.

Put the cubes of tongue into a pot and add all of the remaining ingredients except the vinegar. Partially cover the pot and simmer over medium heat for 35 minutes. Add the vinegar and cook for a further 10 minutes. The sauce should be thick; reduce it over high heat if necessary. Serve hot.

FETTOUMA BENKIRANE
LA NOUVELLE CUISINE MAROCAINE

A Lamb Tongue Pie
Une Tourte de Langues de Mouton

The technique of braising tongue is shown on pages 68-69. To make the short-crust dough, cut about 14 tablespoons [210 ml.] of cold butter into small pieces. Rub the butter into 2 cups [½ liter] of flour and 1 teaspoon [5 ml.] of salt until the mixture resembles fine crumbs. Stir in just enough water—⅓ to ½ cup [75 to 125 ml.]—to form a dough that can be gathered into a firm ball. Wrap the dough in plastic wrap or foil and chill it for at least 30 minutes before use.

To serve 6

six 5 oz.	braised lamb tongues, braising liquid strained and reserved	six 150 g.
1 lb.	short-crust dough	½ kg.
3 or 4	slices lean bacon	3 or 4
2 tbsp.	butter, cut into pieces	30 ml.
2 tbsp.	fresh lemon juice	30 ml.
Chicken and mushroom stuffing		
¼ lb.	chicken breast, poached for 10 minutes, skinned, boned and chopped	125 g.
½ lb.	fresh mushrooms, finely chopped	¼ kg.
1½ cups	fresh bread crumbs, soaked in ½ cup [125 ml.] heavy cream	375 ml.
¼ lb.	suet, finely chopped	125 g.
3½ oz.	salt pork, blanched and cut into small cubes	100 g.
1 tbsp.	chopped fresh parsley	15 ml.
8 or 9	scallions, chopped	8 or 9
3 or 4	egg yolks	3 or 4
	salt and pepper	

Slice the tongues lengthwise into strips. Roll out half of the dough and use it to line a 9-inch [23-cm.] deep-dish piepan or a shallow casserole.

To make the stuffing, mix all of the ingredients together. Spread half of the stuffing over the dough in the piepan. Arrange the strips of tongue over the stuffing, then cover them with the remaining stuffing. Lay the bacon strips on top and dot with the pieces of butter. Roll out the rest of the dough and set it loosely over the pie. Bake the pie in a preheated 375° F. [190° C.] oven for about one hour, or until the crust is golden brown.

Meanwhile, boil the braising liquid over high heat until it is reduced to about a third of its original volume. Add the lemon juice. Remove the pie from the oven, lift off the lid, skim off the fat from the surface of the meat and pour in the braising liquid. Before serving, replace the pastry lid, return the pie to the oven and bake it for another 10 minutes, or until golden brown.

PIERRE JOSEPH BUC'HOZ
L'ART DE PRÉPARER LES ALIMENTS

Deviled Lamb Tongues

Langues de Mouton à la Diable

To serve 6

six 5 oz.	lamb tongues, soaked	six 150 g.
1½ quarts	meat stock *(recipe, page 165)*	1½ liters
	salt and pepper	
2 tbsp.	olive oil	30 ml.
2 tbsp.	prepared mustard	30 ml.
1¾ cups	dry bread crumbs	425 ml.
Deviled sauce		
3 tbsp.	chopped shallots	45 ml.
1 cup	dry white wine	¼ liter
½ cup	white wine vinegar	125 ml.
	salt and cayenne pepper	
1 tbsp.	chopped fresh parsley	15 ml.

Simmer the tongues in the stock for about one hour, or until they are tender. Let them cool in the stock before removing them and peeling them. Reserve the stock.

To make the sauce, put the shallots, white wine and vinegar into a nonreactive saucepan. Boil over high heat until the liquid is reduced by two thirds. Add 1 cup [¼ liter] of the reserved stock, reduce the heat and simmer for 10 minutes. Season with salt and a large pinch of cayenne. If you like, strain the sauce. Add the parsley and keep the sauce warm.

Split each tongue lengthwise and season it with salt and pepper. In a bowl, beat the olive oil and mustard together. Dip each tongue half in the oil mixture, then roll it in the bread crumbs. Place the tongues about 5 inches [13 cm.] from the heat source of a preheated broiler and broil them for about 10 minutes on each side, or until nicely browned. Pour the sauce into a sauceboat and serve it with the tongues.

IRENE LABARRE AND JEAN MERCIER
LA CUISINE DU MOUTON

Marinated Lamb Tongues in Batter

Langues de Mouton Marinées

To serve 4

four 5 oz.	lamb tongues, soaked, poached for 30 minutes and peeled	four 150 g.
½ lb.	lard, or 8 tablespoons [120 ml.] butter and ⅓ cup [75 ml.] vegetable oil	¼ kg.
8	sprigs parsley	8
White wine marinade		
2	lemons, the peel cut into strips, the juice strained	2
½ cup	white wine vinegar	125 ml.
	salt and pepper	
5	whole cloves	5
1-inch	strip dried orange peel	2½-cm.
1	bay leaf	1
1 tsp.	rosemary	5 ml.
1 tbsp.	chopped fresh thyme	15 ml.
1	small onion, chopped	1
2	scallions, chopped	2
1 tbsp.	capers, rinsed and drained	15 ml.
White wine batter		
1 cup	flour	¼ liter
¼ tsp.	salt	1 ml.
2	egg yolks	2
¾ cup	dry white wine	175 ml.

Put the marinade ingredients into a bowl. Add the tongues and marinate them for 15 minutes; because tongues have a spongy consistency they will absorb all the marinade they can hold in that time. Drain them and wipe them dry.

To make the batter, mix the flour and salt with the egg yolks and wine. The batter should have the consistency of a thick cream. Soak the tongues in the batter for five minutes.

In a large skillet, heat the lard or butter and oil over high heat. Place the tongues in the fat, making sure that they do not touch each other, and fry them on both sides until they are evenly browned. Drain them on paper towels, then move them to a warmed platter. Garnish with the parsley sprigs.

L. S. ROBERT
L'ART DE BIEN TRAITER

Lamb Tongues with Lentil Purée

Langues de Mouton à la Purée de Lentilles

If the tongues are small, use 12 instead of six. A single piece of salt pork weighing about ¾ pound [350 g.] will supply both the diced fat and rind for the tongues and the sliced salt pork that flavors the lentils. The rind may be cut into pieces and rolled into scrolls as demonstrated on pages 68-69.

	To serve 6	
5 oz.	lamb tongues, soaked, poached for 30 minutes and peeled	150 g.
2 oz.	pork fatback, or salt pork with the rind removed, diced	60 g.
1	carrot, sliced into rounds	1
1	medium-sized onion, thinly sliced and separated into rings	1
1	bouquet garni	1
¼ lb.	salt-pork rind, blanched for 3 minutes	125 g.
1 cup	dry white wine	¼ liter
2 cups	veal stock (recipe, page 165)	½ liter
Lentil purée		
1 lb.	dried lentils	½ kg.
	salt	
1	onion, stuck with 1 whole clove	1
1	small carrot, split in half	1
½	garlic bulb, unpeeled	½
1	small bouquet garni	1
5 oz.	lean salt pork with the rind removed, blanched in boiling water for 3 minutes, drained	150 g.
2 tbsp.	butter, cut into small pieces	30 ml.
	freshly ground black pepper	

Choose a pan big enough to hold the tongues in one layer. Fry the diced salt pork until it renders its fat, then brown the sliced carrot and onion in it. Take out the vegetables and set them aside. Add the tongues and brown them lightly. Set them aside. Now make a layer of the carrots and onions in the bottom of the pan, add the bouquet garni and cover with the blanched pork rind. Place the tongues on top.

Pour in the white wine, and boil to reduce the wine by two thirds. Heat the stock to the boiling point and pour it into the pan. Place a piece of buttered parchment paper cut the same size as the pan over the tongues, cover the pan with a lid and cook in a preheated 300° F. [150° C.] oven for two hours.

To make the lentil purée, place the lentils in a saucepan, cover them with cold water and boil them for five minutes; drain them. Pour just enough water into the saucepan to cover the lentils. Add ½ tablespoon [7 ml.] of salt for each quart [1 liter] of water. Add the onion stuck with the clove, the carrot, garlic, small bouquet garni and the salt pork. Bring to a boil, skim, and reduce the heat; simmer over the lowest possible heat for one and three quarters to two hours.

Drain the lentils; discard the onion, carrot, garlic and bouquet garni; and reserve the salt pork. Rub the lentils, while still very hot, through a fine-meshed sieve. Pour the purée into a saucepan and reduce it over high heat, stirring and scraping the bottom of the pan with a wooden spatula. When the purée has thickened, return it to a thick pouring consistency by adding about ½ cup [125 ml.] of braising liquid from the tongues. Remove the pan from the heat and stir in the butter. Grind pepper over the top.

Uncover the tongues, discard the pork rind and increase the oven heat to its highest temperature. Baste the tongues repeatedly with their juices. The juices will caramelize slightly and cover the tongues with a shiny coating.

Pile the lentil purée into a shallow dish and arrange the tongues on top with the glazed side uppermost. Strain the braising liquid and baste each tongue with a tablespoon [15 ml.] of it. Cut the reserved pork into six pieces and place each piece at the base of a tongue. Serve with the remaining braising juices from a sauceboat.

PAUL BOCUSE
PAUL BOCUSE'S FRENCH COOKING

Lamb Tongues with Onions

Langues de Mouton aux Oignons en Crépines

A velouté, poulette or tomato sauce (recipes, page 166) will complement the tongues.

	To serve 4	
four 5 oz.	lamb tongues, soaked, poached for 30 minutes and peeled	four 150 g.
6 tbsp.	butter	90 ml.
12	large onions, coarsely chopped	12
2	salt anchovies, filleted, soaked in water for 30 minutes and drained	2
2	shallots, chopped	2
1 tbsp.	chopped fresh fennel leaves	15 ml.
2 tbsp.	chopped fresh parsley	30 ml.
3	egg yolks, 1 beaten	3
	salt and coarsely ground pepper	
½ lb.	caul, soaked, drained and cut into 4 equal-sized pieces	¼ kg.
1 cup	dry bread crumbs	¼ liter

Melt the butter and cook the onions over low heat until they are transparent and golden brown—about 30 minutes. Add the anchovies, shallots, fennel, parsley and two egg yolks and mix thoroughly. Season with salt and pepper. Spread out the pieces of caul. Spread a layer of the onion mixture in the center of each piece, place a tongue on top and cover with more of the onion mixture. Wrap the caul around the tongue-and-onion assembly. Dip the caul packages in the beaten egg yolk and then in the bread crumbs.

Lay the packages in a buttered shallow ovenproof dish and bake them in a preheated 400° F. [200° C.] oven until they are golden—about 30 minutes, or place them under a preheated broiler for about 10 minutes on each side. Serve them with any sauce you consider suitable.

MENON
LES SOUPERS DE LA COUR

Sweetbreads, Brains and Fries

Sweetbreads Morris Flexner

To serve 4

1½ lb.	veal sweetbreads, soaked, parboiled, membrane removed, pressed under weights	¾ kg.
3 cups	water	¾ liter
2	celery ribs, leafy tops included	2
2 or 3	sprigs parsley, plus 2 tbsp. [30 ml.] chopped fresh parsley	2 or 3
1	small onion, quartered	1
¼ tsp.	peppercorns or freshly ground black pepper	1 ml.
1 tsp.	salt	5 ml.
1	bunch scallions, green tops included	1
½ lb.	fresh mushrooms	¼ kg.
2 tbsp.	butter	30 ml.
1 cup	freshly cooked shelled peas	¼ liter
2	eggs, hard-boiled and coarsely diced	2
¼ cup	heavy cream, mixed with 2 tbsp. [30 ml.] flour	50 ml.
	paprika	

Boil the sweetbreads in the water, with the celery, sprigs of parsley and onion. Add the peppercorns or black pepper, salt and scallions. When the mixture comes to a boil, put a lid on the pot, turn the heat low and cook for 45 minutes, or until

the sweetbreads are tender. Strain the cooking liquor and set it aside. Meanwhile, sauté the mushrooms in the butter for five minutes. Add the peas and hard-boiled eggs. Add the sweetbreads, cut into chunks. Add 1½ cups [375 ml.] of the reserved cooking liquor and the heavy-cream paste. Stir to make a smooth sauce. Taste for seasoning, add more salt and pepper if needed. Pour into a serving dish, sprinkle the surface with the chopped parsley and a dash of paprika. Serve on toast or buttered hot biscuits.

MARION FLEXNER
OUT OF KENTUCKY KITCHENS

Sweetbreads with Peas

Animelle co' Piselli

For a thicker sauce, the sweetbreads may be floured lightly before they are browned. In this case, sauté them in the butter as soon as it is melted and remove them from the pan before adding the onions; return them to the pan when the peas and ham are added. The sliced onions called for in this recipe may be replaced by about ½ pound [¼ kg.] of small boiling onions—cooked in butter for 20 minutes and added to the pan with the peas.

To serve 3 or 4

1 lb.	sweetbreads, soaked, parboiled, membrane removed, pressed under weights and sliced	½ kg.
3 tbsp.	butter	45 ml.
2	medium-sized onions, sliced	2
	salt and pepper	
about 1¼ cups	dry white wine	about 300 ml.
½ cup	meat stock (recipe, page 165)	125 ml.
1 lb.	small peas, shelled, boiled for 4 minutes in salted water and drained	½ kg.
¼ lb.	ham, cut into julienne	125 g.

In a deep sauté pan, melt the butter over medium heat and add the onions. Cook the onions until they are lightly browned—about 10 minutes, then add the sweetbreads and salt and pepper. When the sweetbreads are golden brown—after about 10 minutes—add half of the wine and all of the stock. Cook until the liquid is reduced by half, then add the peas, the ham and the rest of the wine. Adjust the seasoning and cook for about five minutes, until the peas and ham are heated through.

GIOVANNI RIGHI PARENTI
LA GRANDE COCINA TOSCANA

Sweetbreads in Scallop Shells

Conchiglie di Animella di Vitello Gratinate

To make the anchovy butter, first fillet one salt anchovy, soak the fillets in water for 30 minutes, then rinse them and pat them dry. In a mortar pound the fillets with 1½ tablespoons [22 ml.] of softened butter. Finally, sieve the mixture.

To serve 6

1 lb.	veal sweetbreads, soaked, parboiled in meat stock (recipe, page 165), membrane removed, pressed under weights and meat cut into walnut-sized pieces, ¾ cup [175 ml.] of the stock reserved	½ kg.
5 tbsp.	butter, 2 tbsp. [30 ml.] cut into small pieces	75 ml.
1 tbsp.	flour	15 ml.
½ cup	dry white wine	125 ml.
1 tsp.	freshly grated nutmeg	5 ml.
1 cup	sliced fresh mushrooms	¼ liter
⅓ cup	freshly grated Parmesan cheese	75 ml.
2 tbsp.	anchovy butter	30 ml.
1 tbsp.	chopped fresh parsley	15 ml.
½ cup	dry bread crumbs	125 ml.

Melt 1 tablespoon [15 ml.] of the butter in a small, non-reactive pan, add the flour and cook over low heat for two minutes, stirring constantly. Add the wine and the reserved stock and cook for six to seven minutes, stirring constantly. Season this sauce with the nutmeg.

In a skillet, sauté the mushrooms in 2 tablespoons [30 ml.] of the remaining butter until they are lightly browned —about three minutes. Add them to the sauce together with the grated cheese and the sweetbreads. Mix well.

Spread 12 scallop shells with the anchovy butter, sprinkle them with the parsley and fill each with about 2 heaping tablespoonfuls of the sweetbread-and-mushroom mixture. Sprinkle with the bread crumbs and dot with the small pieces of butter. Bake the filled shells in a preheated 400° F. [200° C.] oven for 15 minutes until golden brown; serve hot.

NINO BERGESE
MANGIARE DA RE

Braised Sweetbreads with Sorrel Purée

Ris de Veau Classique

To make the sorrel purée, blanch 2 pounds [1 kg.] of sorrel for a few seconds in rapidly boiling salted water, then drain the leaves thoroughly. Stew the sorrel in 2 tablespoons [30 ml.] of butter, stirring until the leaves are very soft—about 10 minutes. Purée the sorrel in a food mill or food processor and season it to taste with salt and pepper.

To serve 4 to 6

2 lb.	sweetbreads, soaked, parboiled, membrane removed, pressed under weights	1 kg.
2 tbsp.	butter	30 ml.
1 cup	meat stock (recipe, page 165)	¼ liter
1½ cups	sorrel purée	375 ml.

Melt the butter in a pan. When the foam subsides, add the sweetbreads and cook them until lightly browned—about 10 minutes. Add the stock to the pan, cover, and simmer until the sweetbreads are tender—about 40 minutes.

To glaze the sweetbreads, transfer them to a fireproof dish. Place the dish about 4 inches [10 cm.] below the heat source of a preheated broiler. Basting the sweetbreads frequently with the cooking liquid, broil for 10 to 15 minutes. Serve them on a bed of sorrel purée.

TANTE MARGUERITE
LA CUISINE DE LA BONNE MÉNAGÈRE

Skewered Sweetbreads

Brochettes de Ris de Veau

To make the maître d'hôtel butter called for in this recipe, beat 2 tablespoons [30 ml.] of fresh lemon juice, 1 tablespoon [15 ml.] of finely chopped fresh parsley, 1 teaspoon [5 ml.] of salt and a small pinch of freshly ground pepper into 14 tablespoons [210 ml.] of softened butter.

To serve 4

2 lb.	veal sweetbreads, soaked, parboiled, membrane removed, pressed under weights, sliced ½ inch [1 cm.] thick and cut into 1-inch [2½-cm.] squares	1 kg.
	salt and pepper	
¼ cup	vegetable oil	50 ml.
¼ cup	chopped fresh parsley	50 ml.
1 lb.	thickly sliced bacon, cut into 1-inch [2½-cm.] squares	½ kg.
3½ cups	fresh bread crumbs	875 ml.
1 cup	*maître d'hôtel* butter	¼ liter
1	lemon, thinly sliced	1

Season the sweetbreads with salt and pepper, brush them with the oil and sprinkle them with the parsley. Thread alternate pieces of sweetbread and bacon onto four skewers. Sprinkle the meat with the bread crumbs, place the skewers across a baking pan and set the pan 6 inches [15 cm.] below the heat source of a preheated broiler. Broil for 15 to 18 minutes, turning the skewers frequently so that all four sides are equally cooked. Transfer the skewered meat to a hot dish and dot with *maître d'hôtel* butter. Garnish the dish with the slices of lemon.

CHARLES RANHOFER
THE EPICUREAN

Veal Sweetbreads in Spinach

Paupiette de Ris de Veau Braisé

To serve 4

1 ¼ lb.	veal sweetbreads, soaked, parboiled, membrane removed, pressed under weights	600 g.
7 tbsp.	butter	105 ml.
2 cups	chopped mixed carrots, onions, shallots and leeks	½ liter
1	garlic clove, chopped	1
1	sprig thyme	1
½	bay leaf	½
1	whole clove	1
½ cup	dry white wine	125 ml.
about 1 quart	meat stock *(recipe, page 165)*	about 1 liter
2 tbsp.	*beurre manié*	30 ml.
1 tsp.	Dijon mustard	5 ml.
	curry powder	
2 cups	heavy cream	½ liter
8	spinach leaves, blanched for a few seconds in salted water	8

Melt 5 tablespoons [75 ml.] of the butter in a saucepan and add the mixed vegetables, garlic, thyme, bay leaf and clove. Stew the mixture very gently until the onions are transparent—about 15 minutes—then place the sweetbreads on top. Moisten the ingredients with the wine and add just enough stock to cover them. Cover the pan and cook over low heat for 15 minutes. Remove the sweetbreads and keep them warm.

To make the sauce, strain the cooking liquid into a clean pan and reduce it by half over high heat. Whisk the pieces of *beurre manié* into the reduced liquid. Add the mustard, a pinch of curry powder and the cream. Reduce this sauce until it is thick enough to coat the back of a spoon.

Cut the sweetbreads into eight equal-sized pieces. Roll each piece in a freshly parboiled spinach leaf and keep the sweetbreads warm in a serving dish. Strain the sauce through a fine-meshed sieve and check the seasoning. Beat in the rest of the butter, pour the sauce over the sweetbreads and serve them at once.

GEORGES BLANC
MES RECETTES

A May Dish of Sweetbreads and Turnips

Ris de Veau aux Navets du Mois de Mai

To serve 4

1 lb.	veal sweetbreads, soaked, parboiled, membrane removed, pressed under weights	½ kg.
10 to 14 tbsp.	butter	150 to 210 ml.
3 lb.	young turnips, cut into 1-inch [2½-cm.] balls	1½ kg.
¼ cup	confectioners' sugar	50 ml.
about 1 ½ cups	water	about 375 ml.
	salt and pepper	
1	carrot, thinly sliced	1
1	onion, thinly sliced	1
1	sprig parsley	1
⅓ cup	dry vermouth	75 ml.
⅓ cup	chopped fresh chervil	75 ml.

In a large saucepan, melt 6 tablespoons [90 ml.] of the butter, add the turnips and sprinkle them with the sugar. Pour in the water and cook the turnips uncovered over low heat for about 20 minutes, or until the water has evaporated and the turnips are tender and glazed with a golden sheen. If the turnips appear to be glazing before they are tender, add a little water to prolong the cooking. Salt and pepper the turnips and reserve them in a warm place.

While the turnips are cooking, melt 4 tablespoons [60 ml.] of the butter in a heavy, nonreactive skillet just large enough to hold the sweetbreads side by side. Add the carrot, onion and parsley and cook over low heat until lightly colored—about 12 minutes. Then put the sweetbreads on top of the vegetables and cook them over low heat for 10 minutes, turning them frequently. Sprinkle the sweetbreads with the vermouth and let the liquid come to a simmer. Add salt and pepper. Cover the skillet and continue cooking the contents over very low heat for 10 minutes.

Arrange the sweetbreads on a serving dish surrounded by the turnips, sprinkle the sweetbreads with the chervil and pour the cooking liquid over them. If you like, you can boil the cooking liquid for a few minutes to reduce it slightly, then thicken it off the heat by beating in the rest of the butter before pouring the liquid over the sweetbreads.

ÉLIANE AND JACQUETTE DE RIVOYRE
CUISINE LANDAISE

Stuffed Sweetbreads

Ris de Veau à la Saint-Cloud

To serve 6

2 lb.	veal sweetbreads, soaked, parboiled, membrane removed, pressed under weights	1 kg.
5 oz.	lean boneless veal, thinly sliced	150 g.
¼ lb.	thinly sliced prosciutto	125 g.
⅔ cup	Champagne or dry white wine	150 ml.
about 2 cups	meat stock (recipe, page 165)	about ½ liter
2 tbsp.	strained fresh lemon juice	30 ml.
	Chicken stuffing	
½ lb.	boned chicken breast, skinned and finely chopped	¼ kg.
2½	thick bacon slices, finely chopped	2½
2 oz.	suet, finely chopped	60 g.
	salt and pepper	
	fines herbes	
6	egg yolks	6

To make the stuffing, mix the chicken, bacon, suet, salt and pepper, fines herbes and egg yolks together.

Slice the sections of sweetbreads nearly in half horizontally and sandwich the stuffing mixture between the sections. Lay half of the sliced veal and prosciutto in a heavy, nonreactive skillet broad enough to hold the sweetbreads in one layer. Lay the stuffed sweetbreads on top. Pour in the wine and enough stock to cover the sweetbreads, then lay the remaining slices of veal and prosciutto on top. Cover the pan, bring the liquid to a boil, then simmer the sweetbreads very gently for 45 minutes, or until they are cooked through.

Transfer the stuffed sweetbreads to a shallow baking dish. Strain the cooking liquid into a small saucepan, and set the skillet aside. Degrease the cooking liquid thoroughly, then boil it until this sauce is syrupy. Glaze the sweetbreads by first pouring a little of the reduced sauce over them. Then put them under a preheated broiler, about 3 inches [8 cm.] from the heat source, and—basting them frequently with the sauce—broil them for five minutes on each side.

Add a few tablespoons of stock to the skillet in which the sweetbreads were cooked. Over medium heat, deglaze the skillet, then add the lemon juice. Strain this liquid through a fine-meshed sieve onto a serving dish and lay the glazed sweetbreads on top.

PIERRE JOSEPH BUC'HOZ
L'ART DE PRÉPARER LES ALIMENTS

Sweetbreads Marinated

To serve 4

2 lb.	veal sweetbreads, soaked, parboiled, membrane removed, pressed under weights	1 kg.
2 tbsp.	butter	30 ml.
1¾ cups	meat stock (recipe, page 165)	425 ml.
	salt and pepper	
1	sprig basil	1
1	onion, sliced	1
¼ cup	white wine vinegar or fresh lemon juice	50 ml.
2	eggs, beaten	2
¾ cup	dry bread crumbs or ½ cup [125 ml.] flour	175 ml.
4 tbsp.	lard	60 ml.
2 cups	fresh parsley leaves, deep fried in hot oil for 10 seconds, drained	½ liter

Slice the sweetbreads into long pieces. Melt the butter in a large pot, add the stock and salt and pepper, the basil, onion and vinegar or lemon juice, and then the sweetbreads. Simmer the mixture over low heat for 15 minutes, or until the sweetbreads are cooked through.

Remove the sweetbreads from the pot, pat them dry and dip them in the beaten eggs. Sprinkle them with the bread crumbs or coat them with the flour. Melt the lard and sauté the sweetbreads for five minutes, or until well browned. Remove the sweetbreads from the pan, arrange them on a serving dish and garnish them with the fried parsley.

VINCENT LA CHAPELLE
THE MODERN COOK

Sweetbreads in Paper Cases

Ris de Veau en Papillotes

To serve 6

1 lb.	veal sweetbreads, soaked, parboiled, membrane removed, pressed under weights and sliced	½ kg.
	salt and pepper	
6 tbsp.	butter	90 ml.
½ cup	Madeira	125 ml.
¼ cup	chicken stock (recipe, page 165)	50 ml.
18	spinach leaves, stems removed	18
6	thin slices baked or boiled ham	6

Sprinkle the sweetbread slices with salt and pepper. Melt 4 tablespoons [60 ml.] of the butter in a sauté pan over medium to low heat, add the sweetbread slices and cook them until they are lightly browned—about 15 minutes.

Remove the sweetbreads from the pan and reserve them in a warm place. Add the Madeira to the pan and deglaze the pan over high heat until the liquid is reduced by two thirds. Stir in the stock.

Sauté the spinach leaves in the remaining butter until softened. Cut six pieces of parchment paper, each about 10 by 12 inches [25 by 30 cm.], into ovals or heart shapes, and butter them. Lay a slice of the ham on one piece of paper, setting the slice to one side of the center. Put three spinach leaves on the ham, add a slice of sweetbread and pour on a bit of the Madeira sauce. Fold the empty side of the paper to cover the ingredients, then fold the edges of the paper together securely, pinching to seal in the contents. Repeat with the remaining paper and the rest of the ingredients.

Place the paper parcels on a wire rack set in a shallow baking pan, and bake in a preheated 375° F. [190° C.] oven for 15 minutes, or until the paper is inflated and browned.

ALEXANDRE DUMAINE
MA CUISINE

Braised Veal Brains in White Wine

Cervelles de Veau en Matelote

To serve 4

1 lb.	veal brains, soaked and membrane removed	½ kg.
1 cup	veal stock *(recipe, page 165)*	¼ liter
1 cup	dry white wine	¼ liter
2 tbsp.	butter	30 ml.
15 to 20	small boiling onions	15 to 20
⅓ lb.	mushrooms, quartered	150 g.
1 tbsp.	flour	15 ml.
	salt and pepper	

Poach the brains by simmering them in the stock and white wine for 20 minutes. Remove the brains.

Melt the butter in a skillet over medium heat and sauté the onions and mushrooms until the onions are lightly browned—about 10 minutes. Stir in the flour, season well with salt and pepper, and moisten the vegetables with about half of the poaching liquid. Stirring frequently, simmer for about 15 minutes.

Slice the brains and arrange them in a shallow baking dish. Pour the onion mixture over them. Bake in a preheated 400° F. [200° C.] oven for about 15 minutes to finish cooking the brains and reduce the sauce. Serve very hot.

JULES BRETEUIL
LE CUISINIER EUROPÉEN

Brain Croquettes

Boudins de Cervelle

To poach the brains, soak them and remove the membrane, then cook them in barely simmering vinegar court bouillon (recipe, page 165) for 25 minutes. Instead of baking the croquettes, you can broil them about 4 inches [10 cm.] from the heat source for four to five minutes on each side; baste them with melted butter when you turn them.

To serve 4 or 5

1 lb.	poached veal brains	½ kg.
about 8 cups	fresh bread crumbs, about 6 cups [1 ½ liters] soaked in milk and squeezed	about 2 liters
7 tbsp.	butter, softened	105 ml.
1	shallot, finely chopped	1
4	fresh mushroom caps, finely chopped	4
	salt and pepper	
	chopped fresh parsley	
3	egg yolks	3
6 oz.	caul, soaked, drained and cut into ten 5-inch [13-cm.] squares	175 g.
1	egg, beaten with a few drops of oil	1
2 tbsp.	clarified butter, melted	30 ml.
1 ¼ cups	tomato sauce *(recipe, page 166)*	300 ml.

Push the brains through a sieve. Add the soaked bread crumbs, the butter, shallot, mushrooms, salt and pepper and a pinch of chopped parsley. Add the egg yolks and mix to form a smooth paste. Refrigerate the mixture for one hour to firm it. Divide the mixture into 10 portions and mold each portion into an oval about 3 inches [8 cm.] long. Wrap each oval in a piece of caul to form a croquette. Dip each croquette in the beaten egg and roll it in the remaining bread crumbs. Refrigerate the croquettes for one half hour.

Lay the croquettes in a buttered shallow baking dish. Sprinkle them with the clarified butter and bake in a preheated 400° F. [200° C.] oven, basting occasionally, until they are golden—about 20 minutes. Serve them very hot, accompanied by the tomato sauce.

PAUL BOUILLARD
LA CUISINE COIN DU FEU

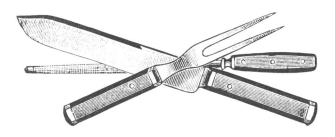

Brain Salad with Eggs

Cervelle à la Cadichonne

	To serve 6	
3 lb.	veal brains, soaked and membrane removed	1½ kg.
4 cups	salted water or meat stock *(recipe, page 165)*	1 liter
1	piece lemon peel	1
3	eggs, hard-boiled and halved	3
6	large lettuce leaves	6
6	fresh tarragon leaves	6
1 cup	mayonnaise *(recipe, page 167)*	¼ liter

Poach the brains for 40 minutes in the salted water or stock with the lemon peel. Allow the brains to cool in their cooking liquor, then drain and dice them. Arrange some of the diced brain and half of a hard-boiled egg on each lettuce leaf. Coat with mayonnaise, decorate each serving with a tarragon leaf and serve.

ROBERT J. COURTINE
LA VRAIE CUISINE FRANÇAISE

Brains Stewed with Tomatoes

Cervelles à la Tomate

Olives and pickled lemon strips may be added as decoration.

	To serve 4	
2 lb.	veal brains, soaked, membrane removed, quartered	1 kg.
3	medium-sized tomatoes, peeled, seeded and chopped	3
½ cup	vegetable oil	125 ml.
5	garlic cloves, crushed to a paste	5
1	sprig coriander, chopped	1
1	sprig parsley, chopped	1
1 tbsp.	paprika	15 ml.
½ tsp.	ground cumin	2 ml.
2 cups	water	½ liter
	salt	
	cayenne pepper	
1 tbsp.	white wine vinegar	15 ml.

Put all the ingredients except the brains and the vinegar into a saucepan with a pinch each of salt and cayenne pepper. Bring the liquid to a boil. Add the brains, reduce the heat and—stirring occasionally—simmer the contents, un-

covered, for about 15 minutes. Add the vinegar and simmer for another five minutes.

Remove the brains and arrange them on a serving dish. If the sauce is not thick, reduce it over high heat. Pour the sauce over the brains. Serve hot or cold.

FETTOUMA BENKIRANE
LA NOUVELLE CUISINE MAROCAINE

Veal Brain Fritters

Cervelle de Veau au Soleil

	To serve 4 to 6	
1½ lb.	veal brains, soaked, membrane removed, parboiled for 10 minutes and drained	¾ kg.
3 cups	chicken stock *(recipe, page 165)*	¾ liter
2 tbsp.	vinegar	30 ml.
3	sprigs parsley	3
3	whole cloves	3
1	garlic clove	1
⅛ tsp.	dried thyme	½ ml.
1	bay leaf	1
	salt and pepper	
	vegetable oil for deep frying	
	Batter	
¾ cup	flour	175 ml.
1 tbsp.	vegetable oil	15 ml.
½ cup	dry white wine	125 ml.
⅛ tsp.	salt	½ ml.

Place the parboiled brains in a nonreactive pot with the stock, vinegar, herbs and seasonings. Bring to a boil over medium heat, reduce the heat and poach the brains, uncovered, for 18 minutes. Drain them and cut them into cubes.

Prepare the batter by blending together the batter ingredients. Pour vegetable oil into a pan to a depth of 3 inches [8 cm.] and heat the oil to 375° F. [190° C.] on a deep-frying thermometer. Coat the cubes of brain—a small batch at a time—with the batter and deep fry them for four minutes, or until nicely browned.

JULIETTE ELKON
A BELGIAN COOKBOOK

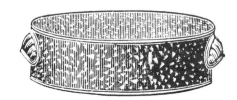

Brains in Red Sauce

Cervelle Sauce Rouge

The volatile oils in hot chilies may make your skin sting and your eyes burn; after handling chilies, avoid touching your face and wash your hands promptly.

	To serve 4	
1 lb.	beef or lamb brains, soaked and membrane removed, split into halves, cut horizontally into 2 slices	½ kg.
1 cup	water	¼ liter
	salt and pepper	
1 tbsp.	chopped fresh coriander leaves or 1 tsp. [5 ml.] ground coriander	15 ml.
4	garlic cloves, crushed to a paste	4
1 tbsp.	paprika, dissolved in ½ cup [125 ml.] oil	15 ml.
2	hot red chilies, stemmed, seeded and chopped	2
4	eggs	4

Put the brains into a large skillet with the water. Season with salt and pepper. Add the coriander, garlic, dissolved paprika and chilies. Cover the skillet and cook over medium heat for 20 minutes. Three minutes before serving, break the eggs one at a time into the skillet, cover, and poach the eggs in the sauce.

IRÈNE AND LUCIENNE KARSENTY
LA CUISINE PIED-NOIR

Baked Brains

Cervelle au Four

	To serve 4	
2 lb.	beef or veal brains, soaked, membrane removed, and split in half, beef brains cut horizontally into 2 slices	1 kg.
3 tbsp.	finely chopped fresh parsley	45 ml.
1	shallot, finely chopped	1
1½ tbsp.	dry bread crumbs, lightly toasted	22 ml.
½ cup	dry white wine	125 ml.
1 cup	meat stock (recipe, page 165)	¼ liter
	salt and pepper	
3 tbsp.	butter, cut into small pieces	45 ml.

Butter an ovenproof dish just large enough to hold the brains side by side and arrange the brains in it. Mix the parsley and shallot and sprinkle the mixture over the brains. Then sprinkle them with the bread crumbs and pour over the wine and stock. Season with salt and pepper. Dot the mixture with the butter and place the dish in a preheated 400° F. [200° C.] oven. Bake the brains for 20 minutes, basting twice with the liquid in the dish to moisten the crust of bread crumbs over the brains. Serve very hot in the baking dish.

RENÉE DE GROSSOUVRE
LES RECETTES D'UNE GRAND'MÈRE ET SES CONSEILS

Brains Poached in Red Wine

Cervelle en Matelote

The technique of poaching brains in a red-wine court bouillon is shown on pages 50-51.

If you wish, add a garnish of glazed boiling onions, and sautéed bacon strips, mushrooms and croutons.

	To serve 6	
1 lb.	beef, veal, lamb or pork brains, soaked, membrane removed	½ kg.
3 cups	red wine	¾ liter
1	onion, sliced	1
1	bouquet garni	1
	salt	
	mixed spices	
4 tbsp.	beurre manié	60 ml.
	pepper	

First make the court bouillon. Pour the wine into a non-reactive pan and add the onion, bouquet garni and a pinch each of salt and mixed spices. Cover, and simmer for 25 minutes. Cool the court bouillon and strain it.

Put the brains into a nonreactive pan and pour the court bouillon over them. Bring the liquid to a boil, then reduce the heat to very low and simmer the brains for 30 minutes if beef, 25 minutes if veal, 20 minutes if pork and 15 minutes if lamb. Remove the brains and drain them, then pat them dry on a towel. Slice them and arrange them on a serving dish. Keep them warm.

Over high heat, reduce the court bouillon to about ¾ cup [175 ml.]. Stir the *beurre manié* into the court bouillon to thicken it into a sauce. Season the sauce to taste with salt and pepper, and pour it over the brains.

FÉLIX BENOIT AND HENRY CLOS JOUVE
LA CUISINE LYONNAISE

Brains in Brown Gravy

Kharoo Bhejoo

The volatile oils in hot chilies may make your skin sting and your eyes burn; after handling chilies, avoid touching your face and wash your hands promptly.

To serve 4

1 lb.	lamb brains, soaked and membrane removed	½ kg.
1½ tsp.	salt	7 ml.
⅓ tsp.	ground turmeric	1 ml.
3 tbsp.	vegetable oil or *ghee*	45 ml.
2	large onions, finely sliced	2
3	garlic cloves, chopped	3
½-inch	piece peeled fresh ginger, chopped	1-cm.
1 tbsp.	finely chopped fresh coriander (optional)	15 ml.
1	hot green chili, stemmed, seeded and coarsely chopped (optional)	1

Poach the brains in 2 cups [½ liter] of water, adding ¾ teaspoon [4 ml.] of the salt and the turmeric. When they are cooked and firm, after about 20 minutes, drain them and let them cool. Cut each brain into six pieces.

In a heavy skillet, heat the oil or *ghee* and fry the onions over medium heat until they are light brown—about 15 minutes. With a mortar and pestle, grind the garlic and ginger to a paste, add the paste to the onions and cook for five minutes, stirring occasionally. Add the brains, the remaining salt and ¾ cup [175 ml.] of water. Bring the mixture to a boil, then simmer, uncovered, for 10 minutes. Add the coriander and the chili, if using, and cook for five minutes more, then remove the skillet from the heat. If you like, sprinkle fried potato cubes over the brains before serving them.

JEROO MEHTA
101 PARSI RECIPES

Lamb Brains Fried with Tomatoes and Peppers

Aijja à la Cervelle de Mouton

Harissa is a spicy paste, obtainable ready-made where Middle Eastern foods are sold. To make it, soak two dried hot chilies in cold water for one hour. Split them and discard the stems and seeds. Grind the chilies in a mortar with 2 to 3 tablespoons [30 to 45 ml.] of caraway seeds, one garlic clove and 1 tablespoon [15 ml.] of coarse salt. Pound the mixture to a thick paste while adding a spoonful of oil, drop by drop.

To serve 2

¼ lb.	lamb brains, soaked, membrane removed, blanched in salted water, drained and cubed	125 g.
3 or 4	garlic cloves	3 or 4
1½ tsp.	caraway seeds	7 ml.
7 tbsp.	olive oil	105 ml.
2	medium-sized tomatoes, peeled, seeded and chopped	2
1 tbsp.	*harissa*	15 ml.
1½ tsp.	paprika	7 ml.
1 cup	water	¼ liter
	salt	
2	green peppers, halved, seeded, deribbed and cut into pieces	2
4	eggs	4

Pound the garlic and caraway seeds together. In a skillet, heat the oil and add the tomatoes, *harissa*, paprika and pounded garlic mixture. Add the water and simmer for a few minutes. Season with salt to taste. Add the peppers and brains. Bring the mixture to a boil and break the eggs one by one into the mixture. Cover and cook over low heat until the eggs are set—about 20 minutes. Serve immediately.

AHMED LAASRI
240 RECETTES DE CUISINE MAROCAINE

Brains Basque-Style

Sesos

To serve 4 to 6

2 lb.	lamb, veal or beef brains, soaked and membrane removed	1 kg.
1 tsp.	salt	5 ml.
1 tbsp.	fresh lemon juice	15 ml.
	flour	
2	eggs, beaten with a pinch of salt	2
2 tbsp.	butter	30 ml.
2 tbsp.	olive oil	30 ml.
2 tbsp.	chopped fresh parsley	30 ml.
2 or 3	lemons, cut into wedges	2 or 3

Drop the brains into boiling water seasoned with the salt and lemon juice. Reduce the heat and simmer gently for 15 minutes for lamb brains, 20 minutes for veal and 30 minutes for beef. Plunge the brains into cold water and let them cool for 15 minutes.

Pat the brains dry and cut them into serving pieces. Dip them in flour and then into the beaten eggs. In a large, heavy skillet melt the butter in the oil over medium heat. Then fry the pieces of brains for about four minutes or until golden brown on both sides. Serve them immediately, sprinkled with the parsley and accompanied by lemon wedges.

ANN ROGERS
A BASQUE STORY COOK BOOK

Baked Brains with Sauce

Inkha Mishwee mi Marqeh

To serve 4 to 6

1½ lb.	brains, soaked, membrane removed, parboiled, drained, cut into small pieces	¾ kg.
2 tbsp.	chopped onion	30 ml.
2 tbsp.	butter	30 ml.
2 tbsp.	flour	30 ml.
	salt and pepper	
½ cup	water or meat stock *(recipe, page 165)*	125 ml.
4	medium-sized tomatoes, peeled, quartered, seeded and sautéed in butter for 15 minutes	4
2 tbsp.	chopped celery	30 ml.
2 tbsp.	chopped green pepper	30 ml.
1	bay leaf	1
1	sprig thyme	1

Over medium heat, brown the onion in the butter. Sift together the flour and salt and pepper to taste, and add to the onion. Stirring constantly, cook until thickened—about two minutes. Add the water or stock and the tomatoes. Stir until blended, then bring the liquid to a boil. Reduce the heat and add the celery, green pepper, bay leaf and thyme. Cook for 10 minutes, stirring occasionally. If the mixture looks dry, add more water. Remove the bay leaf and thyme, and add the brains. Transfer the mixture to a shallow ovenproof dish and bake in a preheated 350° F. [180° C.] oven for 15 minutes.

HELEN COREY
THE ART OF SYRIAN COOKERY

Lamb Fries in Bread Crumbs

Criadillas Fritas

To serve 7

10 oz.	lamb's fries, slit, soaked, peeled, parboiled, halved and cut into wedges the shape of orange segments	300 g.
3	eggs, lightly beaten	3
	salt and pepper	
¾ cup	dry bread crumbs	175 ml.
7 tbsp.	lard	105 ml.
4 to 8 tbsp.	butter	60 to 120 ml.
4	slices firm-textured white bread, crusts removed	4
2	lemons, quartered	2

Season the beaten eggs with salt and pepper and dip the fries into them. Then coat the fries with the bread crumbs. Dip them in the eggs again. Melt the lard and, when it is hot, add the fries and fry them until they are golden brown all over—about 15 minutes. Drain the fries and keep them hot.

In a separate skillet, melt 4 tablespoons [60 ml.] of the butter and fry the bread in it until the slices are golden brown on both sides—adding more butter to the skillet if necessary. Cut the fried bread into triangles and arrange the triangles around a serving dish. Pile the fries in the middle and squeeze the lemons over them before serving.

ANA MARIA CALERA
COCINA CASTELLANA

Fries in Red Spicy Sauce

Rognons Blancs en Sauce

To serve 6

2 lb.	lamb fries, slit, soaked, peeled, parboiled and cut into halves	1 kg.
7 tbsp.	butter	105 ml.
1 tbsp.	paprika	15 ml.
½ tsp.	ground cumin	2 ml.
½ tsp.	ground cinnamon	2 ml.
½ tsp.	salt	2 ml.

In a skillet, melt the butter. Add the fries and brown them quickly over high heat. Reduce the heat, add the remaining ingredients and, stirring often, cook until the fries are tender—15 to 20 minutes. Serve them in their cooking liquid.

FETTOUMA BENKIRANE
LA NOUVELLE CUISINE MAROCAINE

Frivolity Fritters

Beignets d'Animelles

Sweetbreads and brains may be cooked in the same way.

	To serve 4 or 5	
2 lb.	lamb fries, slit, soaked, peeled, parboiled and cut into ¼-inch [6-mm.] slices	1 kg.
1 cup	fritter batter *(recipe, page 167)*	¼ liter
	olive oil for deep frying	
¼ cup	fresh parsley leaves or sprigs	50 ml.
1	lemon, cut into 8 wedges, or 1 cup [¼ liter] tomato sauce *(recipe, page 166)*	1

Olive oil and lemon marinade

1½ tbsp.	strained fresh lemon juice	22½ ml.
1 tsp.	olive oil	5 ml.
	salt and pepper	
1 tbsp.	fines herbes (including tarragon)	15 ml.

Place the sliced fries in a dish, add the marinade ingredients and marinate the fries for 30 minutes to an hour, turning them over a few times. Slip them all at once into the batter.

Pour olive oil into a skillet to a depth of at least ¾ inch [2 cm.]. Set the skillet over high heat. When the oil is hot enough to sizzle as soon as a drop of batter touches the surface, pick the slices out of the batter one by one in a teaspoon. Make certain that each slice is well coated in batter before dropping it into the hot oil. Do not try to fry too many slices at a time. When each slice is golden and crisp on the underside, turn it over with a fork. When golden on both sides, remove the slice with a large, flat wire spoon, first to paper towels to drain, then to a folded napkin arranged on a heated platter. Keep the fritters covered with the napkin while frying the other slices.

When the last fritter is removed from the oil, drop in the parsley, leaving it only long enough to finish sputtering. Drain the parsley for a moment, and place it on the fritters. Arrange the lemon wedges around the fritters or pass a sauceboat of warmed tomato sauce separately.

RICHARD OLNEY
SIMPLE FRENCH FOOD

Sautéed Lamb Fries

Animelles

The author of this recipe specifies flouring the fries without touching them — his way of warning that the flour coating would not be even if patted on by hand. The best technique for coating the fries is to put the flour into a bag, spoon the fries into it and shake them until they are floured.

	To serve 3	
6	lamb fries, slit, soaked, peeled, parboiled and cut into quarters	6
	salt	
¼ cup	flour	50 ml.
3 tbsp.	lard	45 ml.

Salt the fries, wipe them dry and flour them without touching them with your hands. Melt the lard in a skillet and sauté the fries over high heat until they are crisp and golden—about five minutes. Then dish them up and serve them hot for a dainty dish.

VINCENT LA CHAPELLE
THE MODERN COOK

Lamb Fries Clerou

The volatile oils in hot chilies may make your skin sting and your eyes burn; after handling chilies, avoid touching your face and wash your hands promptly.

For a more strongly flavored dish, additional garlic and chilies may be added.

	To serve 6	
2 lb.	lamb fries, slit, soaked, peeled, parboiled and cut into halves lengthwise	1 kg.
2 tbsp.	butter	30 ml.
3	slices bacon, diced	3
1	onion, chopped	1
3	garlic cloves, finely chopped	3
½ cup	chopped fresh parsley	125 ml.
about ½ cup	tomato sauce *(recipe, page 166)*	about 125 ml.
about ½ cup	dry white wine	about 125 ml.
about ½ cup	meat stock *(recipe, page 165)*	about 125 ml.
½ tsp.	savory or rosemary	2 ml.
	salt and freshly ground pepper	
1	dried hot red chili, stemmed, seeded and finely chopped	1
2 tbsp.	Madeira or brandy	30 ml.

In a large skillet, melt the butter over low heat, add the bacon and cook gently until the bacon fat begins to melt. Add the onion, garlic and parsley; increase the heat and sauté the vegetables for five minutes. Add the fries and brown them, stirring occasionally. Combine the tomato sauce, wine and stock, and pour in enough of this liquid to barely cover the fries. Add the savory or rosemary, salt and pepper, and red chili to taste. Simmer the mixture over low heat for 45 minutes, or until the fries are firm; add more of the liquid as necessary to keep the fries covered. At the end of the cooking time, add the Madeira or brandy and simmer for a few minutes. Serve with crusty French bread and a green salad.

JANA ALLEN AND MARGARET GIN
INNARDS AND OTHER VARIETY MEATS

Fries in Red Wine Sauce

Fricassée de Chanterelles d'Ambert en Matelote aux Rognons Blancs

Chanterelles are wild mushrooms that appear in the autumn. About ½ pound [¼ kg.] of dried chanterelles, sold in specialty shops, may be substituted for fresh chanterelles, but must first be soaked in warm water for at least 30 minutes.

	To serve 8	
10 oz.	lamb fries, slit, soaked, peeled and parboiled	300 g.
3 cups	dry red wine	¾ liter
5	shallots, 4 sliced, 1 finely chopped	5
1	bouquet garni	1
1 cup	veal stock (recipe, page 165)	¼ liter
2 tbsp.	beurre manié	30 ml.
6 tbsp.	butter	90 ml.
1¾ lb.	fresh chanterelles, quartered	875 g.
	salt and pepper	

Heat the red wine in a saucepan with the sliced shallots and the bouquet garni. Bring the wine to a boil, and reduce it over high heat until only about 1 cup [¼ liter] is left. Add the veal stock, bind the sauce with the *beurre manié* and simmer it for 20 minutes.

Melt 2 tablespoons [30 ml.] of the butter in a frying pan and sauté the fries for five minutes until lightly browned, then drain them on absorbent paper towels. Add another 2 tablespoons of butter to the pan and sauté the chanterelles until they give up their juices. Add the chopped shallot and strain in the red wine sauce. Reduce the sauce over high heat until it is thick and syrupy. Remove the sauce from the heat, stir in the rest of the butter and add the fries. Season with salt and pepper. Serve very hot.

AMICALE DES CUISINIERS ET PÂTISSIERS AUVERGNATS DE PARIS
CUISINE D'AUVERGNE

Poached Fries in Spicy Sauce

Rognons Blancs en Sauce

	To serve 8	
2 lb.	lamb fries, slit, soaked, peeled, salted for 5 minutes, rinsed and cut into 1½-inch [4-cm.] cubes	1 kg.
1 tsp.	cayenne pepper	5 ml.
½ tsp.	cumin seeds	2 ml.
¼ tsp.	ground cinnamon	1 ml.
4 tbsp.	butter	60 ml.
	salt	

Put the cubed fries into a saucepan with the cayenne pepper, cumin seeds, cinnamon, butter and a little salt. Cover the mixture with water and cook over medium heat until the fries are firm—about 15 minutes. Transfer the fries to a warmed serving dish. Adjust the seasoning of the cooking liquid to taste and boil it until it is reduced to a thick sauce. Pour the sauce over the fries and serve them at once.

AHMED LAASRI
240 RECETTES DE CUISINE MAROCAINE

Fries with Green Peppercorns

Animelles au Poivre Vert

	To serve 6	
12	lamb fries, slit, soaked, peeled, parboiled and split into halves	12
7 tbsp.	butter	105 ml.
2 cups	meat stock (recipe, page 165)	½ liter
½ cup	crème fraîche or heavy cream	125 ml.
2 tbsp.	green peppercorns	30 ml.
	salt	

Heat the butter in a sauté pan and sauté the fries quickly on both sides until lightly colored. Reserve them in the pan.

In a saucepan, boil the stock until it is reduced to about half its original volume. Add the *crème fraîche* or cream and the green peppercorns. Stirring constantly, cook this sauce over fairly high heat until it is as thick as cream—about 10 minutes. Pour the sauce over the fries and simmer for seven to eight minutes. When the fries are tender, correct the seasoning of the sauce. Serve the mixture in a warmed dish.

IRENE LABARRE AND JEAN MERCIER
LA CUISINE DU MOUTON

Tripe, Stomach and Chitterlings

Tripe and Ham Casserole

Tripes à la Paloise

To serve 4 to 6

2 lb.	honeycomb and blanket tripe, rinsed and cut into 2-inch [5-cm.] squares	1 kg.
2	calf's feet, cleaned, rinsed, split and the large bones removed	2
1	ham bone	1
3	onions, 2 finely chopped, 1 stuck with 2 whole cloves	3
1	sprig thyme	1
1	small bay leaf	1
1	garlic bulb, outer skin removed	1
12	peppercorns	12
	salt	
1 cup	wine vinegar	¼ liter
1¾ cups	dry white wine	425 ml.
about 2 quarts	water	about 2 liters
2 tbsp.	rendered goose fat	30 ml.
1¾ lb.	ham, diced (about 3½ cups [875 ml.])	800 g.
4	shallots, finely chopped	4
1 tbsp.	flour	15 ml.
2 tbsp.	Armagnac	30 ml.
2	medium-sized carrots, grated	2

Put the tripe into a large casserole with the calf's feet, ham bone, the onion stuck with cloves, the thyme, bay leaf, garlic bulb, peppercorns and salt. Sprinkle on half of the vinegar, add the wine and enough water to submerge the contents of the casserole. Cover the casserole and seal it with a strip of paste made from flour, water and a few drops of oil. Bake the casserole in a preheated 250° F. [130° C.] oven for six hours.

Meanwhile, melt the goose fat in a saucepan and fry the ham, chopped onions and the shallots over low heat until the onions are soft—about 10 minutes. Mix in the flour. Stir in the Armagnac and the remaining vinegar, cover the pan and

simmer the mixture over low heat for one hour, stirring it from time to time. Add a spoonful of water when necessary to keep the mixture from sticking to the pan.

Remove the casserole from the oven and break the flour-and-water seal. Remove the calf's feet, pick out and discard the small bones, and dice the meat. Return the meat to the casserole. Stir in the ham-and-onion mixture and the grated carrots. Cover the casserole and bake it for one hour longer.

CÉLINE VENCE
ENCYCLOPÉDIE HACHETTE DE LA CUISINE REGIONALE

Tripe Shadwell-Style

Tripes à la Mode de Shadwell

To serve 4 or 5

2 lb.	tripe, rinsed and cut into 2-inch [5-cm.] squares	1 kg.
2	pig's feet, cleaned and rinsed	2
2 quarts	water	2 liters
½ lb.	sauerkraut, drained (about 1 cup [¼ liter])	¼ kg.
1	large onion, chopped	1
1	celery rib, chopped	1
5	peppercorns	5
2	whole cloves	2
1	garlic clove	1
1	sprig thyme	1
1	bay leaf	1
	salt and freshly ground black pepper	
⅔ cup	dry white wine	150 ml.
¼ to ½ cup	Calvados (optional)	50 to 125 ml.

Put the pig's feet in a large saucepan with the water. Bring to a boil, skim, cover the pan and simmer gently for two hours. Bone the pig's feet, chop the meat and reserve the cooking liquid. Put the meat in a heavy casserole and place the tripe on top. Add the sauerkraut, onion and celery. Tie the peppercorns, cloves, garlic, thyme and bay leaf in a piece of muslin or cheesecloth, and bury this bouquet garni in the casserole. Pour in enough of the reserved cooking liquid to cover the contents of the casserole.

Bring the mixture to a boil on top of the stove, then cover the casserole tightly with foil and a lid. Bake in a preheated 300° F. [150° C.] oven for three hours, or until the tripe is tender. Just before serving, skim any fat from the liquid, adjust the seasoning and stir in the wine and the Calvados, if using. Reheat the casserole and serve the tripe very hot.

SHONA CRAWFORD POOLE
THE LONDON TIMES

Double Tripe the Polish Way, with Saffron

To serve 4

2 lb.	honeycomb and blanket tripe, rinsed and cut into 1-inch [2½-cm.] strips	1 kg.
2 tbsp.	butter	30 ml.
3	small onions, finely chopped	3
2 tbsp.	flour	30 ml.
2½ cups	meat stock (recipe, page 165)	625 ml.
	salt and pepper	
1	bouquet garni	1
3 tbsp.	fresh lemon juice	45 ml.
1 tsp.	powdered saffron, dissolved in ¼ cup [50 ml.] meat stock	5 ml.

In a heavy pot, melt the butter. Add the onions and toss them lightly over a high heat until they are transparent—about two minutes. Add the tripe and toss it lightly for two minutes, then sprinkle it with the flour and moisten it with the stock. Season with salt and pepper and add the bouquet garni. Cover the pan and stew the tripe over low heat for two hours, or until it is tender. Add the lemon juice and diluted saffron, and cook until the sauce is a deep golden color. Transfer the tripe and sauce to a warmed serving dish and serve it at once.

VINCENT LA CHAPELLE
THE MODERN COOK

Baked Tripe

Patsas tou Fournou

To serve 4

2 lb.	tripe, rinsed	1 kg.
½	lemon	½
1	small onion	1
1 or 2	carrots	1 or 2
1	celery rib	1
2	sprigs parsley, plus 1 tsp. [5 ml.] chopped fresh parsley	2
	salt and peppercorns	
3 tbsp.	olive oil	45 ml.
3 tbsp.	fresh lemon juice	45 ml.
3 tbsp.	dry bread crumbs	45 ml.

Rub the tripe well with the half lemon. Put in a saucepan with the onion, carrots, celery and parsley sprigs, and season to taste with salt and peppercorns. Add enough boiling water to cover and simmer gently for about three hours. Remove the tripe from the pan, dry thoroughly and cut into small pieces. In a large bowl mix the oil, lemon juice and chopped parsley, and add the tripe. Stir well and leave for 30 to 40 minutes, turning the tripe pieces occasionally in the liquid. Remove the pieces of tripe carefully and roll them in the bread crumbs. Put them in an oiled ovenproof dish and bake in a preheated 350° F. [180° C.] oven for 15 minutes, or until golden brown.

MARO DUNCAN
COOKING THE GREEK WAY

Tripe with Parmesan Cheese

Trippa alla Toscana

For a stronger cheese flavor, some of the cheese may be added to the tripe with the tomatoes. After the tripe is sprinkled with the cheese, the dish can be baked in a preheated 300° F. [150° C.] oven for 10 minutes, or until the cheese melts.

A calf's foot, parboiled for 30 minutes and boned, may be cooked with the tripe.

To serve 4

2 lb.	tripe, rinsed and cut into thin strips	1 kg.
⅓ cup	olive oil	75 ml.
2 tbsp.	butter	30 ml.
1	celery rib, finely chopped	1
1	carrot, finely chopped	1
1	medium-sized onion, finely chopped	1
1	garlic clove	1
1	bay leaf	1
½ cup	dry white wine	125 ml.
2	tomatoes, peeled, seeded and chopped	2
	salt and pepper	
about 2 cups	meat stock (recipe, page 165)	about ½ liter
5 or 6	fresh basil leaves, chopped	5 or 6
1 cup	freshly grated Parmesan cheese	¼ liter

Heat the oil and butter in a sauté pan, and add the celery, carrot, onion, garlic and the bay leaf. Cook the vegetables over medium heat until the onion is transparent—about 20 minutes. Discard the garlic. Pat the tripe dry with paper towels and add it to the pan. Pour the wine into the pan, increase the heat and cook the mixture until the wine has evaporated. Add the tomatoes and salt and pepper. Pour in enough stock to cover the tripe. Cover the pan and simmer for at least two hours, or until the tripe is tender; stir occasionally and add stock, if necessary, to keep the tripe covered. Add the basil leaves and stir. Sprinkle the dish with the grated Parmesan cheese before serving.

STELLA DONATI (EDITOR)
IL GRANDE MANUALE DELLA CUCINA REGIONALE

Tripe in White Wine Sauce

Gras-double Paulette

To serve 4

2 lb.	tripe, rinsed and cut into 1-inch [2½-cm.] squares	1 kg.
4 tbsp.	butter, 2 tbsp. [30 ml.] cut into small pieces	60 ml.
	salt and pepper	
4	egg yolks	4
2 tbsp.	fresh lemon juice	30 ml.
¼ cup	heavy cream	50 ml.
4	small sour gherkins, sliced	4
2 tbsp.	chopped fresh parsley	30 ml.
White wine sauce		
1¼ cups	dry white wine	300 ml.
2 tbsp.	butter	30 ml.
1	carrot, diced	1
1	onion, diced	1
1 tbsp.	flour	15 ml.
⅔ cup	water	150 ml.
1	bouquet garni	1
6	peppercorns	6
	salt	

To make the sauce, melt the butter in a small nonreactive saucepan, add the carrot and onion, and stew them gently until the onion is transparent but not browned—about 10 minutes. Stir in the flour, then the white wine and water. Add the bouquet garni and peppercorns, and salt the mixture lightly. Stirring continuously, bring the liquid to a boil. Then reduce the heat and simmer the sauce, stirring it occasionally, for 30 minutes to reduce it by about one third.

To cook the tripe, melt 2 tablespoons [30 ml.] of the butter in a large saucepan. Add the tripe and season it with salt and pepper. Cover the pan and stew the tripe over very low heat for 30 minutes. Strain the white wine sauce over the tripe and simmer, covered, for about 15 minutes.

In a bowl, beat the egg yolks with the lemon juice, cream and butter pieces. When the tripe is tender, remove the pan from the heat and stir in the egg-and-cream mixture. Correct the seasoning and pour the tripe into a warmed serving dish. Decorate the tripe with the sliced gherkins and parsley before serving it.

PAUL BOUILLARD
LA GOURMANDISE À BON MARCHÉ

Tripe in Green Sauce

Trippa Verde

To serve 6

2 lb.	tripe, rinsed, poached in salted water for 2 hours, and the liquid reserved	1 kg.
4	garlic cloves, chopped	4
1	onion, chopped	1
1	celery rib, chopped	1
1	carrot, chopped	1
10	sprigs parsley, 8 chopped	10
½ cup	walnuts, chopped	125 ml.
8	basil leaves, chopped	8
	salt and pepper	
¼ cup	olive oil	50 ml.

To the tripe and reserved poaching liquid add half the garlic, the onion, celery, carrot and the two whole parsley sprigs. Bring the mixture to a boil and simmer for about 10 minutes.

Meanwhile, combine the walnuts, basil and the rest of the parsley and garlic in a mortar. Pound the mixture until it forms a smooth, creamy paste, very green and very fragrant. Season it lightly with salt and pepper. Drain the tripe and cut it into thin strips. Place these in a bowl and dress them with the green paste and the olive oil. Mix well.

GIOVANNI RIGHI PARENTI
LA GRANDE CUCINA TOSCANA

Tripe with Onions and Bacon

To serve 4 to 6

2 lb.	tripe, rinsed, cut into 2-inch [5-cm.] squares	1 kg.
4	thick slices lean bacon, diced	4
8	medium-sized onions, sliced	8
½ cup	flour	125 ml.
5 cups	milk	1¼ liters
1 cup	parsley sprigs, plus 2 tbsp. [30 ml.] chopped parsley leaves	¼ liter
1	celery rib, chopped	1
1	sprig thyme	1
2-inch	piece lemon peel	5-cm.
1	bay leaf	1
	salt and freshly ground black pepper	
	grated nutmeg	

Put the bacon in a heavy pan and cook it over low heat until the fat begins to melt. Add the onions, cover the pan and cook them gently until they are transparent. Stir in the flour and cook the mixture for a minute, stirring well. Gradually add the milk, bring it slowly to a boil and stir until the sauce is thick—about two minutes.

Add the tripe to the pan. Tie the parsley sprigs or stems, celery, thyme, lemon peel and bay leaf into a bouquet garni, and add it to the tripe. Season the sauce to taste with salt, pepper and grated nutmeg. Cover the pan and simmer over very low heat until the tripe is tender—about two hours. Serve the tripe at once, sprinkled with the chopped parsley.

SHONA CRAWFORD POOLE
THE LONDON TIMES

Hot Sour Fried Tripe

Goreng Babat Asam Pedas

Tamarind is an astringent fruit, comparable to lemon; salam is a dried Indonesian laurel, or bay, leaf; lemon grass is an aromatic tropical grass. Dried tamarind, salam leaves and lemon grass can be obtained where Indonesian foods are sold. To make the tamarind water, pour ⅓ cup [75 ml.] of boiling water over ½ oz. [15 g.] of dried tamarind pulp and soak for 20 minutes. Strain the liquid. Discard the pulp.

The volatile oils in hot chilies may make your skin sting and eyes burn; after handling chilies, avoid touching your face and wash your hands promptly.

	To serve 4	
2 lb.	tripe, rinsed	1 kg.
5	unpeeled shallots, quartered	5
3	garlic cloves, thinly sliced	3
5	fresh hot green or red chilies, halved and seeded	5
⅓ cup	tamarind water	75 ml.
1 tsp.	ground ginger	5 ml.
½ tsp.	ground coriander	2 ml.
	ground lemon grass (optional)	
1 tsp.	brown sugar	5 ml.
1½ tsp.	salt	7 ml.
2	salam leaves, or substitute bay leaves	2
about 1 cup	vegetable oil	about ¼ liter

Put the tripe into a large saucepan with the shallots, garlic and chilies. To the tamarind water add the ground ginger, coriander, a pinch of lemon grass—if using—the sugar and salt. Pour the mixture over the tripe. Add the salam or bay leaves and simmer the tripe for 30 minutes.

Let the tripe cool in the cooking liquid. When cool, remove and drain the tripe. Pick off the pieces of shallot and garlic and brush away any pieces of herbs. Cut the tripe into small squares and pat them dry.

Heat the oil in a wok or frying pan and fry the tripe squares, a few at a time, until brown—about three minutes. Serve hot.

SRI OWEN
INDONESIAN FOOD AND COOKERY

Tripe Milan-Style

To prepare red kidney beans, cover them with water, bring to a boil and boil them for two minutes. Let the beans soak covered for one hour. Drain them, cover the beans with fresh water, bring to a boil, boil for 10 minutes, then simmer until tender—about one and one half to two hours.

	To serve 4	
2 lb.	tripe, rinsed	1 kg.
2¼ tsp.	salt	11 ml.
1	celery rib	1
2	onions, 1 sliced	2
2	whole cloves	2
4 tbsp.	butter	60 ml.
¼ lb.	salt pork with the rind removed, finely chopped	125 g.
2	carrots, diced	2
1	large celery heart, chopped	1
4	medium-sized tomatoes, peeled, seeded and chopped	4
⅛ tsp.	powdered saffron, dissolved in 1 cup [¼ liter] warm water	½ ml.
1 lb.	dried red kidney beans, cooked	½ kg.
½	small new cabbage, thinly sliced	½
3	large potatoes, boiled, peeled and diced	3
½ tsp.	dried sage	2 ml.
3 tbsp.	freshly grated Parmesan cheese	45 ml.
⅛ tsp.	pepper	½ ml.

Place the tripe in a large pot. Cover it with 8 quarts [8 liters] of water. Add 2 teaspoons [10 ml.] of the salt, the celery rib, whole onion and cloves, and simmer it, uncovered, for two hours. Drain the cooked tripe and cut it into thin strips.

In a large pan, melt the butter, add the salt pork, sliced onion, carrots and celery heart and brown them well. Add the tomatoes and cook over medium heat for five minutes. Add the tripe, the rest of the salt and the diluted saffron and simmer for 30 minutes. Add the beans, cabbage and potatoes and continue simmering for 10 minutes, or until the vegetables are tender. Add the sage, sprinkle the mixture with the Parmesan cheese and pepper and cook for five more minutes. Serve at once.

ADA BONI
THE TALISMAN ITALIAN COOK BOOK

Tripe Andaluz-Style

Menudo Gitano o Callos à la Andaluz

Chorizo is a spicy, garlicky pork sausage available at Latin American food stores. Morcilla is a Spanish blood sausage; if unavailable, any type of blood sausage can be substituted. The technique of peeling peppers is shown on page 54.

To serve 6

3 lb.	veal tripe, rinsed and cut into 2-inch [5-cm.] squares	1½ kg.
3	calf's feet, cleaned, rinsed and chopped into small pieces	3
5 cups	dried chick-peas, soaked overnight and drained	1¼ liters
1	onion, chopped	1
1	ham bone	1
10	garlic cloves, chopped	10
2 tsp.	paprika	10 ml.
2	carrots, chopped	2
2 tsp.	chopped fresh mint leaves	10 ml.
¼ cup	chopped fresh parsley	50 ml.
1	bay leaf	1
	salt	
about 4 cups	water	about 1 liter
½ lb.	*chorizo*	¼ kg.
¼ lb.	*morcilla*	125 g.

Pepper and tomato sauce

2	green peppers, broiled, peeled, halved, seeded, deribbed and chopped	2
2	tomatoes, peeled, seeded and chopped	2
2 tbsp.	vegetable oil	30 ml.
1	onion, chopped	1
¼ lb.	ham, chopped (about ½ cup [125 ml.])	125 g.
1 tsp.	grated nutmeg	5 ml.
1 tsp.	powdered saffron	5 ml.

Place the tripe and calf's feet in a large, heavy pot. Add the chick-peas, onion, ham bone, garlic, paprika, carrots, mint, parsley, bay leaf and a pinch of salt, and cover with water. Bring the water to a boil over high heat and boil for 10 minutes. Then reduce the heat, partly cover the pot and cook until the tripe is tender—about three hours. Add the *chorizo* and the *morcilla* and let the stew simmer slowly while you prepare the sauce.

Heat the oil and fry the peppers, tomatoes, onion and ham with ½ teaspoon [2 ml.] each of the nutmeg and saffron. Stirring occasionally, cook until the onions are transparent—about five minutes.

Remove the *chorizo* and *morcilla* from the pot and slice them. Stir the sauce into the stew and pour it into a warmed serving dish. Arrange the sliced sausages on top of the stew and sprinkle it with the rest of the nutmeg and saffron.

ELIZABETH CASS
SPANISH COOKING

Tripe in Bread Crumbs

Le Tablier de Sapeur de Madame Lea

To serve 4

1 lb.	tripe, rinsed and cut into 2½- to 3-inch [7- to 8-cm.] squares	½ kg.
	salt and pepper	
1	egg, beaten with 1 tsp. [5 ml.] vegetable oil and 1 tsp. water	1
2 cups	fresh bread crumbs	½ liter
4 tbsp.	butter	60 ml.
¼ cup	vegetable oil	50 ml.
2 cups	tartar or *gribiche* sauce (recipe, page 167)	½ liter

Wine-mustard marinade

⅔ cup	dry white wine	150 ml.
1 tsp.	Dijon mustard	5 ml.
2 tbsp.	fresh lemon juice	30 ml.
1 tsp.	vegetable oil	5 ml.
	salt and freshly ground white pepper	

Combine the marinade ingredients and marinate the tripe pieces for three hours. Carefully drain and dry the tripe. Salt and pepper the beaten egg. Dip the pieces of tripe in the egg, then coat them with the bread crumbs. Heat the butter and oil in a cast-iron skillet and sauté the tripe pieces for about six minutes on each side. Then put the skillet under a preheated broiler and brown the tripe well on both sides. Serve with the tartar or *gribiche* sauce.

FÉLIX BENOIT AND HENRY CLOS JOUVE
LA CUISINE LYONNAISE

Tripe in Spicy Tomato Sauce

Ch'mennca

To serve 10

6 lb.	tripe, rinsed and cut into 1-inch [2½-cm.] squares	3 kg.
⅓ cup	vegetable oil	75 ml.
2 cups	tomato sauce *(recipe, page 166)*	½ liter
1 tbsp.	cayenne pepper	15 ml.
5	garlic cloves, chopped	5
	ground coriander	
2	bay leaves	2
1	sprig mint	1
	salt and pepper	
about 2½ quarts	water	about 2½ liters

Heat the oil in a large heavy pot and, when it is very hot, add the tomato sauce, cayenne pepper, garlic, a pinch of coriander, the bay leaves, mint, salt and pepper. Add the tripe and enough water to cover the mixture. Bake the tripe in a preheated 325° F. [170° C.] oven for four hours, or until tender.

LÉON ISNARD
LA GASTRONOMIE AFRICAINE

Kidney Beans and Tripe

To serve 4 to 6

¼ lb.	tripe, rinsed, parboiled for 30 minutes, drained and the cooking liquid reserved	125 g.
1 cup	dried kidney beans, soaked in water overnight and drained	¼ liter
1	large onion, chopped	1
1 tsp.	salt	5 ml.
¼ tsp.	black pepper	1 ml.
¼ tsp.	ground cinnamon	1 ml.
1 tbsp.	rendered bacon or ham fat	15 ml.
2 cups	water	½ liter

Combine all the ingredients in a pot with 1 cup [¼ liter] of the tripe cooking liquid. Bring to a boil over high heat and boil for 10 minutes. Reduce the heat and cover the pot. Simmer for one hour, or until the beans are tender. Add more tripe cooking liquid as needed to keep the tripe and beans covered throughout the cooking time. Correct the seasoning.

HELEN MENDES
THE AFRICAN HERITAGE COOKBOOK

Tripe American-Style

Les Tripes en Amérique

To serve 12

5 lb.	tripe, rinsed, blanched and cut into strips	2½ kg.
8 tbsp.	unsalted butter, softened	120 ml.
2	carrots, thickly sliced	2
2	onions, thickly sliced	2
2	leeks, white parts only, sliced ¼ inch [6 mm.] thick	2
1 lb.	veal shank	½ kg.
2 tsp.	salt	10 ml.
⅓ tsp.	dried thyme	1½ ml.
1	large bay leaf	1
4	whole cloves	4
6	peppercorns	6
½ cup	applejack or Calvados	125 ml.
1 cup	hard cider	¼ liter
2 cups	white wine	½ liter
1 to 3 cups	veal stock *(recipe, page 165)*	¼ to ¾ liter

Cream the butter. With the finger tips rub butter all over the inside surface of a 4-quart [4-liter] New England-style bean pot. Put about one third of the carrots, onions and leeks on the bottom of the bean pot and pack in half of the tripe. Press the veal shank into the mixture. Sprinkle with half of the salt. Add all of the herbs and spices. Add another layer of vegetables, then the rest of the tripe. Sprinkle with the rest of the salt. Finish with a last layer of vegetables. Mix together applejack, hard cider, wine and 1 cup [¼ liter] of the stock. Pour slowly over the contents of the pot. Add more stock if necessary to barely cover the contents of the pot. Close the pot and seal it with a paste made with flour and water. Bake in a 275° F. [140° C.] oven overnight.

To serve, remove the veal shank and spoon the tripe mixture onto very hot plates.

MADELEINE KAMMAN
THE MAKING OF A COOK

Tripe Vinaigrette

To serve 4

1 lb.	honeycomb tripe, or ½ lb. [¼ kg.] each of honeycomb and blanket tripe, rinsed	½ kg.
	salt	
1	small bay leaf	1
3 tbsp.	olive oil	45 ml.
¼ tsp.	dry mustard	1 ml.
¼ tsp.	coarsely ground black pepper	1 ml.
	Tabasco sauce	
2	sweet gherkins, chopped	2
2	scallions, chopped	2
1 tsp.	capers, rinsed and drained	5 ml.
2	eggs, hard-boiled and chopped	2
2 tbsp.	red wine vinegar	30 ml.
2 tbsp.	sour cream	30 ml.

Put the tripe in a saucepan, add cold water to cover, about 1 teaspoon [5 ml.] of salt and the bay leaf. Bring to a boil, reduce the heat, and simmer until the tripe is tender when pricked with a fork—at least one hour.

Meanwhile, make the sauce. Blend together the olive oil, dry mustard and pepper. Add two dashes of Tabasco sauce, the gherkins, scallions, capers, eggs and red wine vinegar.

Drain the tripe and cut it into 1-by-3-inch [2½-by-8-cm.] strips. While it is still warm, toss the tripe with the sauce. Mix well, then add the sour cream. Taste and add more salt if needed. Chill for at least one hour, stirring once or twice.

IRMA GOODRICH MAZZA
ACCENT ON SEASONING

Catalan Tripe

Tripes à la Catalane

To serve 2

1 lb.	tripe, rinsed and cut into small pieces	½ kg.
4 tbsp.	butter or vegetable oil	60 ml.
2	onions, chopped	2
2	tomatoes, peeled and chopped	2
1	small eggplant, peeled and chopped	1
1	small green or red pepper, stemmed, seeded, deribbed and chopped	1
	salt and pepper	

Heat the butter or oil in a pan and add the tripe. Brown the tripe, then remove it from the pan and reserve it. Put the onions into the same pan and sauté them until they are

lightly browned. Add the tomatoes, eggplant, green or red pepper, and salt and pepper. Cover the pan and stew the vegetables for about 15 minutes. Then return the tripe to the pan and simmer it for about two hours.

MARIE THÉRÈSE CARRÉRAS AND GEORGES LAFFORGUE
LES BONNES RECETTES DU PAYS CATALAN

Stewed Tripe from Angoulême

Tripes à la Mode d'Angoulême

To prevent the mixture from sticking to the casserole during the long cooking, the casserole may be lined with blanched pork rinds. Before serving the tripe, the sauce can be strained off, degreased and reduced over high heat.

To serve 6 to 8

2 lb.	tripe, rinsed and cut into 2-inch [5-cm.] squares	1 kg.
1	calf's foot, cleaned, rinsed, large bone removed, the meat split, blanched and cut into pieces	1
1	large carrot, sliced	1
1	large onion, stuck with 2 whole cloves	1
1	bouquet garni	1
20	small shallots, chopped	20
5 or 6	garlic cloves, chopped	5 or 6
	salt and pepper	
2 cups	dry white wine	½ liter
about 2 cups	meat stock *(recipe, page 165)*	about ½ liter
2 or 3	slices firm-textured white bread, crusts removed, toasted and cut into triangles	2 or 3

In an earthenware casserole with a tightly fitting lid, place the carrot, onion, bouquet garni, shallots and garlic, and add salt and pepper. Add the chopped tripe and calf's foot. Pour in the white wine and enough stock to cover the mixture. Make a paste with flour, water and a few drops of oil, and use it to seal the lid of the casserole. Bake the tripe in a 250° F. [120° C.] oven for at least 12 hours. To serve, arrange the toast in a dish. Remove the carrot, onion and bouquet garni and pour the mixture over the toast.

GOMBERVAUX (EDITOR)
LA BONNE CUISINE POUR TOUS

Tripe Sausage, North African-Style

Hasban

The technique of sewing a tripe sausage is shown on pages 64-65. The sausage is usually poached in a stew, but can also be poached in meat stock (recipe, page 165).

	To serve 6	
1	piece of honeycomb or blanket tripe, about 12 by 8 inches [30 by 20 cm.], rinsed	1
2 lb.	mixed honeycomb and blanket tripe, rinsed and chopped	1 kg.
2	garlic cloves, chopped	2
¼ cup	chopped fresh coriander or 1 tsp. [5 ml.] ground coriander	50 ml.
6	mint leaves, chopped	6
	quatre épices	
	caraway seeds	
	salt and pepper	
2 tbsp.	olive oil	30 ml.

In a bowl, combine the chopped, mixed tripe, garlic, coriander and mint. Add a pinch of *quatre épices* and caraway seeds, salt and pepper and the olive oil. Fold the rectangular piece of tripe in half lengthwise and sew up one end and the long open side. Stuff the tripe with the mixture, shape it into a cylinder and sew up the open end. Prick the sausage all over with a needle and poach it for at least three and one half hours, until tender.

IRÈNE AND LUCIENNE KARSENTY
LA CUISINE PIED-NOIR

Tripe with Onions and Wine

Gras Double "Léon de Lyon"

This recipe was invented by Paul Lacombe of the Léon de Lyon Restaurant.

	To serve 8	
4 lb.	tripe, rinsed and cut into thin strips	2 kg.
6 tbsp.	butter	90 ml.
4	large onions, sliced	4
	salt and pepper	
¼ cup	chopped fresh parsley	50 ml.
5	garlic cloves, chopped	5
⅔ cup	dry white wine	150 ml.
½ cup	dry bread crumbs	125 ml.

Melt 4 tablespoons [60 ml.] of the butter and sauté the tripe over high heat until it is golden brown. In another pan, melt the remaining butter and sauté the onions until they are golden. Add them to the tripe. Season with salt and pepper, add the parsley and garlic and pour in the wine, stirring to dislodge any bits that have stuck to the pan.

Transfer the mixture to an ovenproof dish, sprinkle it with the dry bread crumbs and cook in a preheated 400° F. [200° C.] oven for 30 minutes, or until the crumbs are brown.

FÉLIX BENOIT AND HENRY CLOS JOUVE
LA CUISINE LYONNAISE

Tripe Madrid-Style

Callos a la Madrileña

Chorizo is a dried Spanish garlic sausage. If it is not available, substitute any spicy dried garlic sausage.

	To serve 4	
2 lb.	tripe, rinsed and cut into thin strips	1 kg.
2	pig's feet, cleaned, rinsed, poached for 2½ hours and drained	2
4 cups	salted water	1 liter
3 tbsp.	olive oil	45 ml.
1	sweet red pepper, halved, seeded, deribbed and cut into strips	1
1	onion, chopped	1
1	tomato, peeled, seeded and chopped	1
½ lb.	ham, chopped (about 1 cup [¼ liter])	¼ kg.
1	garlic clove, chopped	1
½ tsp.	cayenne pepper	2 ml.
½ lb.	*chorizo*, cut into four pieces	¼ kg.
	salt	

Simmer the tripe and feet together in salted water to cover for one and one half hours, or until both are tender. Remove the feet with a slotted spoon, put them on a plate and separate the tender meat from the bones. Return the meat to the saucepan with the tripe.

Heat the oil and fry the red pepper, onion and tomato until the onion is soft. Add the ham, garlic, cayenne, *chorizo* and salt to taste. Stir well, then pour this sauce into the stewed tripe—by now, the original amount of water will be much reduced—and simmer for another 10 to 15 minutes.

JAN READ AND MAITE MANJÓN
PARADORES OF SPAIN

Tripe in a Spicy, Piquant Broth

Mondongo en Kabik

This is a specialty of the Yucatán peninsula in southern Mexico. Recado rojo is made from ground annatto, peppercorns and oregano, mixed with vinegar, chopped garlic and salt, formed into small balls and dried. It is obtainable where Mexican foods are sold. If it is not available, substitute chili powder. Epazote is a pungent herb that grows in Mexico and in the Southwestern United States. It can be omitted.

The volatile oils in hot chilies may make your skin sting and your eyes burn; after handling chilies, avoid touching your face and wash your hands promptly.

In the instructions for many Yucatán dishes you will see the word "toasted." Toasting onions, garlic, chilies and herbs under the broiler until they are lightly browned gives them a distinctive flavor.

	To serve 6	
1 lb.	blanket tripe, rinsed and cut into 1-inch [2½-cm.] squares	500 g.
1	small calf's foot, cleaned and rinsed	1
2 cups	Seville orange juice	½ liter
½	garlic bulb, unpeeled and toasted	½
1 tsp.	oregano, toasted	5 ml.
	salt	
about 2 quarts	water	about 2 liters
2 tbsp.	peanut or safflower oil	2 tbsp.
1	large tomato, chopped	1
¾ cup	finely chopped onion	175 ml.
1	small green pepper, halved, seeded, deribbed and cut into small squares	1
4	sprigs *epazote*, leaves coarsely chopped, skins discarded	4
9	hot green chilies, stemmed and seeded, 3 toasted and chopped, 6 cut into rounds	9
1 tsp.	*recado rojo*	5 ml.
2 tbsp.	finely cut fresh chives	30 ml.
1	lime, thinly sliced	1

One day ahead, cover the tripe with the orange juice and refrigerate it. Turn the pieces occasionally and let them soak overnight in the refrigerator. Put the pieces of calf's foot into a large saucepan with the garlic, oregano and 1 tablespoon [15 ml.] of salt and cover with the water. Bring the water to a boil, then reduce the heat, cover the pan and cook gently for about four hours, or until the meat is just beginning to get tender. Refrigerate the foot, in its broth, overnight.

The next day, drain the tripe, rinse it and add it to the calf's foot in the broth. Bring the mixture to a boil, cover and cook it slowly until both meats are tender—about an hour.

Meanwhile, heat the oil in a heavy pan and add the tomato, ¼ cup [125 ml.] of the onion, the green pepper and the chopped *epazote*. Fry the mixture, stirring constantly, until the onion is soft. Add the grilled chilies and the *recado rojo*, along with 2 tablespoons [30 ml.] of the broth from the saucepan containing the meats and cook for a few minutes more. Season with salt and set aside.

When the meat is tender, drain it, reserving the broth. Remove the bones from the calf's foot and chop the meat, gristle and skin into large pieces. Put these and the tripe on a warmed serving dish and set aside in a warm place.

If necessary, add water to the reserved broth to make it up to 2 quarts [2 liters]. Add the fried, seasoned vegetables and simmer for about five minutes, or until well flavored. If there is too much fat on top of the broth, skim as necessary. Serve the broth in large soup bowls; serve the meat separately. Present the sliced chilies, the rest of the chopped onion, the chives and lime slices in individual bowls. Accompany the tripe with French bread.

DIANA KENNEDY
RECIPES FROM THE REGIONAL COOKS OF MEXICO

Stewed Tripe

Gras-Double de Montferrand

The authors suggest serving the tripe with Dijon mustard.

	To serve 6	
2 lb.	tripe, rinsed and sliced	1 kg.
2	carrots, sliced	2
2	celery ribs, sliced	2
	thyme	
2	bay leaves	2
2	whole cloves	2
	salt and pepper	
4 cups	dry white wine	1 liter
4	tomatoes, peeled, seeded and chopped	4

Put the tripe, carrots and celery into a large, nonreactive pot. Add a pinch of thyme, the bay leaves, cloves, and salt and pepper to taste. Then add the wine and tomatoes. Cover the contents of the pot with a piece of oiled parchment paper. Cover the pot with a tight-fitting lid, sealed with a paste made from flour, water and a few drops of oil. Simmer the tripe for 12 hours.

AMICALE DES CUISINIERS ET PÂTISSIERS AUVERGNATS DE PARIS
CUISINE D'AUVERGNE

Tripe Toulouse-Style

Gras-Double Toulousaine

To serve 4

2 lb.	tripe, rinsed and cut into 2-inch [5-cm.] squares	1 kg.
4 tbsp.	lard	60 ml.
2	medium-sized onions, chopped	2
1 cup	boiling meat stock *(recipe, page 165)*	¼ liter
¾ cup	milk, scalded	175 ml.
	salt and pepper	
¼ cup	chopped fresh parsley	50 ml.
1	garlic clove, crushed to a paste, or 3 tbsp. [45 ml.] finely cut chives	1
1	egg yolk	1
2 tbsp.	fresh lemon juice	30 ml.

Melt the lard in a saucepan, add the onions and cook over medium heat until the onions are soft and beginning to turn yellow—about 10 minutes. Add the tripe and fry it for a few minutes. Add the boiling stock and scalded milk to the pan; the tripe should be covered with liquid. Season with salt and pepper, cover the pan and simmer over low heat for at least two hours, or until the cooking liquid is reduced by about half. Remove the pan from the heat and stir in the parsley and the garlic or chives. Beat the egg yolk and the lemon juice together and stir them gradually into the mixture.

TANTE MARGUERITE
LA CUISINE DE LA BONNE MÉNAGÈRE

Tripe Casserole

Tripes à la Catalane

To serve 4

2 lb.	tripe, rinsed and cut into 1- to 1½-inch [2½- to 3-cm.] pieces	1 kg.
⅔ cup	olive oil	150 ml.
8	medium-sized potatoes, diced	8
3	onions, sliced	3
5	tomatoes, peeled, seeded and crushed	5
	cayenne pepper	
¾ cup	grated Gruyère cheese	175 ml.

Put the tripe into a pan of salted cold water to cover. Bring to a boil, skim and simmer the tripe for one hour.

While the tripe is cooking, heat half the olive oil and in it fry the potatoes until golden. Drain them, reserving the oil. Fry the onions in the reserved oil until they are brown.

Meantime, warm the rest of the oil in another pan, add the tomatoes and a pinch of cayenne pepper, and cook them over medium heat until their juices have evaporated—about 10 minutes. Add the fried onions to this sauce.

Drain the tripe. Put the tripe and potatoes in an oven-proof dish, cover them with the tomato-and-onion sauce, sprinkle the top with the grated Gruyère, and bake the mixture in a preheated 400° F. [200° C.] oven for 15 minutes, or until the cheese is melted and browned.

IRVING DAVIS
A CATALAN COOKERY BOOK

Stuffed Tripe

Asbane

The technique of preparing and stuffing the tripe is shown on pages 64-65, where half of the ground beef is replaced by finely chopped tripe. The stuffed tripe is usually poached in a stew and served with it.

To serve 6

3 lb.	tripe, in 1 roughly rectangular piece, rinsed	1½ kg.
1½ lb.	ground lean beef	¾ kg.
⅓ cup	raw white rice, cooked and cooled	75 ml.
2	garlic cloves, finely chopped	2
1	large onion, finely chopped	1
3	slices firm-textured white bread, crusts removed, soaked in water and squeezed dry	3
	salt	
	mixed spices	
	mixed herbs	
about 2 quarts	meat stock *(recipe, page 165)*	about 2 liters

For the stuffing, mix the beef, cooked rice, garlic, onion and soaked bread. Add salt and a large pinch each of mixed spices and mixed herbs. The stuffing should be highly spiced.

Fold the tripe in half lengthwise and sew up the edges, leaving one end open. Fill the tripe with the stuffing and tie or sew the open end securely. Simmer the stuffed tripe in stock to cover for at least three and one half hours.

ÉDOUARD DE POMIANE
CUISINE JUIVE: GHETTOS MODERNES

Lamb Tripe
Gumee

To serve 6 to 8

1½ lb.	lamb tripe, rinsed, soaked in salted water with ½ cup [125 ml.] vinegar for 3 hours, drained and cut into 3 pieces	¾ kg.
½ lb.	ground lamb	¼ kg.
½ cup	dried chick-peas, soaked overnight, drained, cooked in water for 1½ hours, drained and coarsely chopped	125 ml.
1 cup	rice, soaked in hot water for 15 minutes and drained	¼ liter
4 tbsp.	butter, melted	60 ml.
	salt and pepper	
	ground cloves and cinnamon	
2 quarts	boiling water	2 liters
2	bay leaves	2

Combine the ground lamb, chick-peas, rice, butter, salt, pepper and a little clove and cinnamon. Spoon the lamb mixture onto the pieces of tripe, wrap the tripe over this filling to form parcels and sew the parcels securely closed. Place the parcels in a pot, cover them with the boiling water and add the bay leaves. Cover and simmer for one and one half hours, or until the tripe is tender. Discard the bay leaves. Transfer the parcels to a warmed platter and cover them to keep them hot. Serve the cooking liquid as a soup, garnished with chopped fresh or dried mint, before presenting the tripe.

HELEN COREY
THE ART OF SYRIAN COOKERY

French Goose (Roasted Pig's Stomach)

To serve 6 to 8

1	pig's stomach, rubbed with vinegar and salt, scrubbed and soaked in several changes of water for 24 hours	1
2 lb.	ground pork	1 kg.
8	medium-sized waxy potatoes, diced	8
8	medium-sized celery ribs, sliced crosswise	8
4 or 5	carrots, sliced	4 or 5
1	small onion, finely chopped (optional)	1
3 tbsp.	chopped fresh parsley	45 ml.
1 tsp.	salt	5 ml.
⅛ tsp.	freshly ground pepper	½ ml.

Combine the ground pork, vegetables and seasonings, mixing well. Stuff the pig's stomach with this mixture and close the openings with string and skewers. Place the stuffed stomach on a rack in a large casserole with a lid, and bake it, covered, in a preheated 350° F. [180° C.] oven for approximately three hours. Remove the lid from the casserole and baste the roast with the drippings that have oozed out. Increase the oven heat to 375° F. [190° C.] and bake the stomach, uncovered, until it is golden brown—about 20 minutes. To serve the stomach, put it on a board or a platter and remove the string and skewers. Cut the stomach into slices 2 inches [5 cm.] thick—no thinner or the stuffing will fall out of the slices.

BETTY GROFF AND JOSÉ WILSON
GOOD EARTH AND COUNTRY COOKING

Stuffed Pig's Stomach, Alsatian-Style
Estomac de Porc Farci

The technique of sewing two stomachs together is shown on page 48. Aromatics can be added to the poaching water for extra flavor. After poaching the stomach, instead of browning it in butter over direct heat, you can rub it with oil and roast it until lightly browned, then baste it with wine and pan juices for a rich glaze, as shown on page 49. The stomach can be served with a poulette sauce (recipe, page 166).

To serve 8 to 10

2	pig's stomachs, rinsed, turned inside out and sewn together	2
7 tbsp.	butter	105 ml.
2¼ cups	finely chopped onions	550 ml.
⅓ cup	finely chopped shallots	75 ml.
3 lb.	potatoes, diced and blanched for 1 minute in boiling salted water	1½ kg.
1¾ lb.	boneless pork blade roast, ground	850 g.
1 lb.	pork tenderloin, diced	500 g.
2	eggs	2
5	sprigs parsley, finely chopped	5
	dried savory leaves, crumbled	
	salt and pepper	
	mixed spices	

Melt half of the butter in a large skillet. Add the onions and shallots, and cook them until they are transparent. Add the diced potatoes and cook the mixture over very low heat for five minutes, tossing it lightly to prevent it from sticking: The potatoes must not be allowed to brown and they must remain intact.

Mix the ground and the diced pork with the eggs, parsley, a pinch of savory, salt and pepper, and mixed spices; with a spatula, work the mixture. Add the potato mixture and stir lightly. Use this stuffing to fill the stomachs without packing them too tightly. Sew up the opening. Use a sharp needle to prick the stomachs in several places to prevent them from bursting during cooking. Place the stomachs in a large pot and cover them with water. Put on a lid and poach the stomachs very gently—the water should tremble but not bubble—for about four hours. Carefully remove the stomachs from the pot and reserve the poaching liquid. Let the stomachs drain thoroughly.

In a heavy saucepan, melt the rest of the butter. Add the poached stomachs and cook them over medium heat, turning them often, until they are golden brown—at least 30 minutes. Cut the stomachs into slices and serve them very hot, accompanied by poaching liquid lightly thickened.

JOSEPH KOSCHER AND ASSOCIATES
LES RECETTES DE LA TABLE ALSACIENNE

Pig's Stomach Stuffed with Pork

Gefüllte Saumagen Pfälzer Art

The technique of cooking a stuffed pig's stomach is shown on pages 48-49. The author suggests serving the stuffed stomach with sauerkraut.

To serve 8 to 10

one 1½ lb.	pig's stomach, rinsed	one ¾ kg.
4	thick slices bacon, cut into pieces	4
3	onions, finely chopped	3
1¼ lb.	ground pork	600 g.
	salt and pepper	
	dried marjoram	
	dried thyme	
	grated nutmeg	
3	potatoes, parboiled for 15 minutes in lightly salted water, peeled and cut into ½-inch [1-cm.] cubes	3
2	hard rolls, soaked in water or milk and squeezed	2
2 tbsp.	chopped fresh parsley	30 ml.
3	eggs, lightly beaten	3
3 cups	water	¾ liter
¼ cup	dry white wine	50 ml.

Melt half of the bacon over low heat and in it fry the onions until they are transparent. Add the ground pork, salt and pepper to taste, and a pinch each of marjoram, thyme and

nutmeg. Add the potatoes. Cook gently for about 20 minutes, then drain off the excess fat. Remove the pan from the heat, stir in the squeezed rolls, the parsley and eggs. Stuff the pig's stomach with this mixture and sew it up.

In a large pot, melt the remaining bacon over medium heat, add the stuffed stomach and brown it on all sides—about 20 minutes. Add the water, bring it to a boil, then cover the pot and simmer the stomach—turning and basting it often—until tender, from two to four hours. Stir in the wine. Serve the stomach accompanied by its cooking liquid.

FRED METZLER AND KLAUS OSTER
AAL BLAU UND ERRÖTHETES MÄDCHEN

Chitlins

To serve 8 to 10

5 lb.	chitterlings, slit, fatty membrane removed, soaked and drained	2½ kg.
about 4 cups	water	about 1 liter
3	garlic cloves	3
1	lemon, halved	1
1 tsp.	freshly ground black pepper	5 ml.
2	whole cloves	2
1 tsp.	dried thyme	5 ml.
2	sprigs parsley	2
2	bay leaves	2
2	onions, quartered	2
¼ cup	cider vinegar	50 ml.
1 tbsp.	dried marjoram	15 ml.
1 tsp.	salt	5 ml.
¼ tsp.	ground mace	1 ml.
¼ tsp.	ground allspice	1 ml.
1¼ cups	tomato sauce *(recipe, page 166)*	300 ml.
	cayenne pepper	

Place the chitterlings in a large pot with water just to cover; add all the ingredients except the tomato sauce and cayenne pepper. Simmer the mixture, covered, for three to four hours, or until tender. The timing will vary, depending on whether fresh or partially cooked chitterlings are used. During the last 30 minutes of cooking, add the tomato sauce to the pot and season with cayenne pepper to taste. Serve with coleslaw and corn bread.

JANA ALLEN AND MARGARET GIN
INNARDS AND OTHER VARIETY MEATS

Head, Ears and Feet

Stuffed Calf's Head
Tête de Veau Farcie

The technique of stuffing a boned calf's head is demonstrated on pages 52-53.

To serve 8

1	calf's head, boned, soaked and cleaned	1
2 tbsp.	coarse salt	30 ml.
1	medium-sized onion	1
2	carrots	2
1	bouquet garni	1
2 tbsp.	butter	30 ml.
¼ cup	flour	50 ml.
2 tbsp.	brandy	30 ml.
1 tbsp.	tomato paste	15 ml.
¼ lb.	ham, cut into julienne	125 g.
¾ cup	ripe olives, rinsed and pitted	175 ml.
Pork and veal stuffing		
¾ lb.	ground pork shoulder	⅓ kg.
½ lb.	ground veal shoulder	¼ kg.
1	egg	1
1 cup	sliced fresh mushrooms	¼ liter
	salt and pepper	
	mixed spices	

Mix the stuffing ingredients, seasoning the mixture fairly heavily. Poach a spoonful of the stuffing and taste it for seasoning. Stuff the head, and roll it and sew it up carefully to hold the stuffing tightly. Wrap the head in muslin or cheesecloth and tie the cloth with string at both ends and in the center.

Put the head in a large pot, pour in enough cold water to cover it, and add the salt, onion, carrots and bouquet garni. Bring to a boil and simmer, partially covered, for five hours.

Remove the head from the pot; strain the cooking liquid. Melt the butter in a pan, stir in the flour, then whisk in the brandy and 4 cups [1 liter] of the cooking liquid, and cook for 10 minutes. Add the tomato paste and simmer for 30 minutes, skimming often. Add the ham and olives. Cook over low heat until smooth and thick. Slice the head into pieces and coat them with the sauce. Serve with mashed potatoes.

EUGÉNIE BRAZIER
LES SECRETS DE LA MÈRE BRAZIER

Poached Calf's Head
Tête de Veau au Naturel

The technique of boning a head is demonstrated on pages 14-15. The head may also be poached in a white court bouillon (recipe, page 165), as shown on pages 46-47.

To serve 4 to 6

1	calf's head, the brain and tongue reserved and soaked, the head boned, soaked, cleaned and halved, each half cut into 3 pieces	1
½ lb.	suet, finely chopped	¼ kg.
1 cup	flour	¼ liter
6 quarts	water	6 liters
1	medium-sized onion, sliced	1
1	large bouquet garni	1
1	garlic clove	1
3	whole cloves	3
2 cups	white wine vinegar	½ liter
3 tbsp.	salt	45 ml.
1 tbsp.	pepper	15 ml.
6 cups	vinegar court bouillon (recipe, page 165)	1 ½ liters
6	sprigs parsley	6

Put the calf's-head pieces and the tongue into a pot of boiling water and parboil for 20 minutes. Drain and rinse them.

In a large, nonreactive pot, melt the suet over low heat. Stir in the flour, water, onion, bouquet garni, garlic, cloves, vinegar and salt and pepper. Bring to a boil over high heat, then add the pieces of head and the tongue. Reduce the heat, cover the meats with a piece of parchment paper, partially cover the pot with a lid and simmer gently for two and one half hours. Remove the tongue from the pot, peel it and return it to the pot. Replace the paper and continue to cook for another hour or so. Meanwhile, remove the membrane from the brain and poach the brain in the vinegar court bouillon for 25 minutes. Drain and keep it warm.

When the calf's-head pieces and tongue are tender, remove them from the pot. Split the tongue in two lengthwise to the base—without completely separating the halves.

To serve the head, fold a napkin to cover the bottom of an oval serving dish. Place the pieces of head with the ears attached at opposite ends of the dish, and lay the remaining pieces around the edge. Lay the tongue, opened out, in the center of the dish with the brain on top. Arrange four sprigs of parsley around the edges of the dish and the remaining two sprigs on each side of the brain.

Eat the head hot with oil and vinegar. Serve chopped parsley, chopped onion and capers on the side.

JULES GOUFFÉ
LE LIVRE DE CUISINE

To Grill a Calf's Head

To serve 6 to 8

1	calf's head, split in half, soaked, cleaned; tongue, soaked; brains, soaked and membrane removed	1
2	egg yolks, lightly beaten	2
	salt and pepper	
¾ cup	dry bread crumbs	175 ml.
2 tsp.	grated lemon peel	10 ml.
¼ cup	finely chopped fresh parsley	50 ml.
6 tbsp.	butter, melted	90 ml.
2	sage leaves	2
2 tbsp.	heavy cream	30 ml.

Poach the calf's head in water for four hours, or until the meat is tender. Poach the tongue separately for two hours.

Strip the meat from one half of the head and chop it fine. Keep the chopped meat warm. Brush the other half of the head with the egg yolks and sprinkle it with pepper and salt. Broil this half, skin side up, about 4 inches [10 cm.] from the heat, basting with a spoonful of the butter, for 10 minutes. Turn the head over and strew over it the bread crumbs, lemon peel and half the parsley. Sprinkle with a spoonful of butter; broil for 10 more minutes. Arrange the chopped meat on a platter and set the broiled half on top. Meanwhile, peel the tongue, split it lengthwise and lay it in a soup plate. Poach the brains in water with salt, the remaining parsley and the sage for 15 minutes. Chop the brains and mix them with the remaining butter and the cream. Heat them briefly and pour half over the tongue. Serve the rest with the head.

F. COLLINGWOOD AND J. WOOLAMS
THE UNIVERSAL COOK

Baked Lamb's Head

Tête d'Agneau Boulangère

To serve 2

1	lamb's head, soaked, cleaned and split in half lengthwise	1
4	large potatoes, quartered	4
	salt and pepper	
½ lb.	butter, melted	¼ kg.
3	garlic cloves, finely chopped	3
2 tsp.	chopped fresh parsley	10 ml.
1½ cups	fresh bread crumbs	375 ml.

Put the lamb's-head halves cut side up in a buttered shallow ovenproof dish. Arrange the potatoes around the head, sea-son with salt and pepper, and pour the melted butter over the meat and potatoes. Bake in a preheated 400° F. [200° C.] oven for about two hours, or until the meat is tender and well browned, basting it every 20 minutes with the cooking juices or more melted butter, if necessary.

Mix the garlic, parsley and bread crumbs, and sprinkle the head with the mixture. Bake the head for a further 10 to 15 minutes, or until the topping is golden brown, basting the meat and potatoes at least once.

LÉON ISNARD
LA GASTRONOMIE AFRICAINE

Stuffed Lamb's Heads

Cabezas de Cordero al Horno

The author suggests serving the lamb's heads with fried pota-toes or boiled new potatoes. Alternatively, potatoes can be added to the dish one hour before the end of the cooking time and baked with the heads.

To serve 4

2	lamb's heads, split into halves, soaked and cleaned	2
	salt	
2 tbsp.	fresh lemon juice	30 ml.
	Pork stuffing	
5 oz.	ground lean pork	150 g.
4 tbsp.	lard	60 ml.
1	garlic clove, chopped	1
¼ cup	chopped fresh parsley	50 ml.
¼ tsp.	cayenne pepper	1 ml.
¼ tsp.	paprika	1 ml.
1	egg, beaten	1

Sprinkle the heads with salt. To make the stuffing, melt the lard in a skillet over medium heat. Mix the ground pork with the garlic, a pinch of salt, the chopped parsley, cayenne pep-per and paprika. Stirring frequently, fry the pork mixture until the pork loses all traces of pink. Drain off the excess fat and reserve it. Transfer the pork mixture to a bowl to cool slightly. Add about half the beaten egg to the pork; save the remaining egg for another use. Mix the egg and pork well and stuff the head cavities with the mixture. Tie the halves of each head together so they resemble complete heads.

Put the heads into an oiled baking dish. Rub the heads with the reserved frying fat and the lemon juice. Cover the heads with oiled parchment paper and bake them in a pre-heated 400° F. [200° C.] oven for one and one half hours. Then remove the parchment paper, baste the heads with the cooking liquid and bake them for another 30 minutes.

MARIA DOLORES COMAS
LO MEJOR DE LA COCINA ESPAÑOLA

Pig's Head Meat in Caul

La Caillette

The technique of boning a head is shown on pages 14-15. The cooking liquid from this dish will serve as a good soup.

To serve 6

2 lb.	pig's head, boned, soaked and cleaned	1 kg.
1 lb.	pork liver, membrane removed, finely chopped	½ kg.
3	garlic cloves, 2 finely chopped	3
	salt and pepper	
½ lb.	spinach, ribs removed	¼ kg.
1	small cabbage, cored and leaves separated	1
½ lb.	lean boneless pork, finely chopped	¼ kg.
½ tsp.	finely chopped fresh parsley	2 ml.
1	egg	1
½ lb.	caul, soaked and drained	¼ kg.
	grated nutmeg	
2 tbsp.	butter	30 ml.
2 oz.	fresh fatback, in 1 piece	60 g.
1	sprig sage	1

Put the head into a heavy pot; add water to cover, the whole garlic clove, and salt and pepper. Bring the water to a boil and simmer the head for about three hours, or until the meat is tender; if necessary, add boiling water to keep the head submerged. Remove the head and let it cool. Bring the cooking liquid to a boil and drop in the spinach. Blanch it for about two minutes. Remove the spinach and drain it. Drop the cabbage leaves into the liquid, blanch them for about five minutes and drain them. Reserve the cooking liquid.

Remove the meat from the head, then chop the meat, spinach and cabbage very fine. Place the mixture in a bowl and add the liver, pork, garlic and parsley. Break the egg over the mixture, grate in a little nutmeg and mix well.

Spread out the caul in a shallow bowl. The edges of the caul should hang over the sides. Place the meat mixture in the center and wrap the edges over it to form a parcel.

Melt the butter in a heavy casserole and add about 2 cups [½ liter] of the reserved cooking liquid. Place the caul parcel in the casserole with the folds downward. Stick the sprig of sage into the fatback and lay it on top of the parcel. Bake the parcel uncovered in a preheated 325° F. [160° C.] oven for about one hour, or until the top is browned. Check at 15-minute intervals to see that the liquid in the casserole has not dried up; if necessary, add more reserved cooking liquid. The parcel is best when served hot, although any leftovers are excellent cold.

EDOUARD NIGNON (EDITOR)
LE LIVRE DE CUISINE DE L'OUEST-ÉCLAIR

Poached Pig's Head

Tête de Cochon au Pot

The poaching broth is served first as a soup, poured over slices of bread. Potatoes or other soup vegetables may be added to the pot 30 minutes before serving.

To serve 6

1	pig's head, soaked, cleaned, encased in spiced salt (recipe, page 167), refrigerated for 3 days and rinsed	1
1 tsp.	peppercorns	5 ml.
2 or 3	whole cloves	2 or 3
2 lb.	green cabbage, cored and halved	1 kg.
1 or 2	garlic cloves	1 or 2
4	slices home-style white bread, crusts removed, torn into pieces (optional)	4
4 tbsp.	butter, cut into pieces	60 ml.

Put the pig's head into a pot and cover it with water. Bring the water to a boil, skim it and add the peppercorns, cloves, garlic and bread, if using. Reduce the heat and simmer the head, partially covered, for two hours. Add the cabbage and simmer for 30 minutes, or until the meat is tender.

Remove the head and bone it. Slice the meat and arrange the pieces in a deep platter. Put the cabbage in a bowl and dot it with the butter. Serve the pig's head and cabbage with vinegar and coarse salt or with vinaigrette sauce.

MAURICE BÉGUIN
LA CUISINE EN POITOU

Calf's Ears with Peas

Oreilles de Veau aux Pois

Although some butchers may be able to obtain them, calf's ears are rarely available in America. Pig's ears make a suitable substitute.

To serve 4

4	calf's ears, cleaned and parboiled	4
2 cups	white court bouillon (recipe, page 165)	½ liter
2 tbsp.	butter	30 ml.
2 lb.	peas, shelled	1 kg.
	salt	
1	bouquet garni, including 2 whole cloves and 1 sprig savory	1
1 tbsp.	flour	15 ml.
1 ½ cups	meat stock (recipe, page 165) or water	375 ml.

Simmer the ears in the white court bouillon for at least three hours, or until they are tender. In a separate pan, melt the butter and add the peas, a pinch of salt and the bouquet garni. Stirring occasionally, cook over low heat for about five minutes. Sprinkle the peas with flour, add the stock or water and increase the heat to medium. When the peas are tender and the liquid slightly reduced—in about 10 minutes—add the cooked ears and heat them through before serving.

MARIN
LES DONS DE COMUS

Beef Cheek Soup or Stew

To serve 8

1	beef cheek, bones broken, washed thoroughly, soaked in warm, salted water for 2 hours to remove slime, washed again	1
4 tbsp.	butter	60 ml.
½ lb.	ham, sliced	¼ kg.
4	bunches celery, sliced	4
3	large onions, sliced	3
2	carrots, sliced	2
1	parsnip, sliced	1
2 or 3	beets, chopped	2 or 3
3	blades mace	3
	salt and pepper	
7 quarts	water	7 liters
	Beef cheek soup garnish	
1	bunch celery, ribs chopped, leaves discarded	1
2 oz.	vermicelli	60 g.
1	end piece of French roll	1
	Beef cheek stew garnish	
1	turnip, boiled and diced	1
1	carrot, boiled and diced	1
1	slice bread, toasted and diced	1
	cayenne pepper	

Take a large pot, put the butter at the bottom of the pot, and lay the cheek in it, flesh side down; add to it the sliced ham, celery, onions, carrots, parsnip, beets, mace, salt and pepper; set the pan over medium heat for 15 minutes; this draws the virtue from the roots, which gives a pleasant strength to the gravy. When the cheek has simmered for 15 minutes, add

the water, and let it stew until the liquid is reduced to 2½ quarts [2½ liters].

If you would have it like soup, remove the meat and vegetables, strain the liquid and add the chopped celery. Cook the vermicelli for three minutes in the liquid and serve it as soup, in a tureen, putting the top of the French roll in the middle just before you serve it up.

If you would have it like stew, remove and drain the cheek, keeping it as whole as possible. Heat the boiled turnip and carrot through in the liquid, drain and remove them, and arrange them on a serving dish with the cheek and the diced bread. Add a little cayenne pepper to the liquid, and strain it through a fine-meshed sieve over the meat, carrot, turnip and bread.

MAY BYRON (EDITOR)
POT-LUCK

Baked Calf's Ears

Oreilles de Veau

Although some butchers may be able to obtain them, calf's ears are rarely available in America. Pig's ears make a suitable substitute.

To serve 4

4	calf's ears, cleaned and parboiled	4
1½ quarts	white court bouillon (recipe, page 165)	1½ liters
½ lb.	roasted chicken breast, skinned, boned and chopped (about 2 cups [½ liter])	¼ kg.
½ lb.	ham, chopped (about 2 cups [½ liter])	¼ kg.
¼ lb.	fresh mushrooms, sautéed in 2 tbsp. [30 ml.] butter and chopped	125 g.
1 cup	velouté sauce (recipe, page 166)	¼ liter
	salt and pepper	
¼ cup	flour	50 ml.
2	eggs, beaten with 1 tbsp. [15 ml.] water	2
1 cup	fresh bread crumbs	¼ liter
4 tbsp.	butter, melted	60 ml.

Put the ears into the white court bouillon and poach them for one and one half hours. Drain them and pat them dry.

Mix the chopped chicken, ham and mushrooms, and bind them with the velouté sauce. Season to taste. Stuff the ears with this mixture and dip the ears first in the flour, then in the beaten eggs and finally in the bread crumbs. Place the ears in a baking dish, pour the butter over them and bake them in a preheated 350° F. [180° C.] oven for 45 minutes, or until golden brown.

ALEXANDRE DUMAINE
MA CUISINE

Stuffed Calf's Ears

Les Oreilles de Veau Farcies

Although some butchers may be able to obtain them, calf's ears are rarely available in America. Pig's ears make a suitable substitute. Instead of being fried, the ears can be baked: Put them in a 450° F. [230° C.] oven for five minutes, then reduce the heat to 350° F. [180° C.] and bake for one hour. Whole beaten eggs may replace the egg whites. If truffles are unavailable, they can be omitted or replaced by mushrooms.

	To serve 6	
6	calf's ears, cleaned and parboiled	6
½	lemon	½
about 3 cups	dry white wine	about ¾ liter
about 3 cups	meat stock (recipe, page 165)	about ¾ liter
1	onion	1
1	carrot, cut into 2 or 3 pieces	1
1	bouquet garni	1
	salt and pepper	
5	egg whites, beaten to soft peaks	5
2 cups	fine dry bread crumbs, sieved	½ liter
1 cup	clarified butter	¼ liter
1½ cups	béarnaise sauce or mayonnaise (recipes, pages 166 and 167)	375 ml.

Sweetbread and chicken stuffing

1 lb.	veal sweetbreads, soaked, parboiled, membrane removed, pressed under weights, diced	½ kg.
1	roasted chicken breast, skinned, boned and diced	1
2 tbsp.	butter	30 ml.
2 tbsp.	flour	30 ml.
2 to 3 tbsp.	heavy cream	30 to 45 ml.
3	truffles, diced	3
	salt and pepper	
1	egg yolk, beaten with 1 tbsp. [15 ml.] heavy cream	1

Rub the parboiled ears with the cut side of the lemon. Wrap each ear tightly in muslin or cheesecloth and sew up the cloth in such a way as to hold each ear in a little bag. Put the ears into a casserole, pour in equal quantities of wine and stock to cover them and add the onion, carrot and bouquet garni. Season with salt and pepper. Bring the liquid to a boil, cover the casserole and simmer the ears for about three hours, adding wine and stock if necessary to keep them covered with liquid. When the ears are cooked, let them cool in the liquid. Drain the ears, unwrap them and pat them dry. Refrigerate them. Reserve the cooking liquid.

To make the stuffing, sauté the diced sweetbreads and chicken breast in the butter. Then sprinkle them with the flour and stir. When the mixture is well browned, stir in about ⅔ cup [150 ml.] of the ear cooking liquid. Add the cream, truffles and salt and pepper. Remove the mixture from the heat and let it cool for two minutes before adding the beaten egg yolk. Chill the stuffing before using it.

Stuff each ear from the base right up to the tip. Then dip the base and stuffed part of the ear first into the beaten egg white and then into the bread crumbs; repeat the operation so that there is a sufficiently thick coating to hold in the stuffing. The coating will adhere better if the coated ears are refrigerated for five to six hours before they are fried.

In a deep pan, heat the clarified butter. Add the ears, stuffed side upwards, and fry them until they are golden brown, about 10 minutes. Then turn them over and fry the stuffed side for 10 minutes. Remove the ears, drain them and serve them with the béarnaise sauce or mayonnaise.

LUCIEN TENDRET
LA TABLE AU PAYS DE BRILLAT-SAVARIN

Stewed Pig's Ears

Orelhas de Porco

	To serve 4	
4	pig's ears, cleaned and parboiled	4
5 tbsp.	lard	75 ml.
3 tbsp.	vegetable oil	45 ml.
1	large onion, sliced	1
1	sprig parsley, chopped	1
4	garlic cloves, crushed	4
	pepper	
4	medium-sized tomatoes, peeled, seeded and chopped	4
2	green peppers, halved, seeded, deribbed and sliced into strips	2
2 cups	dry white wine	½ liter
⅔ cup	port	150 ml.

In a nonreactive saucepan, heat the lard and oil, and lightly fry the onion, parsley and garlic. When the onion is golden, add the pig's ears, season with pepper and cook until the ears begin to color. Add the tomatoes and green peppers, then pour in the white wine and port. Cover the pan and simmer the contents over low heat for one and one half to two hours, or until the ears are tender.

MARIA ODETTE CORTES VALENTE
COZINHA REGIONAL PORTUGUESA

Pig's Ears with Cheese

Oreilles de Porc "Cantalienne"

To serve 6

4	pig's ears, cleaned and parboiled	4
¼ tsp.	salt	1 ml.
6	sprigs parsley	6
2	leeks, chopped	2
1	onion, studded with 3 whole cloves	1
1	sprig thyme	1
1	bay leaf	1
2 cups	white sauce *(recipe, page 167)*	½ liter
¼ lb.	Cantal cheese, grated or thinly sliced	125 g.

Place the pig's ears in a pan with enough water to cover them and add the salt, parsley, leeks, onion, thyme and bay leaf. Bring to a boil, reduce the heat and simmer, uncovered, for three to four hours. Drain the ears and cut them into fairly thin strips, place them in a deep gratin dish, pour the white sauce over them and sprinkle with the grated or sliced cheese. Bake in a preheated 400° F. [200° C.] oven for 30 minutes, or until the cheese is golden brown.

ROGER LALLEMAND
LA VRAIE CUISINE DE L'AUVERGNE ET DU LIMOUSIN

Pig's Ears in Caper Sauce

Oreille de Porc à la Barbe Robert

To serve 4

4	pig's ears, cleaned, parboiled, poached in meat stock *(recipe, page 165)* and white wine for 3 hours, or until tender, drained and sliced, ¼ cup [50 ml.] poaching liquid reserved	4
2 tbsp.	butter	30 ml.
8	scallions, chopped	8
2 tbsp.	white wine vinegar	30 ml.
1 tbsp.	capers, rinsed and drained	15 ml.
½ tsp.	freshly grated nutmeg	2 ml.
	salt and pepper	
1 tsp.	Dijon mustard	5 ml.

Melt the butter in a skillet, add the pig's-ear slices and sauté them until lightly browned—about five minutes. Transfer the ears to a serving dish and keep them warm. Add the

scallions to the butter remaining in the skillet and cook them over low heat for about two minutes. Then increase the heat and add the reserved poaching liquid, the wine vinegar, capers, nutmeg, salt and pepper. Boil for about two minutes, or until the liquid is slightly reduced. Stir in the mustard and pour this sauce over the ears.

PIERRE DE LUNE
LE NOUVEAU CUISINIER

Hog's Ears Farce

This recipe is adapted from a cookbook first published in 1857, when "farce" was clearly understood to mean force-meat—a stuffing mixture of finely chopped ingredients.

To serve 4

4	pig's ears, cleaned and parboiled in salted water for 3 hours, or until tender	4
6 tbsp.	butter	90 ml.
¼ cup	flour	50 ml.
1 ⅓ cups	meat stock *(recipe, page 165)*	325 ml.
⅓ cup	sherry	75 ml.
1 tbsp.	prepared mustard	15 ml.
1	onion	1
	black or cayenne pepper	
	Anchovy forcemeat	
1	salt anchovy, filleted, soaked in water for 30 minutes, drained and patted dry	1
4 to 6	fresh sage leaves, chopped	4 to 6
¼ cup	chopped fresh parsley	50 ml.
¼ lb.	suet, finely chopped	125 g.
2 cups	fresh bread crumbs	½ liter
	salt and pepper	
2	egg yolks	2

Mix the forcemeat ingredients together, using only a little salt. Raise the skin on the upper side of each ear and stuff the cavity with the forcemeat. Fry the ears in 4 tablespoons [60 ml.] of the butter for 10 minutes on each side; pour off the excess fat and drain the ears on paper towels.

In a large pot, melt the rest of the butter and work the flour into it. Add the stock, sherry, mustard, whole onion and a little black or cayenne pepper. Add the ears to the pot and cover it tightly.

Stew the ears gently for 30 minutes, shaking the pot often. When the ears are tender, remove the onion, place the ears carefully in a dish and pour the sauce over them.

MRS. RUNDELL
MODERN DOMESTIC COOKERY

Pig's Ears with Yellow Peas

Loffelerbsen nach Berliner Art

To serve 6

1 lb.	pig's ears, scrubbed and rinsed, parboiled for 5 minutes, drained and diced	½ kg.
1	onion, chopped	1
1	leek, chopped	1
1	small celeriac, cut into julienne	1
2 tbsp.	lard	30 ml.
2 cups	dried yellow peas, soaked overnight and drained	½ liter
1 tbsp.	dried thyme	15 ml.
1 tbsp.	dried marjoram	15 ml.
	salt and pepper	
2	potatoes, diced	2

Fry the onion, leek and celeriac in the lard in a large saucepan. Add the peas, cover generously with water, and bring to a boil. Add the diced meat and the herbs, season with salt and pepper, cover and simmer for 40 minutes. Add the potatoes and cook, covered, for a further 20 minutes, or until the potatoes and peas are tender.

ELIZABETH SCHULER
MEIN KOCHBUCH

Calf's Feet in Batter

Nóżki Cielęce Smażone W Cieście

To serve 2

4	calf's feet, cleaned, rinsed, blanched and split lengthwise	4
	salt and pepper	
1½ cups	sliced carrot, leek, celeriac and parsnip	375 ml.
1	bay leaf	1
1 tsp.	allspice berries	5 ml.
2 cups	flour	½ liter
2	eggs, the yolks separated from the whites	2
2 tbsp.	vegetable oil	30 ml.
½ cup	water	125 ml.
about 1 lb.	lard	about ½ kg.

Simmer the calf's feet in boiling salted water to cover for one and one half hours. Add the mixed vegetables, bay leaf and allspice berries, and continue cooking for about one and one half hours more, or until the meat is tender and separates from the bones. Drain the calf's feet and bone them. Trim the meat into eight neat rectangles, spread these on a board, place another board over them and put a heavy weight on top. Let the meat stand for about two hours.

To make the batter, mix the flour with the egg yolks, oil and water. Let the mixture stand for an hour. Beat the egg whites until stiff, add salt and fold them into the batter. Slice the pieces of pressed meat into halves, sprinkle them with salt and pepper and dip them in the batter. In a skillet over medium heat, melt enough lard to make a layer about ½ inch [1 cm.] deep. Fry the meat pieces, a small batch at a time, until golden brown—about four minutes on each side. Add more lard to the skillet as needed.

ANNA ROŚCISZEWSKA-STOYANOW (EDITOR)
DOBRA KUCHNIA

Calf's Feet Stew

Tagine de Pieds de Veau

Bulgur is made by steaming, drying and cracking wheat kernels. It is obtainable at health-food stores and where Middle Eastern or North African foods are sold.

To serve 6

3	calf's feet, cleaned, rinsed and chopped into pieces	3
1 lb.	bulgur, soaked in water for 20 minutes and squeezed dry	½ kg.
2½ cups	dried chick-peas, soaked in water overnight and drained	625 ml.
¾ cup	olive oil	175 ml.
4	onions, chopped	4
4	garlic cloves, crushed	4
2 tbsp.	paprika	30 ml.
½ tsp.	cayenne pepper	2 ml.
1 tsp.	ground cumin	5 ml.
1 tsp.	ground ginger	5 ml.
½ tsp.	powdered saffron	2 ml.
1 tsp.	salt	5 ml.
2 quarts	water	2 liters

Put all the ingredients into a deep pot. Bring the mixture to a boil, reduce the heat to low, cover tightly and simmer until the meat comes away from the bones—about four hours. Stir occasionally, adding water if necessary. To serve, spread the bulgur and chick-peas in a large, deep platter, arrange the calf's feet on top and pour the cooking liquid over them.

FETTOUMA BENKIRANE
LA NOUVELLE CUISINE MAROCAINE

Braised Pig's Feet
Daube de Pieds de Porc

To serve 4

2	pig's feet, cleaned, rinsed and blanched	2
14 oz.	lean salt pork with the rind removed, chopped	400 g.
4	medium-sized carrots, sliced	4
2	medium-sized onions, sliced	2
½ lb.	pork rind	¼ kg.
⅓ cup	brandy, warmed	75 ml.
1 cup	dry red wine	¼ liter
	salt and pepper	

In a heavy pot, heat the salt pork until the fat begins to melt. Add the carrots and onions. Place the pig's feet and pork rind on the bed of vegetables, pour in the brandy and set it alight. When the flame dies, moisten the mixture with the red wine. Season with salt and pepper to taste. Cover the pot and seal the lid with a paste made from flour, water and a few drops of oil. Simmer the mixture for a minimum of four hours so that the meat is completely tender.

AMICALE DES CUISINIERS ET PÂTISSIERS AUVERGNATS DE PARIS
CUISINE D'AUVERGNE

Deviled Pig's Feet
Fricassée de Pieds de Porc

To poach the pig's feet, first clean, rinse and blanch them. Then simmer them in meat stock (recipe, page 165) to cover for four hours, or until the meat separates from the bones.

To serve 4

4	poached pig's feet, boned and the meat sliced	4
	salt and pepper	
	mixed spices	
2 tbsp.	butter	30 ml.
¼ lb.	lean salt pork with the rind removed, chopped	125 g.
2	onions, finely chopped	2
2 to 3 tbsp.	meat stock (recipe, page 165) or pig's-feet cooking liquid	30 to 45 ml.
1 tsp.	prepared mustard	5 ml.
1 tbsp.	fresh lemon juice	15 ml.
2 tbsp.	white wine vinegar	30 ml.

Season the pig's-feet meat with salt and pepper and a large pinch of mixed spices. Melt the butter in a skillet and sauté the salt pork over high heat until it is browned. Add the pig's feet and chopped onions, and cook for about five minutes, or until the meat is lightly browned. Add the meat stock or pig's-feet cooking liquid and let it come to a boil.

Mix the mustard with the lemon juice and vinegar. Add the diluted mustard to the skillet, stir well and bring the mixture to a boil once more. Serve hot.

L. S. ROBERT
L'ART DE BIEN TRAITER

Baked Corned Pig's Feet
Chispes Afiambrados

To serve 4

4	pig's feet, cleaned and rinsed	4
about 1¾ quarts	water and wine, in equal parts	about 1¾ liters
3 tbsp.	vinegar	45 ml.
2	bay leaves	2
1	sprig marjoram	1
1	sprig parsley	1
3	onions	3
6	whole cloves	6
10	peppercorns	10
2	eggs, beaten	2
1 cup	dry bread crumbs	¼ liter
Brine		
2 lb.	coarse salt	1 kg.
½ cup	sugar	125 ml.
5 quarts	water	5 liters

To make the pickling solution, add the salt and sugar to the water and bring the water to a boil. Pour the brine into a large crock and let the brine cool completely. Add the pig's feet, cover them with a plate and weight the plate with a water-filled jar. Refrigerate the pig's feet for eight or nine days. Remove them from the brine, place them in fresh water to cover and soak them in the refrigerator for 24 hours.

Drain the pig's feet and put them in a nonreactive pan with equal quantities of water and wine to cover them. Add the vinegar, bay leaves, marjoram, parsley, onions, cloves and peppercorns. Cook the pig's feet for four hours, or until tender. Cool the pig's feet in the liquid, then remove them from the pan and bone them.

Dip the boned pig's feet in the beaten eggs, then roll them in the bread crumbs and arrange them in one layer in a shallow pan. Bake them in a preheated 400° F. [200° C.] oven until they are golden—about 10 minutes on each side.

MARIA ODETTE CORTES VALENTE
COZINHA REGIONAL PORTUGUESA

Székely Pig's Feet in Sauerkraut

To serve 4

4	pig's feet, cleaned, rinsed and sprinkled with salt	4
4 tbsp.	lard	60 ml.
1 cup	finely chopped onions	¼ liter
2	garlic cloves, chopped	2
	caraway seeds	
½ tsp.	paprika	2 ml.
2 cups	water	½ liter
2 lb.	sauerkraut, rinsed and drained	1 kg.
2 tsp.	flour	10 ml.
2½ cups	sour cream	625 ml.
¼ cup	finely cut fresh dill	50 ml.

Heat the lard in a heavy casserole and put in the pig's feet. Roast the pig's feet in a preheated 350° F. [180° C.] oven—turning them over halfway through the cooking time—for about 20 minutes, or until they are lightly browned. Remove the pig's feet from the casserole. In the remaining fat, fry the onions over medium heat; add the garlic, a pinch of caraway seeds and the paprika, pour in the water and stew for five minutes. Return the pig's feet to the casserole and cover the casserole. Simmer the mixture for about 40 minutes, then add the sauerkraut and continue cooking for about three hours. When the meat is tender, mix the flour with the sour cream and stir the mixture into the stew; add the dill, cover and simmer for another 10 minutes.

Before serving, bone each pig's foot and cut the meat into three pieces. Place the sauerkraut in a deep dish and arrange the pieces of meat on top of it.

JÓZSEF VENESZ
HUNGARIAN CUISINE

Pig's Feet in Thick Gravy

Les Pieds de Porc

To serve 4

4	pig's feet, cleaned, rinsed and split lengthwise	4
5	onions, 3 quartered, 2 diced	5
1	bouquet garni	1
about 2 quarts	water	about 2 liters
	salt and pepper	
5 tbsp.	butter	75 ml.

Put the pig's feet in a heavy pot and add the quartered onions and the bouquet garni. Pour in enough cold water to cover

the contents well. Season with salt and pepper. Over high heat bring the liquid to a boil, skimming it. Then reduce the heat, partially cover the pot, and simmer the contents for five hours, or until the bones separate easily from the meat and the cooking liquid is reduced by half. Remove the pig's feet from the liquid with a skimmer, bone them and place them in a large bowl. Strain the cooking liquid and pour it over them. Refrigerate the pig's feet overnight.

The next day, melt the butter in a saucepan over medium heat. Add the diced onions and stir with a wooden spoon until they are soft and golden—about 10 minutes. Lift the pig's feet out of the jellied cooking liquid and lay them on top of the onions, then spoon enough jelly over them to barely cover the pig's feet. Partially cover the pan and simmer the contents for one hour to reduce the liquid to a thick gravy. Serve the pig's feet and gravy from a warmed dish and accompany them with a pot of mustard.

RENÉE DE GROSSOUVRE
LES RECETTES D'UNE GRAND'MÈRE ET SES CONSEILS

Pig's Feet with Sauerkraut

Varkenspoten met Zuurkool

To serve 4 to 6

4	pig's feet, cleaned, rinsed and blanched	4
4 tbsp.	lard	60 ml.
1 cup	chopped onion	¼ liter
3 lb.	sauerkraut, rinsed and drained	1½ kg.
1 tbsp.	cumin seeds	15 ml.
1 tbsp.	juniper berries	15 ml.
	salt and pepper	
about 1 quart	unsweetened apple juice or cider	about 1 liter
½ cup	Calvados	125 ml.
	sugar	

Melt the lard in a heavy, nonreactive pot and fry the onion over medium heat until golden—about 10 minutes. Stir in the sauerkraut, cumin seeds and juniper berries, then add salt and pepper. Pour in the apple juice or cider and add the pig's feet, covering them with some of the sauerkraut. Quickly bring the liquid to a boil. Cover the pot and bake it in a preheated 350° F. [180° C.] oven for two and one half to three hours, or until the meat is tender. Turn the pig's feet from time to time and make sure there is enough liquid in the pot. Add a little more apple juice or cider, if necessary. When the meat is tender, add the Calvados and a pinch of sugar and cook, uncovered, for another five minutes. Serve with mashed potatoes.

HUGH JANS
VRIJ NEDERLAND

Pig's Feet with Noodles

Schweinsfuss mit Nudeln

To cook the egg noodles, put them into plenty of water and boil them until they are just tender to the bite—from two to 10 minutes, depending on whether they are fresh or dried. If celeriac is not available, four celery ribs can be substituted.

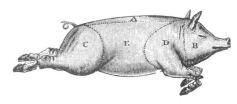

	To serve 4	
4	pig's feet, cleaned, rinsed, split lengthwise and soaked in cold water for 30 minutes	4
1	large onion, coarsely chopped	1
2	carrots, coarsely chopped	2
½	celeriac, coarsely chopped	½
about 2 cups	dry white wine	about ½ liter
4	peppercorns	4
3	bay leaves	3
1 tsp.	dried marjoram	5 ml.
	salt	
2 tbsp.	butter	30 ml.
4	medium-sized tomatoes, peeled, seeded and chopped	4
⅓ cup	Madeira	75 ml.
1 lb.	egg noodles, cooked	½ kg.
⅔ cup	heavy cream	150 ml.

Put the pig's feet, onion, carrots and celeriac into an earthenware bowl and pour in enough white wine to cover them. Add the peppercorns, bay leaves, marjoram and a little salt. Cover the bowl and let the mixture marinate in the refrigerator for three days.

Remove the pig's feet from the marinade, drain them and pat them dry. In a heavy pot, melt the butter and sauté the pig's feet over high heat for about 10 minutes. Strain the marinade and discard the peppercorns and bay leaves. Reserve the marinade liquid and add the marinade vegetables to the pot. Sauté them with the pig's feet for about 10 minutes. Add the tomatoes and increase the heat; stirring occasionally, cook until all the liquid in the pot evaporates.

Pour in the marinade liquid, cover the pot and bake in a preheated 325° F. [160° C.] oven for two and one half to three hours, or until the meat is very tender.

Remove the pig's feet from the pot and arrange them on a serving dish. Strain the cooking liquid, stir in the Madeira and pour the liquid over the pig's feet. Sprinkle the egg noodles with the cream and serve them with the pig's feet.

LILO AUREDEN
DAS SCHMECKT SO GUT

Pig's Feet Stew

Fresh pig's feet may be used, in which case the author recommends coating them liberally with salt and refrigerating them in the salt overnight.

The volatile oils in hot chilies may make your skin sting and your eyes burn; after handling chilies, avoid touching your face and wash your hands promptly.

	To serve 6	
2	corned pig's feet, cut into chunks, soaked in water for 3 hours and drained	2
½ lb.	dried chick-peas, soaked in water overnight and drained	¼ kg.
4 cups	water	1 liter
2 tbsp.	lard	30 ml.
1	fresh hot red chili, stemmed, seeded and chopped	1
1 cup	chopped onions	¼ liter
2	tomatoes, peeled, seeded and chopped	2
½ cup	chopped ham	125 ml.
½ lb.	*chorizo,* sliced	¼ kg.
2	sprigs coriander, chopped	2
2 tsp.	salt	10 ml.
2	medium-sized potatoes, cut into chunks	2
1 lb.	pumpkin or winter squash, halved, seeded, peeled and the flesh cut into 1-inch [2½-cm.] cubes	½ kg.
	cayenne pepper	
1 tbsp.	*annatto,* diluted in ¼ cup [50 ml.] water	15 ml.

Poach the pig's feet and chick-peas in the water until they are almost tender—about three hours. Melt the lard and gently fry the chopped chili, onion, tomatoes and ham. Add this mixture to the pig's feet with the *chorizo,* coriander and salt. Cook over medium heat for 15 minutes.

Add the potatoes and pumpkin, season to taste with cayenne pepper and stir in the *annatto* coloring. Remove the pan from the heat when the potatoes and pumpkin are cooked—about 20 minutes.

BERTA CABANILLAS AND CARMEN GINORIO
PUERTO-RICAN DISHES

Pig's Feet with Pine Nuts and Peas

Pies de Cerdo con Piñones y Guisantes

To serve 4

2	pig's feet, cleaned, rinsed and split lengthwise	2
2	bay leaves, 1 halved lengthwise	2
about 2 quarts	water	about 2 liters
2	medium-sized onions, 1 cut into quarters, 1 finely chopped	2
1	celery rib, cut into 2 or 3 pieces	1
1	carrot, cut in half	1
1	bouquet garni	1
5 or 6	peppercorns	5 or 6
	salt	
5 tbsp.	lard	75 ml.
2	large ripe tomatoes, peeled, seeded and chopped	2
½ cup	dry white wine	125 ml.
1 tbsp.	flour	15 ml.
1 cup	freshly shelled peas	¼ liter
2 tbsp.	pine nuts	30 ml.
	saffron threads	
1	garlic clove	1
3 tbsp.	chopped fresh parsley	45 ml.
¼ cup	dry bread crumbs	50 ml.
1 tsp.	vegetable oil	5 ml.

Sandwich half a bay leaf between the two halves of each pig's foot and tie the two halves together with string. Put the pig's feet in a heavy pot with water to cover and add the quartered onion, the celery, carrot, bouquet garni, peppercorns and salt. Simmer gently until the pig's feet are very tender—about four hours. If necessary, add hot water during the cooking to keep the contents covered.

In a large, nonreactive saucepan, melt the lard and fry the chopped onion with the remaining bay leaf. When the onion begins to brown, add the tomatoes. Add the wine and let it reduce a little, then sprinkle in the flour and cook for a few minutes longer. Add 1 cup [¼ liter] of the pig's-feet cooking liquid and let the mixture simmer over low heat.

Drain the pig's feet, reserving the cooking liquid; discard the strings and bay-leaf halves and add the pig's feet to the tomato mixture. Add the peas and pine nuts and, if necessary, more of the reserved cooking liquid to ensure that the pig's feet are just covered. Cover the pan and simmer the pig's feet for 20 minutes. Using a mortar and pestle, pound a few saffron threads, the garlic and 1 tablespoon [15 ml.] of the chopped parsley to a paste. Add the bread crumbs, oil and enough of the reserved cooking liquid to dilute the paste to a pourable consistency. Pour the paste over the pig's feet and correct the seasoning. Cook for 10 minutes, then remove the pan from the heat, discard the bay leaf and sprinkle the contents of the pan with the rest of the chopped parsley. There should be just enough sauce to cover each pig's-foot half. If the sauce is too plentiful, cook it for a little longer—uncovered—to reduce it. Transfer the pig's feet and sauce to a warmed serving dish.

MARIA DOLORES COMAS
LO MEJOR DE LA COCINA ESPAÑOLA

Pig's Feet Sultana

The volatile oils in hot chilies may make your skin sting and your eyes burn; after handling chilies, avoid touching your face and wash your hands promptly.

To serve 3 or 4

2	pig's feet, cleaned, rinsed and blanched	2
	salt	
1	bay leaf	1
2 tsp.	peppercorns	10 ml.
¼ cup	oil	50 ml.
1	large onion, chopped	1
2	garlic cloves, chopped	2
2	fresh hot red chilies, stemmed, seeded and chopped	2
2	ripe tomatoes, peeled, seeded and chopped	2
½ cup	dried chick-peas, soaked overnight, drained, boiled in unsalted water for 1½ to 2 hours or until tender, and drained	125 ml.
2	potatoes, boiled for 15 minutes, peeled and diced	2
2 tbsp.	chopped fresh parsley	30 ml.

Combine the pig's feet, bay leaf and peppercorns in a pot. Add salted water to cover, bring to a boil and simmer until the feet are tender—four to six hours. Remove the meat from the bones and cut it into pieces.

Heat the oil, add the onion, garlic and chilies, and sauté them over medium heat for about 10 minutes, until the onion is soft but not brown. Add the tomatoes and cook the mixture for 20 minutes over low heat. Add the meat from the pig's feet, the chick-peas and potatoes, and cook for about five minutes. Before serving, sprinkle the top with the chopped parsley.

INDAY CAMARA-GUMBAN
"WHAT'S COOKING?"

Spiced Pig's Feet Stew

Ragoût de Pattes

To serve 4 to 6

6	pig's feet, cleaned and rinsed	6
2	garlic cloves, cut into slivers	2
1 tbsp.	salt	15 ml.
½ tsp.	pepper	2 ml.
¼ tsp.	each ground cloves, allspice, cinnamon and nutmeg	1 ml.
4 tbsp.	lard	60 ml.
4	onions, sliced	4
2 tbsp.	flour	30 ml.
about 4 cups	boiling water	about 1 liter

Slit each foot in several places and insert the garlic slivers. Combine the salt, pepper and spices. Roll the feet in this mixture, pressing it on firmly. Heat the lard in a heavy pot just large enough to hold the feet in one layer. Fry the feet over medium heat until they begin to brown. Add the onions and let them brown, then add the flour and brown it. Add boiling water just to the top of the meat, cover the pot partway, and cook over low heat until the pork is very tender—about two hours. Serve with mashed potatoes.

MORTON G. CLARK
FRENCH-AMERICAN COOKING

Lamb's Feet in Egg and Lemon Sauce

Podarakia Arniou Avgolemono

To serve 4 to 8

8	lamb's feet, cleaned, split almost in half and rinsed	8
1	onion	1
2	carrots	2
2 or 3	celery ribs	2 or 3
2 or 3	sprigs parsley, plus 2 tbsp. [30 ml.] chopped fresh parsley	2 or 3
	salt and pepper	
6 cups	water	1½ liters
4 tbsp.	butter	60 ml.
3 tbsp.	flour	45 ml.
2	egg yolks	2
3 tbsp.	fresh lemon juice	45 ml.

Put the feet in a saucepan with the onion, carrots, celery and sprigs of parsley, and season to taste. Add water to cover, bring to a boil and simmer uncovered for three hours, or until the meat is tender and there is about 1 cup [¼ liter] of liquid left. Transfer the feet to a dish and keep them warm.

Strain the cooking liquid and return it to the pan. Melt the butter in a small, nonreactive saucepan and stir in the flour. Cook over gentle heat for two to three minutes and gradually pour in the hot stock, stirring constantly. Simmer until the sauce thickens, then adjust the seasoning. Lightly beat the egg yolks with the lemon juice and mix them into the sauce. Do not boil again. Pour the sauce over the feet and sprinkle with the chopped parsley.

MARO DUNCAN
COOKING THE GREEK WAY

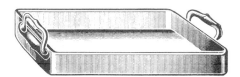

Lamb's Feet, Majorcan-Style

Pies de Carnero en Salsa Cames Seques

To cook the feet, poach them in white court bouillon (recipe, page 165) for three and one half to four hours, or until the meat comes away easily from the bones.

To serve 2

4	lamb's feet, cleaned, rinsed, cooked, boned and cut into pieces	4
3 tbsp.	vegetable oil	45 ml.
2	tomatoes, peeled, seeded and chopped	2
1	small onion, chopped	1
1	sprig parsley, chopped	1
2	garlic cloves, chopped	2
2 cups	fresh bread crumbs, soaked in water and squeezed dry	½ liter
	water	
	pepper	

Put 2 tablespoons [30 ml.] of the oil into a skillet, and fry the tomatoes, onion and parsley over medium heat until the vegetables are soft—about 10 minutes. Add the meat and stir thoroughly.

In a mortar, pound the garlic and bread crumbs, then add the rest of the oil and just enough water to form a paste. Season with pepper. Add this paste to the meat and cook until the sauce has thickened—about 30 minutes.

GABRIEL SASTRE RAYÓ AND ANTONIA ORDINAS MARÍ (EDITORS)
LIBRE DE CUINA DE CA'N CAMES SEQUES

Lamb's Feet in Poulette Sauce

Pieds d'Agneau Poulette

Calf's feet may be prepared in the same way, as shown on pages 52-53. If you use calf's feet, you will need only 12, but you must increase the cooking time to four hours. To ensure that the feet remain white, substitute 2 quarts [2 liters] of white court bouillon (recipe, page 165) for the water, aromatic vegetables and bouquet garni called for in this recipe.

To serve 6

24	lamb's feet, cleaned, rinsed and blanched	24
2 quarts	lightly salted water	2 liters
2	carrots	2
2	garlic cloves	2
2	onions, 1 stuck with 3 whole cloves	2
1	bouquet garni	1
½ lb.	button mushrooms, trimmed	¼ kg.
3 tbsp.	fresh lemon juice	45 ml.
	salt	
9 tbsp.	butter	135 ml.
2 tbsp.	flour	30 ml.
2	egg yolks, lightly beaten	2
	cayenne pepper	
2 tbsp.	finely chopped fresh parsley	30 ml.

Put the feet into a large pot, cover them with salted water, and add the carrots, garlic, onions and bouquet garni. Bring to a boil and simmer, partially covered, for three hours.

Drain the feet, reserving and straining 2 cups [½ liter] of their poaching liquid. Split the feet and remove the bones. Place the meat in a saucepan and cover it to keep it warm.

Put the mushrooms into a pan with ⅓ cup [75 ml.] of water, 2 tablespoons [30 ml.] of lemon juice, and salt to taste. Add one third of the butter and bring to a boil. Cover and simmer for one to two minutes. Strain the mushrooms, reserving the liquid, and add them to the feet.

To make the poulette sauce, melt the rest of the butter in a saucepan and stir in the flour. Add the reserved mushroom cooking liquid and the strained poaching liquid from the feet. Bring the sauce to a boil, whisking constantly, reduce the heat and simmer for about 40 minutes, stirring occasionally. Remove the pan from the heat. Whisk about ½ cup [125 ml.] of the sauce into the beaten egg yolks and add the rest of the lemon juice and the chopped parsley. Gradually whisk the egg-yolk mixture into the remaining sauce. Season with a little salt and a very small pinch of cayenne pepper.

Cook the sauce gently for three to five minutes, or until it begins to thicken. Pour it over the feet and mushrooms, and simmer until they are heated through. Serve immediately.

LÉON ISNARD
LA CUISINE FRANÇAISE ET AFRICAINE

Tails

Old-fashioned Oxtail Stew

Terrine de Queue de Boeuf à l'Ancienne

Fatback lardons can be used to lard the oxtails before they are browned in butter. For extra flavor, first roll the lardons in persillade (recipe, page 166).

To serve 6

two 3 lb.	oxtails, cut into sections	two 1½ kg.
	salt and freshly ground pepper	
8 tbsp.	butter	120 ml.
2	carrots, quartered	2
4	large onions, halved	4
1	bouquet garni	1
¾ cup	eau de vie or other brandy	175 ml.
3	garlic cloves, unpeeled	3
⅓ cup	flour	75 ml.
6 cups	red wine	1½ liters
2 cups	meat stock (recipe, page 165)	½ liter
1 lb.	bacon, thickly sliced and cut into strips ¼ inch [6 mm.] wide	½ kg.
2 lb.	fresh mushrooms, stems removed	1 kg.

Salt and pepper the oxtails. Melt half of the butter in a deep, nonreactive and ovenproof pot and add the oxtails, carrots and onions. When the meat and vegetables are lightly browned—in 20 to 30 minutes—pour the *eau de vie* or other brandy into the pot and set it alight. When the flames die, stir in the garlic and flour. Add the bouquet garni, wine and stock, and stir constantly until the liquid boils. Put the pot in a preheated 300° F. [150° C.] oven for two hours.

In a skillet, melt the rest of the butter and sauté the bacon for five minutes over high heat; drain. In a separate skillet, sauté the mushrooms until they have given up their liquid—about five minutes. Transfer the oxtails to an earthenware casserole. Strain the cooking liquid into a nonreactive saucepan and let it cool for 30 minutes. Cover the oxtails with the mushrooms and bacon.

Degrease the liquid in the saucepan and reduce it over high heat to thicken it slightly. Pour this sauce over the oxtail mixture and cover the casserole. Put it in a preheated 300° F. oven for two hours to complete the cooking. Serve the stew very hot, accompanied, if you like, by noodles.

ACADÉMIE DES GASTRONOMES, ACADÉMIE CULINAIRE DE FRANCE
LA HAUTE CUISINE FRANÇAISE

Pig's Tails and Turnips

To serve 4 to 6

2 to 3 lb.	pig's tails, cut into 2-inch [5-cm.] pieces, scrubbed, patted dry and seasoned with ¾ tsp. [4 ml.] salt	1 to 1½ kg.
1 tbsp.	lard	15 ml.
2	medium-sized onions, chopped	2
2	garlic cloves, finely chopped	2
1 tbsp.	flour	15 ml.
2 cups	water	½ liter
8	turnips, cut into ½-inch [1-cm.] slices	8
1 tsp.	finely chopped celery	5 ml.
1 tsp.	finely chopped fresh parsley	5 ml.
½ tsp.	finely chopped fresh thyme	2 ml.
1	bay leaf	1

In a pan with a lid, melt the lard. Add the pig's tails and brown them on all sides; remove them from the pan. Add the onions and garlic. Cook them until golden—about 10 minutes. Add the flour and, stirring constantly, brown it.

Return the pig's tails to the pan and add the water, turnips, celery and herbs. Bring the liquid to a boil. Reduce the heat. Cover the pan and simmer the contents for one hour, or until the meat is tender when pricked with a fork.

HELEN MENDES
THE AFRICAN HERITAGE COOKBOOK

Oxtails Alsatian-Style

Queues de Boeuf à l'Alsacienne

To serve 4 to 6

6 lb.	oxtail, cut into 2-inch [5-cm.] sections between the vertebrae	3 kg.
¼ lb.	ham, chopped (about ½ cup [125 ml.])	125 g.
¼ lb.	lean salt pork with the rind removed, chopped	125 g.
3	carrots, chopped	3
2	medium-sized turnips, chopped	2
2	onions, sliced	2
6 cups	meat stock (*recipe, page 165*)	1½ liters
⅓ cup	brandy	75 ml.
4 tbsp.	butter, melted	60 ml.
	fresh bread crumbs	

Put the pieces of ham and salt pork into a heavy pot and heat until the salt-pork fat melts. Add the carrots, turnips and onions. Set the pieces of oxtail on top and cover them completely with the meat stock. Add the brandy. Bring the liquid to a boil and skim it. Cover the pot, put it into a preheated 350° F. [180° C.] oven and cook for at least four hours, or until the meat is tender.

Strain the cooking liquid through a fine sieve and remove all the fat. Pour the liquid over the oxtails and let them stand until nearly cold. Lift out the oxtails; bone and trim the meat. Dip the pieces in the melted butter and roll them in the bread crumbs. Broil them about 6 inches [15 cm.] from the heat source for about 10 minutes on each side, or until golden brown.

CHARLES RANHOFER
THE EPICUREAN

Stewed Oxtail with Black Olives

Queue de Boeuf aux Olives Noires

This dish can, of course, be cooked in one operation, but for those who don't like very fat, rich food, the system of getting rid of most of the fat from the sauce makes a better dish. The flaming with brandy does much to strengthen the flavor of the sauce, but it can be omitted if brandy seems an extravagant ingredient in a dish that should really be cheap.

To serve 6 to 8

two 3 lb.	oxtails, cut into 1-inch [2½-cm.] sections, soaked in cold water for 2 hours and drained	two 1½ kg.
3 tbsp.	olive oil	45 ml.
⅓ cup	brandy, warmed	75 ml.
1 cup	dry white wine	¼ liter
about 2½ cups	meat stock (*recipe, page 165*) or water	about 625 ml.
1	large bouquet garni: bay leaves, thyme and parsley sprigs, a strip of dried orange peel and 2 crushed garlic cloves	1
1½ cups	pitted ripe olives	375 ml.

Heat the oil in a big heavy pot or *daubière*. Put in the pieces of oxtail and let them sizzle gently for a few minutes. Pour in the brandy and set it alight. When the flames have died down, add the wine. Let it bubble fiercely for a minute or so. Add just enough stock or water to come level with the top of the pieces of oxtail. Bury the bouquet garni in the center. Cover the pot. Bake in a preheated 290° F. [145° C.] oven for about three hours. Pour off all the liquid and refrigerate the liquid and oxtails separately until the next day. Remove and discard the fat from the surface of the jelled liquid. Melt the liquid in a pan and add the oxtail and olives. Cook an hour or so on top of the stove, until the oxtail meat is coming away from the bones. Serve with boiled rice.

ELIZABETH DAVID
FRENCH PROVINCIAL COOKING

Burgundian Oxtail Stew

To serve 6

4 to 5 lb.	lean oxtail, cut into 2-inch [5-cm.] pieces	2 to 2½ kg.
2 tbsp.	butter	30 ml.
1 tbsp.	vegetable oil	15 ml.
½ lb.	salt pork with the rind removed, cubed, blanched for 3 minutes and drained	¼ kg.
1 cup	finely chopped onions	¼ liter
1 cup	finely chopped carrots, plus 4 or 5 carrots, peeled and cut into julienne 2 inches [5 cm.] long	¼ liter
½ cup	finely chopped celery	125 ml.
2	large garlic cloves, finely chopped	2
1½ tbsp.	tomato paste	22 ml.
	salt and freshly ground pepper	
3 cups	Burgundy	¾ liter
about 3 cups	beef stock (recipe, page 165)	about ¾ liter
1	bouquet garni	1
12 to 16	small boiling onions, peeled	12 to 16
12 to 16	small new potatoes, peeled	12 to 16
12 to 16	tiny turnip balls, peeled	12 to 16
1 tbsp.	cornstarch, mixed into a paste with a little cold stock (optional)	15 ml.

Heat the butter and oil in a large, heavy, heatproof casserole. Add the salt-pork cubes and sauté over medium heat until almost crisp; then remove them with a slotted spoon to a side dish and set them aside. Discard all but 2 tablespoons [30 ml.] of fat from the casserole. Add a few pieces of oxtail at a time and brown them on all sides, seasoning them with salt and pepper. Transfer them to the side dish.

Discard all but 3 tablespoons [45 ml.] of fat from the casserole, add the chopped onions, chopped carrots, the celery and garlic, and cook the mixture for three to four minutes, until nicely browned. Add the tomato paste, and salt and pepper to taste. Return the salt pork and oxtail to the casserole. Add the wine and stock, bring to a boil, and bury the bouquet garni among the oxtail pieces. Cover the casserole and place in a preheated 350° F. [180° C.] oven. Braise the oxtail for two hours, or until almost tender. Remove the casserole from the oven. Carefully degrease the cooking juices. Add the peeled onions, potatoes, julienned carrots and the turnips. Return the casserole to the oven and continue cooking until all the vegetables are tender.

Remove the casserole from the oven. With a slotted spoon transfer the oxtail pieces and vegetables to a deep dish. Place the casserole over high heat and reduce the cooking juices by a third. For a thicker sauce, beat in the cornstarch mixture—the sauce must heavily coat the spoon. Taste and correct the seasoning. Pour the sauce over the oxtail and vegetables and serve accompanied by French bread; follow it with a well-seasoned salad.

PERLA MEYERS
THE PEASANT KITCHEN

Mixed Variety Meats

Turkey Giblets with Turnips

Les Abatis de Dinde aux Navets

An alternative technique for cooking turkey giblets is shown on pages 70-71.

To serve 4

1	turkey gizzard, cleaned, rinsed and quartered	1
1	turkey heart, trimmed and quartered	1
1	turkey liver, trimmed and quartered	1
1	turkey neck, skin removed, cut into 4 pieces	1
2	turkey wings, each cut into 3 pieces at the joints	2
2	turkey feet, singed, skinned, trimmed and halved lengthwise	2
¼ cup	finely chopped pork fatback	50 ml.
3 tbsp.	beurre manié	45 ml.
	salt	
1 tsp.	sugar	5 ml.
2 cups	meat stock (recipe, page 165)	½ liter
1	bouquet garni	1
2	onions, 1 stuck with a whole clove	2
3	medium-sized turnips, quartered	3
8	small waxy potatoes	8
1	carrot, sliced	1
1	celery heart, quartered	1

In a saucepan over low heat, melt the fatback until it renders its liquid fat. Then add the *beurre manié* and, when the *beurre manié* begins to brown, add the turkey pieces, except the liver. Season with salt and sauté the turkey pieces until well browned—seven to eight minutes. Add the sugar.

Heat the stock and slowly pour it into the pan, stirring constantly. Add the bouquet garni and the onions. Simmer the mixture over low heat for about 45 minutes. Add the turnips, potatoes, carrot and celery. Cover the pan and simmer until the meats are tender—about 30 minutes. Add the liver and cook for a further 10 minutes.

Remove the turkey pieces and arrange them in a serving dish, with the wings on top. Arrange the turnips, potatoes, carrot and celery around the meats. Discard the bouquet garni and the onion and clove. Strain the sauce, pressing the other onion through the sieve. Return the sauce to the saucepan. Degrease the sauce and reduce it if necessary. Pour the sauce over the meats and vegetables.

CHARLES MONSELET
LETTRES GOURMANDES

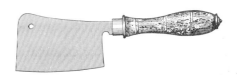

Duck Giblets and Livers

The technique of preparing a gizzard is shown on page 10.

To serve 4

1 lb.	duck gizzards, rinsed, gravel sacs cleaned, meat finely chopped	½ kg.
½ lb.	duck or chicken livers, trimmed and finely chopped	¼ kg.
3 tbsp.	fresh lemon juice	45 ml.
1 tbsp.	soy sauce	15 ml.
1 tsp.	brown sugar	5 ml.
1 tbsp.	water	15 ml.
1 tbsp.	flour	15 ml.
3 tbsp.	lard	45 ml.
1	small onion, chopped	1
2	garlic cloves, finely chopped	2
	salt	

Combine the lemon juice, soy sauce and brown sugar with the water. Thicken this sauce with the flour.

Heat the lard in a skillet over high heat and stir fry the onions and the garlic for one to two minutes. Add the chopped gizzards and salt and, constantly stirring, fry for five minutes. Now fry the livers, but only until they change color. Add the sauce, and stir fry until the sauce is thick.

MARIA KOZSLIK DONOVAN
THE FAR EASTERN EPICURE

Haggis

The oatmeal called for in this recipe is coarsely ground oat kernels; it is obtainable at health-food stores. If not available, rolled oats may be substituted.

Some cooks shake a little flour into the haggis bag before filling. Some add a little grated nutmeg or a pinch of dried herbs to the stuffing. The usual accompaniments to haggis are mashed potatoes and mashed turnips or, better still, the two mashed together.

To serve 12

1	large lamb's stomach	1
2 lb.	lamb liver, membrane removed	1 kg.
1 lb.	lamb heart, fat, tubes and fibrous tissue removed	½ kg.
1 lb.	lean boneless lamb shoulder	½ kg.
½ lb.	coarse oatmeal	¼ kg.
½ lb.	suet, finely chopped	¼ kg.
2	medium-sized onions, finely chopped	2
	black pepper and salt	
	cayenne pepper (optional)	
about 4 cups	boiling water or meat stock (recipe, page 165) (optional)	about 1 liter
1 cup	milk (optional)	¼ liter

Put the lamb meats on to boil, covered with cold water. Let the meats poach for one and one half hours, then remove them from the pot. Reserve the cooking liquid and leave it to cool. Grate the liver and finely chop the heart and lean lamb.

Spread the oatmeal out in a roasting pan and put it into a preheated 350° F. [180° C.] oven to toast for 20 to 30 minutes, stirring it occasionally to color it evenly.

Put the liver, heart, and lean lamb into a bowl with the minced suet, onions and toasted oatmeal, and season liberally with black pepper and salt—and a pinch of cayenne pepper, if you like. Mix well and add enough of the cooled cooking liquid—about 1 cup [¼ liter]—to give the mixture a smooth, soft consistency. Use the mixture to fill the stomach rather more than half full—say five eighths—leaving the stuffing plenty of room to swell. Sew up the stomach securely and place the haggis on a rack set in a pot.

Add enough boiling water to submerge the haggis (the milk can be added to the water) or, better still, add stock. Over high heat, return the liquid to a boil—then reduce the heat to low. As soon as the haggis begins to swell, prick it all over with a skewer to prevent it from bursting. Adding boiling water as required to keep the haggis submerged, simmer it, uncovered, for six hours. Serve it very hot.

F. MARIAN MCNEILL
THE SCOTS KITCHEN

Pig's Feet, Tails and Ears in Sweet-and-Sour Sauce with Polenta

Piedini, Codini e Orecchie di Maiale in Agrodolce con Polenta

To serve 6

1 lb.	pig's feet, cleaned, rinsed, split and parboiled for 10 minutes in salted water	½ kg.
1 lb.	pig's tails, scrubbed, rinsed, cut into 2-inch [5-cm.] sections and parboiled for 10 minutes in salted water	½ kg.
½ lb.	pig's ears, cleaned and parboiled for 8 minutes in salted water	¼ kg.
2	carrots, sliced	2
1	onion, stuck with a whole clove	1
1	bouquet garni	1
	salt	
2½ cups	cornmeal	625 ml.
6 cups	water	1½ liters

Sweet-and-sour sauce

7 tbsp.	lard	105 ml.
¼ cup	finely chopped ham fat	50 ml.
⅓ cup	chopped onion	75 ml.
1	garlic clove, finely chopped	1
½ cup	superfine sugar	125 ml.
½ cup	golden raisins	125 ml.
⅓ cup	pine nuts	75 ml.
¾ cup	white wine vinegar	175 ml.
	salt and pepper	
1 tbsp.	potato flour, dissolved in 2 cups [½ liter] warm water	15 ml.

Put the parboiled pig's feet, tails and ears into a heavy pot. Add the carrots, whole onion and bouquet garni and season with salt. Add water to cover. Bring the water to a boil and cook, partially covered, over medium heat for 45 minutes. Remove the ears and drain them. Cook the tails for another 45 minutes before removing and draining them. Let the feet cook until the meat comes away from the bones—about three and one half hours. Drain the feet and bone them.

To make the sauce, heat the lard in a saucepan. Mix together the ham fat, chopped onion and garlic, and fry them gently for about 10 minutes, until the onion is transparent. Add the well-drained meat, the sugar, golden raisins and pine nuts. Pour in the vinegar, season with salt and pepper and simmer, uncovered, until the vinegar has completely evaporated—about 15 minutes. Remove the pan from the heat and stir in the diluted potato flour. Return the pan to the heat, bring the liquid to a boil and continue cooking, stirring occasionally, until the sauce has reduced to about 1 cup [¼ liter] and is slightly syrupy—about 30 minutes.

To make the polenta, boil the water with a pinch of salt. Stirring continuously, sprinkle the cornmeal into the water. Reduce the heat and, stirring continuously with a wooden spoon, cook for at least 30 minutes, or until the mixture comes away from the sides of the pan.

To serve, spoon the polenta into six soup bowls, put pieces of the meat in the bowls and pour the sauce over them.

LUIGI CARNACINA AND VINCENZO BUONASSISI
IL LIBRO DELLA POLENTA

Roast Chicken Pieces

Menudillos de Pollo "Rustidos"

The technique of preparing poultry feet is shown on page 10. To make the aïoli, pound a chopped garlic clove in a mortar with 1 teaspoon [5 ml.] of coarse salt. Add two egg yolks and stir until the mixture turns pale. Stirring constantly, add 1 cup [¼ liter] of olive oil, drop by drop. When the sauce is quite thick, stir in 2 teaspoons [10 ml.] of fresh lemon juice and 2 teaspoons of water.

To serve 4

12	chicken livers, trimmed	12
12	chicken gizzards, cleaned and rinsed	12
8	chicken feet, singed, skinned and trimmed	8
12	chicken necks, skinned	12
	salt	
5 tbsp.	lard	75 ml.
1	garlic clove	1
¼ cup	chopped fresh parsley	50 ml.
1 tbsp.	fresh bread crumbs	15 ml.
8	almonds, blanched, peeled and toasted	8
¼ cup	water	50 ml.
1 cup	aïoli	¼ liter

Sprinkle all the chicken pieces with salt. Melt the lard in a skillet and fry the pieces until they are evenly browned. In a mortar, pound the garlic with the chopped parsley, the bread crumbs and the toasted almonds. Dilute the paste with the water and add it to the chicken. Reduce the heat under the mixture and simmer for 30 minutes, or until the chicken pieces are tender. Transfer them to a serving dish and pour the aïoli over them just before serving.

ANA MARIA CALERA
365 RECETAS DE COCINA CATALANA

Calf's Head

The technique of stuffing and braising tripe is demonstrated on pages 64-65.

	To serve 10	
1	calf's head, boned, soaked and cleaned	1
3 lb.	tripe in 1 piece, rinsed	1½ kg.
	salt and freshly ground black pepper	
1	garlic bulb, cloves separated and peeled	1
½ lb.	lean salt pork with the rind removed, cut into small pieces	¼ kg.
2 or 3	carrots, thinly sliced	2 or 3
½ lb.	lard	¼ kg.
1 lb.	lean ground beef or veal	½ kg.
2 lb.	onions, chopped (about 6 cups [1½ liters])	1 kg.
½ lb.	walnuts, ground (about 2 cups [½ liter])	¼ kg.
4 cups	parsley sprigs	1 liter
1 cup	dry white wine	¼ liter
	paprika	
about 1 cup	meat stock (recipe, page 165)	about ¼ liter

Sprinkle the head and tripe with salt and black pepper. Place the garlic cloves, salt pork and carrot slices in the meaty parts of the head. Set aside.

Melt 7 tablespoons [105 ml.] of the lard in a skillet and fry the ground beef or veal over medium heat, stirring constantly until it is lightly browned. Pour the meat and fat into a bowl and reserve them. Melt an additional 7 tablespoons of the lard in the same skillet and fry the onions, walnuts and parsley until the onions are transparent—about five minutes. Add the wine and cook for a few minutes before combining the onion mixture with the ground meat.

Lay the tripe, smooth side uppermost, on a work surface. Place the head on the tripe and spread the ground meat mixture over it. Wrap the tripe around the head and sew up the parcel. Rub the tripe well with the remaining lard and sprinkle it with a little paprika.

Put the parcel in an earthenware casserole and pour in the stock. Cover and braise in a preheated 350° F. [180° C.] oven, basting every 30 minutes, for three to four hours, or until the tripe is tender when pierced with a small, sharp knife. Twenty minutes before the end of the cooking time, remove the lid and let the tripe brown.

EMIL MARKOV
RESORTS IN BULGARIA

Liver and Pig's Feet Pudding
Cruibin Ciste

	To serve 6 to 8	
1 lb.	pork liver in 1 piece, membrane removed	½ kg.
4	pig's feet, cleaned, rinsed and blanched	4
¼ lb.	lean salt pork with the rind removed, blanched for 3 minutes and drained	125 g.
1	onion, sliced	1
1	carrot, sliced	1
4	sprigs thyme	4
1 tbsp.	finely chopped fresh parsley	15 ml.
4 cups	meat stock (recipe, page 165)	1 liter
2 to 4 tbsp.	*beurre manié*	30 to 60 ml.

Suet dough		
2 cups	flour	½ liter
¼ lb.	suet, finely chopped	125 g.
½ tsp.	salt	2 ml.
1 tsp.	baking powder	5 ml.
½ cup	dried currants, soaked in warm water for 15 minutes and drained	125 ml.
½ cup	milk	125 ml.

Put the liver, pig's feet, salt pork, vegetables and herbs into a large saucepan. Cover the contents with the meat stock and simmer, with the lid ajar, until the liver is firm—about 30 minutes. Take out the liver, chop it very fine and set it aside. Cover the saucepan and gently stew the contents for another 30 minutes.

Meanwhile, mix the flour, suet, salt and baking powder. Stir in the currants and make the whole into a stiff dough by adding the milk gradually while mixing. Then form the dough into a flat cake just large enough to fit inside the saucepan. Lay the cake on top of the meat. Cover the pan tightly and cook gently until the pastry is cooked through—about one hour. Loosen the pastry by running a knife around the sides of the saucepan. Remove the pastry and cut it into six to eight wedges. Keep it very hot.

Put the chopped liver back in the pan. Thicken whatever gravy is left with the *beurre manié* and simmer for three minutes, stirring all the time. Split the feet and cut the salt pork into six to eight pieces. Arrange the feet in a deep plate with the salt pork, chopped liver and the gravy. Arrange the wedges of pastry around the plate.

IRISH RECIPES TRADITIONAL AND MODERN

Liver and Kidney
Shao Shih Chien

To serve 4

½ lb.	veal kidney, outer fat and membrane removed, halved, cored and cubed	¼ kg.
½ lb.	veal liver, membrane removed, cubed	¼ kg.
2	cucumbers, peeled, halved, seeded and diced	2
	salt	
1 tsp.	cornstarch	5 ml.
2 tbsp.	soy sauce	30 ml.
1½ tbsp.	fresh lemon juice	22½ ml.
3 tbsp.	lard	45 ml.

Sprinkle the diced cucumbers liberally with salt and let them stand for half an hour. Drain the cucumbers, rinse them and dry them well. Moisten the cornstarch with the soy sauce and lemon juice.

Heat the lard in a heavy iron skillet. Stir fry the kidney for a few minutes. Move the kidney to one side of the skillet and add the liver. Stir and fry until it changes color. Add the cucumbers and fry them for a few minutes. Pour the thickened soy sauce into the skillet and stir until the sauce thickens. Serve at once.

MARIA KOZSLIK DONOVAN
THE FAR EASTERN EPICURE

Polish Stuffed Pig's Stomach
Salceson Bialy

To serve 12

1	pig's stomach, rinsed	1
1	pig's head, boned, soaked, cleaned, tongue and brains removed, brains reserved for other use, head meat cut into pieces	1
one ¾ lb.	pork heart, fat, tubes and fibrous tissue removed	one 350 g.
¼ lb.	pork belly	125 g.
¾ lb.	pork rind	350 g.
2 tbsp.	salt	30 ml.
½ tsp.	freshly grated nutmeg	2 ml.
	pepper	
	mixed dried herbs	

Combine the head meat, tongue, heart, pork belly, pork rind and 1 tablespoon [15 ml.] of the salt in a large pot. Add water to cover and bring to a boil. Reduce the heat and simmer uncovered. Remove the pork belly after 30 minutes. Continue cooking the other meats until they are tender but not falling to pieces, about one to one and one half hours for a small pig's head, two hours for a larger—and older—one. Remove the meats and drain them. Reduce the cooking liquid to about 4 cups [1 liter], then strain it.

Peel the tongue. Cut the tongue and pork belly into large cubes. Slice the other meats thin. Cut the rind into julienne. Put the meats into a bowl and add the remaining salt, the grated nutmeg and the herbs. Pour in enough reserved cooking liquid to moisten the mixture and combine the meats well. Stuff the mixture loosely into the pig's stomach and sew the stomach shut. Prick the stomach with a skewer. Immerse the stomach in a pot of hot water, bring the water to just below a boil and simmer the stuffed stomach, uncovered, until it is tender. This may take six hours. Add water if necessary to keep the stomach submerged.

Remove the stuffed stomach from the pot and rinse it in cold water. Wrap it in a cloth, set it on a tray, lay a board on top and weight the board with two or three cans of food. Refrigerate the stomach for about 12 hours before slicing and serving it. It can safely be kept in the refrigerator for about three days.

MARIA DISSLOWA
JAK GOTOWAĆ

Veal Kidney Meatballs
Krusteln von Kalbsniere

To serve 4 to 6

1 lb.	veal kidneys, outer fat and membrane removed, halved, cored and finely chopped	½ kg.
½ lb.	veal sweetbreads, soaked, parboiled, membrane removed, pressed under weights and finely chopped, or ½ cup [125 ml.] finely chopped roast veal	¼ kg.
1	lemon, peel grated, juice strained	1
	freshly grated nutmeg	
1	onion, finely chopped	1
6 tbsp.	butter	90 ml.
1 cup	dry bread crumbs	¼ liter
1 cup	gelatinous veal stock *(recipe, page 165)*	¼ liter
3	eggs, beaten	3
	salt	

Combine the kidney and sweetbreads or veal. Season the meat with the lemon peel and a pinch of nutmeg. Brown the onion in 4 tablespoons [60 ml.] of the butter, and stir in half of the bread crumbs. Add the veal stock and lemon juice and simmer this sauce until it is well reduced and very thick—about 15 minutes. Remove the pan from the heat and let the sauce cool. Stir in two thirds of the beaten eggs and the chopped meat; season lightly with salt. Form the mixture into small oval balls. Roll them in the remaining beaten egg and bread crumbs, and sauté the balls in the remaining butter until they are golden brown—about seven minutes.

HENRIETTE DAVIDIS
PRAKTISCHES KOCHBUCH

Pig's Feet and Ear Stew
Ragôut de Pieds et d'Oreilles
To serve 6

3	pig's feet, cleaned, rinsed, split, large bones removed, the meat cut into pieces	3
4 or 5	pig's ears, cleaned, parboiled and cut into pieces	4 or 5
2	carrots, cut into halves	2
2	large onions, quartered	2
2	leeks, cut into halves	2
	salt and pepper	
	mixed spices	
1	bouquet garni	1
about 2 quarts	water	about 2 liters
1 tbsp.	butter or lard	15 ml.
12	small boiling onions, peeled	12
1 tbsp.	flour	15 ml.
4	medium-sized potatoes, quartered	4
2	shallots	2
2	garlic cloves	2
2 tbsp.	chopped fresh parsley	30 ml.
2 tbsp.	chopped fresh chervil	30 ml.

Put the pig's feet and ears into a large pot with the carrots, the large onions and the leeks. Season with salt, pepper and a pinch of mixed spices and add the bouquet garni. Cover the contents of the pot with water and bring it to a boil. Reduce the heat to medium, cover the pot and cook for one hour.

Melt the butter or lard in a large skillet and sauté the small onions until they are golden. Meanwhile, strain the stew, reserving the cooking liquid. Pat the pig's feet and ears dry with paper towels. Add them to the onions and lightly brown them all over—about 15 minutes. Stir in the flour, then stir in 1 to 2 cups [¼ to ½ liter] of the cooking liquid—the meat should barely be covered. Bring the liquid to a boil, stirring. Add the potatoes, season again with salt and pepper and another pinch of mixed spices, and add the shallots and garlic. Cover the skillet and cook over medium heat for 30 minutes; the potatoes should be tender but intact. Just before serving, sprinkle the stew with the parsley and chervil.

LA CUISINE DU PÉRIGORD

Feet and Tripe Packets, Avignon-Style
Pieds et Paquets à la Tricastine

The onion and tomatoes can be replaced by 1 cup [¼ liter] of tomato sauce (recipe, page 166).

To serve 6

2	lamb's feet, cleaned and rinsed	2
3 lb.	lamb tripe, rinsed and sliced into twenty 6-inch [15-cm.] squares	1½ kg.
2 or 3	fennel branches	2 or 3
1	large onion, chopped	1
2 or 3	tomatoes, peeled, seeded and chopped	2 or 3
3 or 4	medium-sized carrots, sliced	3 or 4
1	bay leaf	1
1	small bunch fresh thyme or savory	1
1 cup	water	¼ liter
1 cup	dry white wine	¼ liter
¾ cup	grated Gruyère cheese	175 ml.

Pork and garlic stuffing

1 lb.	ground pork	½ kg.
2	garlic cloves, finely chopped	2
¼ cup	chopped fresh parsley	50 ml.
	salt and pepper	

Thoroughly mix together the stuffing ingredients. Divide the stuffing among the 20 pieces of tripe and roll them up. Tie the packets securely with thread, or make a small slit near one end of each packet and pass the packet halfway through the slit so that it is held firmly in the middle.

Cover the bottom of a heavy casserole with the fennel branches in such a way as to prevent the packets, which will be laid on top, from sticking. Lay the packets on the fennel, and add the feet. Sprinkle the chopped onion and tomatoes over the packets, then add the sliced carrots, bay leaf and thyme or savory. Pour in the water, cover the casserole and simmer over very gentle heat for four to five hours. Add the wine and simmer for another five to six hours.

Discard the bay leaf and the bunch of herbs. Bone the feet and place their meat, and the rest of the contents of the casserole, in a large gratin dish. Sprinkle with the grated cheese. Bake in a preheated 350° F. [180° C.] oven for 10 to 15 minutes, or until the cheese is melted. Serve immediately.

RUDOLPHE BRINGER
LES BONS VIEUX PLATS DU TRICASTIN

Tripe Polish-Style with Meatballs

To serve 8 to 10

3 lb.	tripe, rinsed	1½ kg.
about 2 quarts	salted water or meat stock *(recipe, page 165)*	about 2 liters
¾ cup	dry white wine (optional)	175 ml.
6 tbsp.	butter	90 ml.
2	carrots, cut into julienne	2
½	celeriac, cut into julienne	½
2	leeks, trimmed to 1 inch [2½ cm.] above the white part, washed and thinly sliced	2
1	onion, finely chopped	1
⅓ cup	flour	75 ml.
¼ tsp.	ground ginger	1 ml.
1 tsp.	paprika	5 ml.
1	small bay leaf, crushed	1
3 to 4 tsp.	dried marjoram	15 to 20 ml.
	freshly grated nutmeg	
	ground allspice	
	salt and pepper	
Meatballs		
10 oz.	veal or pork liver, membrane removed	300 g.
2 tbsp.	finely chopped suet or bone marrow	30 ml.
1	egg	1
about 1¾ cups	fresh bread crumbs	about 425 ml.
1 tbsp.	finely chopped fresh parsley	15 ml.
	salt	

Put the tripe into a large pan and cover it with salted water or stock. Add the wine, if using, and simmer for approximately four hours, adding boiling water or stock as the liquid in the pan evaporates. When cooked, the tripe should be so tender that you can crush it between your fingers. Cut the tripe into thin strips and put it back into the cooking liquid. There should be not less than 6 cups [1½ liters] of liquid.

Meanwhile, in a saucepan, melt 2 tablespoons [30 ml.] of the butter, add 2 to 3 tablespoons [30 to 45 ml.] of water and the carrots, celeriac and leeks. Cook them over low heat. When the water has evaporated and the vegetables are tender, add them to the tripe.

Melt the remaining butter, add the onion and cook over low heat until the onion is lightly browned. Add the flour. Be careful not to let lumps form. Stir in some of the tripe cooking liquid and then pour the mixture into the pan with the tripe. Flavor the tripe with the ginger, paprika, bay leaf and

marjoram. Add nutmeg, allspice, salt and pepper to taste, and simmer the tripe over low heat for 20 minutes to let the aroma of the spices and herbs develop and blend.

For the meatballs, chop the liver to a pulp with the suet or bone marrow. Add the egg and enough bread crumbs to give the mixture a firm consistency. Add the parsley and salt to taste. Make the meatballs the size of walnuts. Place them in the pan with the tripe and simmer for 10 minutes.

MARIA LEMNIS AND HENRYK VITRY
OLD POLISH TRADITIONS IN THE KITCHEN AND AT THE TABLE

Feet and Tripe Packages

Les Pieds et Paquets

If lamb's feet are not available, substitute four calf's feet.

To serve 6

3 lb.	lamb tripe, rinsed, cut into about 30 diamond-shaped pieces with 3- to 4-inch [8- to 10-cm.] sides, trimmings reserved	1½ kg.
8	lamb's feet, cleaned, rinsed and boned	8
4 to 5 tbsp.	olive oil	60 to 75 ml.
2	onions, chopped	2
2	medium-sized carrots, chopped	2
	salt and pepper	
1 tbsp.	crumbled dried oregano	15 ml.
3	firm, ripe tomatoes, peeled, seeded and chopped	3
	cayenne pepper	
1	bouquet garni	1
3 cups	dry white wine	¾ liter
about 2½ cups	veal stock *(recipe, page 165)* or water	about 625 ml.
Bacon stuffing		
½ lb.	thickly sliced lean bacon, blanched for 3 minutes and cut crosswise into ½-inch [1-cm.] strips	¼ kg.
4	garlic cloves	4
¼ cup	chopped fresh parsley	50 ml.
	salt and pepper	
	trimmings from the stomachs, finely chopped	

For the stuffing, pound the garlic to a purée in a large mortar, add the parsley, the bacon, a little salt and plenty of pepper, plus the trimmings from the stomachs. Mix well, so that the bacon strips are thoroughly coated. Spread out the diamond-shaped pieces of tripe. Use a small, sharp knife to make a diagonal slit about ½ inch [1 cm.] long near the top point of each diamond. Slightly below the center of the diamond, place one or two of the coated bacon strips. Fold the two sides of the diamond to the center, fold the bottom to the center and roll up the diamond to enclose the bacon strips in a neat package. Fold the top of the diamond over the package and pass its tip through the slit.

Pour the olive oil into a heavy 3½-quart [3½-liter] pot and set it on a heat-diffusing pad over low heat. Add the onions, carrots, salt and pepper and the oregano. Stirring occasionally with a wooden spoon, cook for 20 to 30 minutes, or until softened. Stir in the tomatoes. Fit the tripe packages and the lamb's feet into the pot; make sure there are no empty spaces between them, so that they can be well moistened with a minimum of liquid. Season with salt and a pinch of cayenne pepper, push the bouquet garni into the center and pour in the white wine.

Add enough stock or water to barely submerge the meats; cover and seal the lid with foil or a paste of flour and water. Simmer the mixture over very low heat on top of the stove or in an oven at its lowest setting for eight hours. Shake the pot from time to time to keep the meats evenly moistened. Before serving, skim off as much fat as possible from the surface of the liquid.

This dish will come to no harm if chilled, reheated and served the next day. On the contrary, the sauce will become more concentrated and the tripe packages and the feet more succulent. The best accompaniment is a crusty loaf of bread.

RICHARD OLNEY
CUISINE ET VINS DE FRANCE

Lamb's Feet, Country-Style
Hardjama Fallâhiyya

To serve 6

2	lamb's feet, cleaned and rinsed	2
1	lamb's head, soaked and cleaned	1
1	garlic bulb, the cloves separated, peeled and finely chopped	1
1 tsp.	ground caraway	5 ml.
10	slices firm-textured white bread	10
7 tbsp.	vegetable oil or butter	105 ml.
¼ tsp.	powdered saffron	1 ml.
	salt and pepper	
½ cup	flour	125 ml.
4	eggs	4
¼ cup	wine vinegar	50 ml.

Place the feet, head, garlic and caraway in a pot of boiling water and poach uncovered until the meats are tender—about three hours. Remove the feet and head, bone them and slice the meat into pieces. Strain and reserve 3 cups [¾ liter] of the cooking liquid. Fry the bread slices in the oil or butter. Arrange a layer of fried bread in the bottom of a heavy casserole and cover it with a layer of meat. Arrange alternate layers of meat and fried bread until all are used up.

Dilute the saffron in a spoonful of the cooking liquid and add it to the remaining liquid with salt and pepper. Moisten the flour with a little of the liquid, then add it to the mixture. Beat the eggs with the vinegar and stir them in. Pour this sauce into the casserole. Bake in a preheated 350° F. [180° C.] oven for 40 minutes, or place the casserole on a heat-diffusing pad over very low heat and simmer for 30 minutes.

RENÉ R. KHAWAM
LA CUISINE ARABE

Beef Heart Casserole
Coeur de Boeuf Bourgeoise

To serve 8 to 10

one 4 lb.	beef heart, fat, tubes and fibrous tissue removed	one 2 kg.
1 lb.	tripe, rinsed and sliced into strips	½ kg.
1	calf's foot, cleaned, rinsed, split and blanched	1
½ lb.	lean salt pork with the rind removed, thinly sliced, half the slices cut into lardons	¼ kg.
1	large onion, stuck with 3 whole cloves	1
1	garlic clove, finely chopped	1
1	sprig thyme	1
2	bay leaves	2
2 tsp.	black peppercorns	10 ml.
	salt	
1 tsp.	freshly grated nutmeg	5 ml.
about 3 cups	dry white wine	about ¾ liter
about 3 cups	water	about ¾ liter

With a sharp-pointed knife, make slits in the outer surfaces of the heart, and lard it with the salt-pork lardons. Place the heart in a heavy 5-to-6-quart [5-to-6-liter] casserole and add the onion, garlic, thyme, bay leaves, peppercorns, salt, nutmeg, and the tripe and the calf's foot. Cover the ingredients with the salt-pork slices. Press the ingredients down. Pour in equal quantities of white wine and water so that the liquid covers the ingredients. Cover the casserole, seal it with a flour paste and bake in a 250° F. [130° C.] oven for seven to eight hours, or until the meats are tender.

GASTON DERYS
LES PLATS AU VIN

Sausages

Herbed Chitterling Sausages
Andouilles aux Fines Herbes

Mesentery is a fatty membrane that holds intestines in place. If it is not available, use 1 pound [½ kg.] of cooked tripe, sliced into strips. To cook mesentery, soak it in acidulated water for two hours, drain it, slice it into strips and poach it for two hours in a white court bouillon (recipe, page 165).

To make 6 sausages

2 lb.	chitterlings, slit, fatty membrane removed and soaked	1 kg.
1 lb.	cooked, sliced mesentery	½ kg.
	salt and pepper	
½ tsp.	freshly grated nutmeg	2 ml.
	mixed spices	
4 tbsp.	butter	60 ml.
3	shallots, chopped	3
1½	onions, quartered, half finely chopped	1½
¾ cup	chopped fresh mushrooms	175 ml.
¼ cup	gelatinous veal stock (recipe, page 165)	50 ml.
¼ cup	velouté sauce (recipe, page 166)	50 ml.
2	truffles, diced	2
1	carrot, coarsely chopped	1
1	celery rib	1
1	turnip, coarsely chopped	1
1	bouquet garni	1
1¼ cups	water	300 ml.
⅔ cup	dry white wine	150 ml.

Madeira and vegetable marinade

⅓ cup	Madeira	75 ml.
1	medium-sized onion, thinly sliced	1
1	carrot, thinly sliced	1
2	sprigs each, thyme and parsley	2
1	bay leaf	1

Reserve six lengths of chitterlings, each about 15 inches [38 cm.] long, choosing pieces without holes in the sides. Cut the rest of the chitterlings into strips and put them in a bowl with the mesentery. Season with salt and pepper, the nutmeg and mixed spices. Add the marinade ingredients. Cover and refrigerate for seven to eight hours. Drain off the liquid through cheesecloth and discard the vegetables and herbs.

Melt the butter in a sauté pan and add the shallots and chopped onion. Cook them over low heat for 10 minutes, or until transparent. Add the mushrooms, cook for another two minutes, then add the marinated meats and cook until the moisture evaporates. Sprinkle the stock and velouté sauce over the meats, add the truffles and season well. Bring to a boil, pour the mixture into a bowl and let it cool.

To make the sausages, first tie with string one end of each of the reserved lengths of chitterlings, then fill each length with the mixture, taking care not to overfill. As soon as each length is full, tie the open end.

Prick the sausages and arrange them in a large pot. Add the carrot, celery, turnip and the onion quarters, a pinch of salt and the bouquet garni. Pour in the water and white wine. Bring the liquid to a boil, then reduce the heat to just below the boiling point and simmer, uncovered, for three to four hours—adding water as the liquid evaporates. Remove the pan from the heat and let the sausages cool in their cooking liquid. Drain them, place them side by side under a board and refrigerate them overnight to straighten them.

Fry the sausages over low heat until lightly browned, about five minutes on each side, and serve on heated plates.

URBAIN DUBOIS AND ÉMILE BERNARD
LA CUISINE CLASSIQUE

Chitterling Sausage with Sorrel Purée
Andouille à l'Oseille

The technique of making chitterling sausages is demonstrated on pages 82-84.

To serve 4

4	chitterling sausages, each sliced into 3 pieces	4
8 tbsp.	butter	120 ml.
2 lb.	sorrel, stems removed and leaves chopped	1 kg.
	salt	
⅓ cup	heavy cream	75 ml.

Heat 5 tablespoons [75 ml.] of the butter in a broad saucepan. Add the sorrel and a pinch of salt, cover and simmer over low heat for 30 minutes. Meanwhile, heat the remaining butter in a skillet, add the sausage slices and—turning them frequently—fry them for five minutes, or until they are lightly browned. When the sorrel is cooked, stir in the cream, mixing it thoroughly. Transfer the sorrel to a warmed serving dish and place the sausage slices on top.

MARIE BISSON
LA CUISINE NORMANDE

Troyes Chitterling Sausages
Andouillettes de Troyes

The technique of making these sausages is shown on pages 82-84. Instead of being chilled in the stock, the sausages can be wrapped in plastic wrap and chilled. The stock, degreased and strained, can be used in another dish. To crisp the surfaces of the poached sausages, broil them before serving.

	To make 8 to 10 sausages	
2 lb.	chitterlings, slit, fatty membrane removed, soaked, cut into long thin strips	1 kg.
4 yards	hog casings, washed, drained and cut into 6- to 8-inch [12- to 15-cm.] lengths	4 meters
	salt and ground white pepper	
	grated nutmeg	
½ lb.	fresh fatback with the rind removed, cut into strips ¼ inch [6 mm.] wide	¼ kg.
2 or 3	shallots, finely chopped	2 or 3
¼ cup	finely chopped fresh parsley (optional)	50 ml.
4 cups	gelatinous veal stock (recipe, page 165)	1 liter
Vegetable and wine marinade (optional)		
2	onions, chopped	2
2	carrots, chopped	2
3 or 4	sprigs thyme	3 or 4
1	bay leaf	1
4 cups	dry white wine	1 liter

Season the chitterlings with salt, pepper and a pinch of nutmeg. If they are to be marinated, mix the marinade vegetables and crumble the thyme and bay leaf into them. In a bowl, arrange a layer of vegetables, then a layer of chitterlings, then a layer of vegetables, and so on until all the ingredients have been used up. Pour in the white wine, cover, and marinate the chitterlings in the refrigerator overnight. Drain them, reserving the liquid and vegetables.

To make each sausage, first wind several chitterlings around your hand, one after the other, to make a looped bundle 6 to 8 inches [15 to 20 cm.] long and 1½ to 2 inches [4 to 5 cm.] wide. Continue making looped bundles until all of the chitterlings are used up. Lay a strip of fatback—flat or folded double—over each looped bundle of chitterlings. Insert a piece of string about 10 inches [25 cm.] long through the center of each bundle. Loop the string through the bundle, leaving the two ends free but together. Twist the loops into a figure eight. Sprinkle the twisted loops with the chopped shallot and parsley, if using. Pull a piece of casing over your thumb and index finger, pushing it well down to leave the finger ends free. With the same two fingers, grip the ends of the string of a twisted loop and use your other hand to slide the casing off your fingers and onto the bundle of chitterlings. Pull out the string and use a knife or fork handle to tuck the ends of the casing into the sausage. Prick each sausage several times with a fork.

If a marinade was used, add the marinade ingredients to the stock. Heat the stock to a boil. Add the sausages and reduce the heat. Skimming occasionally, simmer the sausages for four to five hours. Carefully remove the sausages with a skimmer and wrap each one separately in wax paper. Degrease the stock, bring it to a boil and strain it. Arrange the sausages in one or more deep dishes and pour the stock over them. Chill them until they are to be broiled.

A. DELPLANQUE AND S. CLOTEAUX
LES BASES DE LA CHARCUTERIE

Lorraine Chitterling Sausages
Andouille Lorraine

The technique of making chitterling sausages is demonstrated on pages 82-84.

Chitterling sausages are delicious when broiled and served with mashed potatoes, but they are most exquisite cold, eaten with no other addition than a little mustard.

	To make two 4-pound [2-kg.] sausages	
2½ lb.	chitterlings, slit and fatty membrane removed	1¼ kg.
1 cup	wine vinegar	¼ liter
4	sprigs thyme	4
2	bay leaves	2
1 cup	fresh basil leaves	¼ liter
½ lb.	pork fatback, finely chopped	¼ kg.
⅓ cup	fines herbes	75 ml.
6 cups	milk	1½ liters
	salt and pepper	
4 tbsp.	lard	60 ml.

Combine the wine vinegar, two of the thyme sprigs, one bay leaf and half of the basil with 2 quarts [2 liters] of water. Soak the chitterlings in this liquid for several hours. Then discard the soaking liquid.

Choosing the fattest ends, cut about one third of the chitterlings into 12-inch [30-cm.] lengths to use as casings. Cut the remaining chitterlings into very small pieces. Combine the pork fat with the fines herbes and add them. Fill the casings with the mixture. Tie both ends of each sausage and prick the sausages all over.

Combine the milk with an equal quantity of water; add salt and pepper, the remaining thyme, bay leaf, basil and the lard, and bring the liquid to just below the boiling point. Poach the sausages in the liquid for about five hours, or until soft to the touch.

J. BERJANE
FRENCH DISHES FOR ENGLISH TABLES

Truffled Tongue Sausage

Langue Farcie aux Truffes

The technique of cooking a tongue in a sausage casing is demonstrated on pages 80-81. An equal number of calf's feet may replace the pig's feet.

To serve 6

one 3 lb.	beef tongue, soaked, poached for 1½ hours and peeled	one 1½ kg.
2	pig's feet, cleaned and rinsed	2
¼ lb.	pork fatback, sliced into ¼-by-1½-inch [6-mm.-by-4-cm.] lardons	100 g.
¼ cup	spiced salt *(recipe, page 167)*	50 ml.
1	large truffle, peeled and julienned	1
about 1 yard	hog casing, washed and drained	about 1 meter
1	onion, chopped	1
1	carrot, diced	1
about 4 cups	veal stock *(recipe, page 165)*	about 1 liter

Toss the fatback lardons with 1 tablespoon [15 ml.] of the spiced salt to coat them. Lard the tongue along its entire length by inserting the lardons and the truffle julienne. Stuff the tongue into the hog casing and tie the casing at both ends. Rub the casing with the rest of the spiced salt. Prick the casing thoroughly all over, cover the sausage with plastic wrap and refrigerate it for two to three days, turning it daily. Unwrap the sausage and rinse it.

Put the onion and carrot into a long, narrow cooking vessel, such as a fish poacher. Lay the sausage on top of the vegetables, add the pig's feet and pour in enough stock to cover the sausage. Cover the vessel with a sheet of buttered parchment paper and the lid, and simmer the sausage over low heat for five hours. Let the sausage cool slightly in the cooking liquid before transferring it to a platter.

Strain the cooking liquid, degrease it, and boil it until only 2 cups [½ liter] of liquid remain. Slice the sausage, pour a little of the reduced liquid over the slices and serve the rest from a sauceboat.

CHARLES DURAND
LA CUISINIER DURAND

Sweet Liver Sausages

Mazzafegati Dolci

To make savory liver sausages, omit the fatback, sugar and orange peel, use only ¼ cup [50 ml.] of raisins, and add 10 oz. [300 g.] of ground pork and salt to taste. Fill the casings and cook the sausages in the same way as the sweet liver sausages.

To make about 12 sausages

2 lb.	pork liver, membrane removed, finely chopped	1 kg.
5 oz.	pork fatback, finely diced	150 g.
½ cup	pine nuts	125 ml.
¾ cup	seedless white raisins, soaked in warm water for 15 minutes and drained	175 ml.
⅓ cup	sugar	75 ml.
2 tbsp.	finely diced fresh orange peel	30 ml.
	salt and pepper	
2 yards	hog casings, washed and drained	2 meters

Put all the ingredients except the hog casings into a bowl and mix thoroughly. Using a funnel, pack the mixture loosely into the casings and knot the sausages at 4- to 5-inch [10- to 13-cm.] intervals. The sausages can be grilled, baked or fried in a little oil.

GUGLIELMA CORSI
UN SECOLO DI CUCINA UMBRA

Spicy Liver Sausage

Saucisses de Foie

The technique of making sausages is shown on pages 78-79.

To make 10 to 12 sausages

2 lb.	veal liver, membrane removed, finely chopped	1 kg.
5 oz.	suet, finely chopped	150 g.
2 or 3	garlic cloves, finely chopped	2 or 3
2 tsp.	ground cumin	10 ml.
1 tsp.	paprika	5 ml.
	salt and pepper	
about 3 yards	hog casing, washed and drained	about 3 meters
1 tbsp.	olive oil	15 ml.

Mix together the liver, suet, garlic, cumin, paprika, salt and pepper. Use a funnel to fill the sausage casings without packing them too tightly—they should remain supple. Tie up the ends, and twist each filled casing into a string of four or five sausages. Prick the sausages with a skewer. Pour the oil into a skillet, add the sausages, and put the skillet over very low heat. Turning the sausages frequently, fry them until they are evenly browned and the casings are crisp—about 30 minutes.

IRÈNE AND LUCIENNE KARSENTY
LA CUISINE PIED-NOIR

Liver Sausage

The pork rinds can be omitted and chopped pork fat added to the ground meats with the rest of the stuffing ingredients. The technique of making a liver sausage is shown on pages 78-79.

To make about sixteen 5-inch [13-cm.] sausages

2 lb.	pork liver, membrane removed, cut into pieces	1 kg.
4 lb.	pork heart, fat, tubes and fibrous tissue removed	2 kg.
2 lb.	pig's cheek	1 kg.
¾ lb.	pork rinds	750 g.
2 cups	raw white rice, boiled in lightly salted water for 15 minutes and drained	½ liter
⅔ cup	salt	150 ml.
1 tsp.	paprika	5 ml.
1 tsp.	freshly ground black pepper	5 ml.
	white pepper	
	marjoram	
10 tbsp.	lard	150 ml.
2 cups	finely chopped onions	½ liter
about 5 yards	sausage casings	about 5 meters

Bring the heart, pig's cheek and pork rinds to a boil in slightly salted water to cover—skimming off and discarding the scum. Reduce the heat and cook them for one and one half hours, skimming off the fat as it rises to the surface and reserving it. Remove the heart and cheek from the liquid and set them aside to cool. Cook the rinds for another one and one half hours, adding more water if necessary, and skimming and reserving the fat. Let the rinds cool in the liquid.

Put the heart, cheek and rinds through a food grinder with the liver. Place the mixture in a large bowl. Add the rice, salt, paprika, black pepper and a pinch each of white pepper and marjoram.

Melt 4 tablespoons [60 ml.] of the lard and add the fat reserved from skimming the cooking liquid. When the fat is hot, add the onions and sauté them over medium heat until they are golden. Add the onions to the meat mixture. Fill the sausage casings loosely with the mixture, tying them at 5-inch [13-cm.] intervals. Prick the sausages with a needle. Bring a pan of water to a boil, reduce the heat and add the sausages. Keeping the water just below the boiling point, poach the sausages for 30 minutes. Drain them, then cover and refrigerate them.

To fry the sausages, melt the rest of the lard and sauté them until they are evenly browned, turning frequently. Serve them with potatoes, fried onions and braised cabbage.

JÓZSEF VENESZ
HUNGARIAN CUISINE

Scrapple

To serve 12

one 12 lb.	pig's head, cut into thirds and soaked in acidulated water for 2 hours, parboiled in fresh water for 10 minutes and rinsed	one 6 kg.
about 1 tsp.	salt	about 5 ml.
6	peppercorns	6
3	whole cloves	3
1	bay leaf	1
2 cups	cornmeal	½ liter
1	onion, finely chopped	1
¼ tsp.	cayenne pepper	1 ml.
½ tsp.	freshly grated nutmeg	2 ml.
½ tsp.	rubbed sage	2 ml.
	freshly ground pepper	

In a heavy pot, combine the parboiled pig's head, 1 teaspoon [5 ml.] of the salt, the peppercorns, cloves and bay leaf. Bring to a boil, cover, and simmer for three hours, or until the meat falls off the bones easily. Strain this stock and reserve it. Remove the meat from the bones and chop it; reserve it.

Reheat the stock. Gradually add the cornmeal, stirring constantly until thick—about 15 to 30 minutes. Add the meat, onion, cayenne, nutmeg and sage; season with salt and pepper. Pour the mixture into two greased 8-by-3-inch [20-by-8-cm.] loaf pans. Refrigerate the scrapple until it is set. It will keep in the refrigerator for up to one week. To serve, slice the scrapple and fry it.

JANA ALLEN AND MARGARET GIN
INNARDS AND OTHER VARIETY MEATS

Lamb's Feet Baked in Caul

Pieds de Mouton à Rouennaise

To serve 4

8	lamb's feet, cleaned, rinsed, parboiled in salted water for 20 minutes and drained	8
2 cups	Madeira	½ liter
1½ cups	chopped onions	375 ml.
10 tbsp.	butter	150 ml.
2 tbsp.	chopped fresh parsley	30 ml.
1½ lb.	ground pork	¾ kg.
5 tbsp.	brandy	75 ml.
¾ lb.	caul, cut into eight 6-inch [15-cm.] squares	350 g.

Put the lamb's feet into a heavy, nonreactive pot. Add the Madeira. Bring to a boil, cover and simmer over low heat for one and one quarter hours, or until the meat is tender. Meanwhile, gently fry the onions in 4 tablespoons [60 ml.] of the butter for 10 minutes, or until golden. Add the onions and parsley to the ground pork. Mix well.

Remove the cooked feet from the pot and set them aside. Add 4 tablespoons of the cooking liquid to the pork mixture. Add the brandy and mix thoroughly. Bone the lamb's feet and halve the meat of each foot lengthwise.

Spread out the squares of caul on a work surface. In the center of each square, place a layer of pork mixture, half a lamb's foot, another layer of pork, another half lamb's foot and a final layer of pork. Wrap each caul around the meat to form a well-sealed parcel.

Put the parcels into a roasting pan. Melt the remaining butter and pour it over them. Bake them on the top shelf of a preheated 400° F. [200° C.] oven, turning the parcels from time to time, until well browned—about 25 minutes.

MARIE BISSON
LA CUISINE NORMANDE

Truffled Pig's Feet

Pieds de Porc Truffés

The technique of making truffled pig's feet is demonstrated on pages 76-77. For a leaner forcemeat, use 2 pounds [1 kg.] of lean pork and 1 pound [½ kg.] of pork fat. Finely chop and mix them. Pound a garlic clove to a paste with 5 tablespoons [75 ml.] of coarse salt and add it to the pork with two chopped truffles. Add a large pinch of mixed herbs and 1 cup [¼ liter] of brandy. Refrigerate the forcemeat for several hours.

To serve 10

10	pig's feet, cleaned, rinsed and blanched	10
1 cup	Madeira	¼ liter
about 4 cups	veal stock (recipe, page 165)	about 1 liter
1	truffle, sliced	1
½ lb.	caul, soaked, drained and cut into 10 equal-sized pieces	¼ kg.
8 tbsp.	butter, melted	120 ml.
1 cup	dry bread crumbs	¼ liter

Fine truffled forcemeat

1½ lb.	lean pork, finely chopped	¾ kg.
1½ lb.	pork fat, finely chopped	¾ kg.
2	truffles, finely chopped	2
	salt and white pepper	
	mixed spices	
	brandy	

Place the pig's feet in a shallow pan, add the Madeira and enough stock to cover them. Bring the liquid to a simmer, cover and cook the feet until very tender—at least four hours. Leave the feet in the liquid until they are cold, then drain and bone them. Reserve the liquid. Slice half the foot meat into 10 equal-sized pieces. Chop the remaining meat.

To make the fine truffled forcemeat, mix the lean pork and pork fat and rub them through a sieve. Combine the pork mixture with the truffles, salt and white pepper, mixed spices, a dash of brandy and the chopped foot meat.

Skim the fat from the reserved cooking liquid and reduce it over high heat for about 10 minutes. Strain about ½ cup [125 ml.] of the liquid and add it to the forcemeat mixture.

Divide the forcemeat into 20 equal-sized pieces. Shape a piece of forcemeat into a triangular sausage, top it with a piece of the sliced foot meat and cover with another piece of forcemeat. Press two or three slices of truffle into the sausage and wrap it in a piece of caul. Repeat the procedure with the rest of the ingredients. Brush the sausages with the melted butter, coat them in the bread crumbs and broil for about 10 minutes on each side. Serve with mashed potatoes.

PROSPER MONTAGNÉ
NEW LAROUSSE GASTRONOMIQUE

Standard Preparations

Meat Stock

This general-purpose strong stock will keep for up to a week if refrigerated and brought to a boil every two days.

To make about 3 quarts [3 liters] stock

2 lb.	beef shin	1 kg.
2 lb.	veal shank	1 kg.
2 lb.	chicken backs, necks, feet and wing tips	1 kg.
about 5 quarts	water	about 5 liters
1	bouquet garni, including leek and celery	1
1	garlic bulb	1
2	medium-sized onions, 1 stuck with 2 whole cloves	2
4	large carrots	4

Place a rack in the bottom of a large stockpot to prevent the ingredients from sticking. Fit all the meat, bones and chicken pieces into the pot and add water to cover by about 2 inches [5 cm.]. Bring slowly to a boil and, with a slotted spoon, skim off the scum that rises. Keep skimming, occasionally adding a glass of cold water, until no more scum rises—after about 10 to 15 minutes.

Add the bouquet garni, garlic, onions and carrots, and skim once more as the liquid returns to a boil. Reduce the heat to very low, cover the pot with the lid ajar and simmer for at least five hours. If the meat is to be eaten, remove the veal after one and one half hours, the beef after three hours.

Ladle the stock into a colander lined with dampened muslin or cheesecloth and set over a large bowl. Let the stock cool, then remove the last traces of fat from the surface with a skimmer and a paper towel; if the stock has been refrigerated to cool, lift off the solidified fat with a knife.

Veal stock. Omit the beef shin and chicken pieces and substitute about 4 pounds [2 kg.] of meaty veal trimmings: neck, shank or rib tips. For a richer, more gelatinous stock, add a calf's or pig's foot, cleaned, rinsed, split and blanched for five minutes in boiling water.

Beef stock. Substitute 4 pounds of beef tail, shank or chuck for the veal shank and the chicken pieces, and simmer the stock for five hours. For a more gelatinous stock, add a calf's foot, chicken wing tips or pork rinds.

Chicken stock. Old hens and roosters yield the richest stock. Omit the beef and veal and substitute about 5 pounds [2½ kg.] of chicken carcasses, necks, feet, wings, gizzards and hearts. Simmer for about two hours.

Wine Court Bouillon

To make about 2 quarts [2 liters] court bouillon

2 cups	dry white or red wine	½ liter
1	large onion, sliced	1
1	large carrot, sliced	1
2	garlic cloves, crushed	2
1	celery rib, diced	1
1	leek, white part only, sliced	1
½ cup	parsley sprigs	125 ml.
1	bay leaf	1
6 cups	water	1½ liters
	salt	
5 or 6	peppercorns	5 or 6

Put the vegetables, herbs and water into a large nonreactive pan and season with a pinch of salt. Bring to a boil, then reduce the heat, cover and simmer for 15 minutes. Pour in the wine and simmer for a further 10 minutes. Add the peppercorns, then simmer for five minutes longer.

Vinegar court bouillon. Substitute 1 cup [¼ liter] of wine vinegar for the 2 cups [½ liter] of wine.

Lemon court bouillon. Substitute 1 cup of fresh lemon juice for the 2 cups of wine.

White Court Bouillon

To make about 6 quarts [6 liters] court bouillon

½ cup	flour	125 ml.
6 quarts	water	6 liters
3	carrots, coarsely chopped	3
2	onions, each studded with a whole clove	2
1	bouquet garni	1
¼ lb.	suet, finely chopped	125 g.
⅓ cup	fresh lemon juice	75 ml.

Mix the flour with enough of the water to form about ½ cup [125 ml.] of thin paste. Put the carrots, onions and bouquet garni into a deep pot. Pour in the rest of the water and whisk the flour-and-water paste into it. Add the suet and lemon juice. Bring the liquid to a boil, cover the pot and simmer for 10 minutes.

Béarnaise Sauce

To make about 1 cup [¼ liter] sauce

½ cup	dry white wine	125 ml.
¼ cup	white wine vinegar	50 ml.
2	shallots, finely chopped	2
	cayenne pepper	
1	sprig tarragon, plus 1 tsp. [5 ml.] finely chopped	1
1	sprig chervil, plus 1 tsp. [5 ml.] finely chopped	1
3	egg yolks	3
½ lb.	unsalted butter, cut into small pieces and softened	¼ kg.
	salt and freshly ground pepper	

Put the wine, vinegar and shallots in a heatproof earthenware casserole, a heavy enameled saucepan, or the top part of a glass or stainless-steel double boiler set over boiling water. Add a pinch of cayenne, and the sprigs of tarragon and chervil. Place the pan over low heat and simmer the mixture for 15 to 20 minutes, or until only 3 to 4 tablespoons [45 to 60 ml.] of syrupy liquid remain. Strain the liquid into a bowl, pressing the juices from the herbs, then return the liquid to the pan.

Reduce the heat to very low and whisk in the egg yolks. After a few seconds, whisk in one third of the butter and continue whisking until it is absorbed. Repeat this procedure twice more, whisking until the sauce begins to thicken. Remove the pan from the heat and continue whisking; the heat of the pan will continue to cook and thicken the sauce. Stir in the chopped herbs and season with salt and pepper.

Persillade

To make about ½ cup [125 ml.] persillade

3 or 4	garlic cloves	3 or 4
½ tsp.	coarse salt	2 ml.
½ cup	finely chopped fresh parsley	125 ml.

Pound the garlic cloves and salt in a mortar until they form a smooth paste. Add the chopped parsley and mix it in well with your fingers. Use the persillade within a few hours; it will lose its fresh green color if kept longer.

Velouté Sauce

To make about 1¼ cups [300 ml.] sauce

2 tbsp.	butter	30 ml.
2 tbsp.	flour	30 ml.
2½ cups	meat stock *(recipe, page 165)*	625 ml.

Melt the butter in a heavy saucepan over low heat. Stir in the flour to make a roux and cook, stirring, for three to four minutes. Whisking constantly, pour the stock into the pan. Increase the heat and continue to whisk until the sauce comes to a boil. Reduce the heat to low, and move the saucepan half off the heat so the liquid on only one side of the pan simmers. A skin of fat and impurities will form on the still side. Remove the skin periodically with a spoon. Cook the sauce for about 40 minutes to reduce it and eliminate all taste of flour.

Poulette sauce. Make a velouté sauce, remove it from the heat and let it cool for a few minutes. Using a fork, beat two egg yolks with 2 tablespoons [30 ml.] of fresh lemon juice and 2 tablespoons of chopped parsley; stir in a little velouté sauce. Gradually whisk the yolk mixture into the velouté sauce and continue whisking until it is well blended. Return the pan to low heat and, whisking constantly, simmer for three to five minutes, or until the sauce is thick and smooth.

Tomato Sauce

When fresh, ripe summer tomatoes are not available, use canned Italian-style plum tomatoes.

To make about 1¼ cups [300 ml.] sauce

1	medium-sized onion, diced	1
1 tbsp.	olive oil	15 ml.
5	medium-sized very ripe tomatoes, quartered	5
2	garlic cloves, chopped	2
1 tsp.	chopped fresh parsley	5 ml.
1 tsp.	mixed basil, marjoram and thyme	5 ml.
1	bay leaf	1
1 to 2 tsp.	sugar (optional)	5 to 10 ml.
	coarse salt and freshly ground pepper	

In a large enameled or stainless-steel saucepan, gently fry the diced onion in the oil until soft but not brown. Add the other ingredients and simmer for 20 to 30 minutes, or until the tomatoes have been reduced to the desired consistency. Sieve, using a wooden pestle or spoon. Return the sauce to the heat to warm through. If a thicker consistency is required, simmer the sauce, uncovered, for 20 to 30 minutes, stirring frequently to prevent sticking. Season the sauce with salt and pepper to taste just before using or serving it.

Mayonnaise

To prevent curdling, all ingredients should be at room temperature and the oil should be added very gradually at first. Mayonnaise will keep for several days in a covered container in the refrigerator. Stir it well before use.

To make about 1 ½ cups [375 ml.] mayonnaise

2	egg yolks	2
	salt and white pepper	
2 tsp.	white wine vinegar or fresh lemon juice	10 ml.
1 tsp.	Dijon mustard (optional)	5 ml.
1 to 1½ cups	oil	250 to 375 ml.

Put the egg yolks in a warmed dry bowl. Season with salt and pepper; add 1 teaspoon [5 ml.] of the vinegar or lemon juice, and mustard, if you wish. Mix thoroughly with a small whisk. Whisking constantly, add the oil, drop by drop to begin with. When the sauce starts to thicken, pour in the remaining oil in a thin, steady stream, whisking rhythmically. The mayonnaise should be firm enough to hold its shape on the whisk. Whisk in the remaining vinegar or lemon juice and taste for seasoning.

Tartar sauce. Stir about 1 teaspoon [5 ml.] each of finely chopped sour gherkins, capers and fines herbes into the mayonnaise.

Gribiche sauce. Stir two chopped hard-boiled eggs into the tartar sauce.

White Sauce

To make about 1 ½ cups [375 ml.] sauce

2 tbsp.	butter	30 ml.
2 tbsp.	flour	30 ml.
2 cups	milk	½ liter
	salt	
	white pepper	
	freshly grated nutmeg (optional)	
	heavy cream (optional)	

Melt the butter in a heavy saucepan. Stir in the flour and cook, stirring, over low heat for two to five minutes. Pour in the milk, whisking constantly to blend the mixture smoothly. Increase the heat and continue whisking while the sauce comes to a boil. Season with a little salt. Reduce the heat to very low and simmer for about 40 minutes, stirring occasionally. Add pepper and a pinch of nutmeg, if you like; taste for seasoning. Whisk again until the sauce is perfectly smooth and add cream if you prefer a richer and whiter sauce.

Fritter Batter

For a batter that is less rich but crisper, omit the egg yolks. The quantity of liquid may be varied according to taste; a thicker batter will coat the food better, but a thinner batter will produce a crisper surface.

To make 1 cup [¼ liter] batter

¾ cup	flour	175 ml.
	salt	
2 tbsp.	olive oil	30 ml.
2	eggs, the yolks separated from the whites	2
¾ cup	tepid beer	175 ml.

Put the flour and a pinch of salt into a large bowl. Make a well in the center of the flour, pour the oil into the well and add the egg yolks and beer. Working from the center outward, whisk just long enough to produce a smooth batter. Let the batter stand in a warm place for at least one hour. Just before using the batter, beat the egg whites to stiff peaks and fold them gently into it.

Spiced Salt
Sel Épicé

Ingredients and proportions may be varied to taste.

To make about ½ cup [125 ml.] seasoning

2 tbsp.	coarse salt	30 ml.
4	whole cloves	4
1	blade mace or ¼ tsp. [1 ml.] ground mace	1
10	peppercorns	10
¼ tsp.	ground cinnamon	1 ml.
¼ tsp.	grated nutmeg	1 ml.
¼ tsp.	cayenne pepper or ½ dried hot chili	1 ml.
10	whole allspice	10
¼ tsp.	anise seeds	1 ml.
1 tsp.	mixed herbs	5 ml.

Pound and grind all of the ingredients to a coarse powder in a mortar. Store in a tightly sealed jar. The seasoning should be used within six months.

Recipe Index

All recipes in the index that follows are listed by their English titles. Entries are organized by the types of variety meats and also by the major ingredients specified in the recipe titles. Sauces, stuffings and marinades are listed separately. Foreign recipes are listed by country or region of origin. Recipe credits appear on pages 173-175.

General Index/Glossary

Included in this index to the cooking demonstrations are definitions, in italics, of special culinary terms not explained elsewhere in this volume. The Recipe Index begins on page 168.

Recipe Credits

The sources for the recipes in this volume are shown below. Page references in parentheses indicate where the recipes appear in the anthology.

Académie des Gastronomes, Académie Culinaire de France, *La Haute Cuisine Française.* © Jean-Pierre Delarge, Le bélier prisme, 1975. Published by Éditions Universitaires, Jean-Pierre Delarge, Éditeur, Paris.

Translated by permission of Jean-Pierre Delarge, Éditeur(150).
Allen, Jana and Margaret Gin, *Innards and Other Variety Meats.* Copyright © 1974 by Jana Allen and Margaret Gin. Reprinted by permission of the publisher, 101 Productions, San Francisco(103, 124, 137, 163).
Amicale des Cuisiniers et Pâtissiers Auvergnats de Paris, *Cuisine d'Auvergne (Cuisines du Terroir).* © 1979 Denoël-Paris. Published by Éditions Denoël, Paris. Translated by permission of Éditions Denoël(125, 134, 145).
Aureden, Lilo, *Das Schmeckt So Gut.* © 1965 by Lichtenberg Verlag, München. Published by Lichtenberg Verlag, Munich. Translated by permission of Kindler

Verlag GmbH(147).
Beard, James A., *The Fireside Cook Book.* Copyright © 1949, 1976 by Simon and Schuster, Inc., and Artists and Writers Guild, Inc. Published by Simon and Schuster, New York. By permission of Simon and Schuster, Inc., a division of Gulf & Western Corporation(87).
Béguin, Maurice, *La Cuisine en Poitou.* Published by La Librairie Saint-Denis, Niort, 1932(140).
Benkirane, Fettouma, *La Nouvelle Cuisine Marocaine.* © All rights reserved for all countries by Fettouma Benkirane, 24, bd Roosevelt, Casablanca Anfa, Morocco and SEFA International, 27, Rue de Marignan, 75008 Paris—France. Published by Jean Pierre Taillandier, 1979. Trans-

lated by permission of SEFA International(112, 120, 123, 144).

Benoit, Félix and Henry Clos Jouve, *La Cuisine Ly-onnaise.* © Solar, 1975. Published by Solar, Paris. Translated by permission of Solar, Paris(121, 130, 133).

Bergese, Nino, *Mangiare da Re.* © Giangiacomo Feltrinelli Editore, Milano, 1969. Published by Giangiacomo Feltrinelli Editore S.p.A. Translated by permission of Giangiacomo Feltrinelli Editore S.p.A.(116).

Berjane, J., *French Dishes for English Tables.* Copyright Frederick Warne & Co., Ltd., London 1931. Published by Frederick Warne & Co., Ltd., London. By permission of Frederick Warne (Publishers) Ltd.(161).

Bisson, Marie, *La Cuisine Normande.* © Solar, 1978. Published by Solar, Paris. Translated by permission of Solar(95, 160, 164).

Blanc, Georges, *Mes Recettes.* Copyright by Georges Blanc. Published by Édition COGEP, Lyon, 1980. Translated by permission of the author(117).

Bocuse, Paul, *Paul Bocuse's French Cooking.* Translated by Colette Rossant. Copyright © 1977 by Random House, Inc. Reprinted by permission of Pantheon Books, a division of Random House, Inc.(114).

Boni, Ada, *The Talisman Italian Cook Book.* Translated and augmented by Matilde La Rosa. Copyright 1950, 1977 by Crown Publishers, Inc. Published by Crown Publishers, Inc., New York. By permission of Crown Publishers, Inc., New York(129).

Borer, Eva Maria, *Tante Heidi's Swiss Kitchen.* English text copyright © 1965 by Nicholas Kaye Ltd. Published by Kaye & Ward Ltd., London. First published under the title *Die Echte Schweizer Küche* by Mary Hahns Kochbuchverlag, Berlin W., 1963. By permission of Kaye & Ward Ltd.(106).

Bouillard, Paul, *La Cuisine au Coin du Feu.* Copyright 1928 by Albin Michel. Published by Éditions Albin Michel, Paris. Translated by permission of Éditions Albin Michel(108, 128). *La Gourmandise à Bon Marché.* Copyright 1935 by Éditions Albin Michel. Published by Éditions Albin Michel, Paris. Translated by permission of Éditions Albin Michel(119).

Brazier, Eugenie, *Les Secrets de la Mère Brazier.* © Solar, 1977. Published by Solar, Paris. Translated by permission of Solar(138).

Breteuil, Jules, *Le Cuisinier Européen.* Published by Garnier Frères Libraires-Éditeurs, Paris, 1860(119).

Bringer, Rudolphe, *Les Bons Vieux Plats du Tricastin.* Published by Éditions Daniel Morcrette, France. By permission of Éditions Daniel Morcrette(157).

Břízová, Joza and Maryna Klimentová, *Tschechische Küche.* Published by PRACE, Prague and Verlag für die Frau, Leipzig, 1977. Translated by permission of DILIA, Theatrical and Literary Agency, Prague, for the authors(87).

Buc'hoz, Pierre Joseph, *L'Art de Préparer les Aliments.* Second edition. Published by the author, Paris, 1787(112, 118).

Bugialli, Giuliano, *The Fine Art of Italian Cooking.* Copyright © 1977 by Giuliano Bugialli. Published by Times Books, a division of Quadrangle/The New York Times Book Co., Inc., New York. By permission of Times Books, a division of Quadrangle/The New York Times Book Co., Inc.(92).

Byron, May (Editor), *Pot-Luck.* Published by Hodder and Stoughton Ltd., London, 1914. By permission of Hodder and Stoughton Ltd.(141).

Cabanillas, Berta and Carmen Ginorio, *Puerto-Rican Dishes.* Copyright 1956 by Berta Cabanillas and Carmen Ginorio. Published by Editorial Universitaria, Universidad de Puerto Rico, 1974. Translated by permission of University of Puerto Rico Press(147).

Calera, Ana Maria, *Cocina Castellana.* © Ana M. Calera, 1974. Published by Editorial Bruguera, S.A. Barcelona. Translated by permission of Editorial Bruguera S.A.(154). *365 Recetas de Cocina Catalana.* © Ana Maria Calera. © Editorial Everest. Published by Editorial Everest S.A., Leon. Translated by permission of Editorial Everest S.A.(123).

Camara-Gumban, Inday, *"What's Cooking?"* Copy-

right by Inday Camara-Gumban. Published by The Cebu Star Press, Cebu City, Philippines, c. 1966. By permission of the author(148).

Carnacina, Luigi and Vincenzo Buonassisi, *Il Libro Della Polenta.* © by Aldo Martello Editore. By permission of Giunti Publishing Group Italy(154).

Carréras, Marie-Thérèse and Georges Lattorgue, *Les Bonnes Recettes du Pays Catalan.* © Presses de la Renaissance, 1980. Published by Presses de la Renaissance, Paris. Translated by permission of Presses de la Renaissance(132).

Cass, Elizabeth, *Spanish Cooking.* Copyright © Elizabeth Cass, 1957. First published by André Deutsch Ltd., 1957. Also published by Mayflower Books Ltd., 1970. By permission of André Deutsch Ltd.(90, 130).

Chu, Grace Zia, *Madame Chu's Chinese Cooking School.* Copyright © 1975 by Grace Zia Chu. Published by Simon and Schuster, New York. By permission of Simon and Schuster, Inc., a division of Gulf & Western Corporation(99).

Clark, Morton G., *French-American Cooking.* Copyright © 1967 by Morton Clark. Originally published by J. B. Lippincott. Reprinted by permission of Harper & Row, Publishers, Inc.(103, 149).

Collingwood, F. and J. Woolams, *The Universal Cook.* Fourth Edition, 1792. Published by Scatchard and Whitaker(107, 139).

Comas, Maria Dolores, *Lo Mejor de la Cocina Española.* © Geocolor, S.A. Published by Geocolor S.A., Barcelona 1979. Translated by permission of Ediciones Grijalbo S.A., Barcelona(139, 148).

Corey, Helen, *The Art of Syrian Cookery.* Copyright © 1962 by Helen Corey. Published by Doubleday & Company, Inc., Garden City, New York. Reprinted by permission of Doubleday & Company, Inc.(123, 136).

Corsi, Guglielma, *Un Secolo di Cucina Umbra.* Published by Tipografia Porziuncola, Assisi, 1968. Translated by permission of Tipografia Porziuncola(162).

Courtine, Robert J., *La Vraie Cuisine Française.* © 1953, 1963 by Éditions Gerard & Co., Verviers. Published by S.A. Les Nouvelles Éditions Marabout, Brussels. Translated by permission of S.A. Les Nouvelles Éditions Marabout(120).

Crawford Poole, Shona, *The Times.* © Times Newspapers Limited. Published March 20, 1980. By permission of Times Newspapers Limited(126, 128).

La Cuisine Lyonnaise. Published by Éditions Gutenberg, Lyon, 1947(92).

La Cuisine du Périgord (L'Encyclopédie de la Cuisine Régionale). © Presses Pocket, 1979. Published by Presses Pocket, Paris. Translated by permission of Les Presses de la Cité, Paris(157).

Cutler, Carol, *The Six-Minute Soufflé and Other Culinary Delights.* Copyright © 1976 by Carol Cutler. Published by Clarkson N. Potter, Inc. By permission of Clarkson N. Potter(90, 109).

David, Elizabeth, *French Provincial Cooking.* Copyright © Elizabeth David, 1960, 1962, 1967, 1969. Published by Penguin Books Ltd., London. By permission of the author(96, 151). *Summer Cooking.* © Elizabeth David, 1950, 1951, 1955, 1958, 1965, 1980. Published in 1980 under the title *Elizabeth David Classics,* comprising *A Book of Mediterranean Food, French Country Cooking* and *Summer Cooking,* by Jill Norman Ltd., London. By permission of Jill Norman Ltd.(90, 94).

Davidis, Henriette, *Praktisches Kochbuch.* Newly revised by Luise Holle. Published in Bielefeld and Leipzig, 1898(87, 89, 156).

Davis, Irving, *A Catalan Cookery Book.* Lucien Scheler, Paris, 1969. By permission of Lucien Scheler(135).

de Grossouvre, Renée, *Les Recettes d'une Grand'mère et Ses Conseils.* © Hachette 1978. Published by Librairie Hachette, Paris. Translated by permission of Librairie Hachette(105, 121, 146).

Delfs, Robert A., *The Good Food of Szechwan.* Copyright © in Japan 1974 by Kodansha International Ltd. Published by Kodansha International Ltd., Tokyo. By permission of Kodansha International Ltd.(100).

Delplanque, A. and S. Cloteaux, *Les Bases de la Charcuterie.* © 1975 Éditions Jacques Lanore C.L.T.

Published by Éditions Jacques Lanore C.L.T., Malakoff. Translated by permission of Éditions Jacques Lanore C.L.T.(161).

de Lune, Pierre, *Le Nouveau Cuisinier.* Paris, 1656(143).

de Périgord, A.-B., *Le Trésor de la Cuisinière et de la Maîtresse de Maison.* Published by Garnier Frères, Libraries-Éditeurs, Paris, 1852(102).

de Pomaine, Édouard, *Cuisine Juive: Ghettos Modernes.* Copyright 1929 by Albin Michel. Published by Albin Michel, Éditeur, Paris. Translated by permission of Éditions Albin Michel(135).

de Rivoyre, Eliane and Jacquette, *La Cuisine Landaise (Cuisines du Terroir).* © 1980 by Éditions Denoël, Paris. Published by Éditions Denoël, Paris. Translated by permission of Éditions Denoël(106, 117).

Derys, Gaston, *Les Plats au Vin.* © Éditions Albin Michel, 1937. Published by Éditions Albin Michel, Paris, 1937. Translated by permission of Éditions Albin Michel(110, 159).

Disslowa, Maria, *Jak Gotowac.* Published by Wydawnictwo Polskie, R. Wegnera, Poznan, Poland. By permission of Agencja Autorska, Poland(157).

Donati, Stella (Editor), *Il Grande Manuale della Cucina Regionale.* © Copyright 1979 Euroclub Italia S.p.A., Bergamo. Published by SugarCo Edizioni S.r.l., Milan. Translated by permission of Euroclub(88, 127).

Donovan, Maria Kozslik, *The Far Eastern Epicure.* Copyright © by Maria Kozslik Donovan. Originally published by Doubleday & Company, Inc., Garden City, New York. Reprinted by permission of Maria Kozslik Donovan(98, 153, 156).

Dorset Federation of Women's Institutes, *What's Cooking in Dorset.* Published by The Dorset Federation of Women's Institutes, 1972. By permission of The Dorset Federation of Women's Institutes(92).

Dubois, Urbain and Émile Bernard, *La Cuisine Classique*(160).

Dumaine, Alexandre, *Ma Cuisine.* © 1972 by Pensée Moderne, Paris. Published by Éditions de la Pensée Moderne, Paris. Translated by permission of Jacques Grancher, Éditeur, Paris(119, 141).

Duncan, Maro, *Cooking the Greek Way.* © Paul Hamlyn Limited 1964. Spring Books, London. By permission of the Hamlyn Publishing Group Limited, Feltham, Middlesex, England(101, 108, 127, 149).

Durand, Charles, *La Cuisinier Durand (Cuisine du Midi et du Nord).* Newly revised eighth edition. Nîmes, 1863(162).

Eldon, Juliette, *A Belgian Cookbook.* Reprinted by permission of Farrar, Straus and Giroux, Inc. Copyright © 1958 by Farrar, Straus and Cudahy, Inc. (now Farrar, Straus and Giroux, Inc.)(120).

Flexner, Marion, *Out of Kentucky Kitchens.* Copyright © 1949 by Marion Flexner. Used by permission of Franklin Watts, Inc.(115).

Gombervaux (Editor), *La Bonne Cuisine pour Tous.* Published by Presses de la Renaissance, Paris, 1979(91, 132).

Gouffé, Jules, *Le Livre de Cuisine.* Fifth Edition. Published by Librairie Hachette, Paris, 1881(138).

Gould-Marks, Beryl, *Eating the Russian Way.* Copyright © 1963 by Beryl Gould-Marks. Published by Holt, Rinehart and Winston, New York. Reprinted by permission of Holt, Rinehart and Winston Publishers(89, 94).

Grigson, Jane, *English Food.* Copyright © Jane Grigson, 1974. Published by Macmillan London Ltd., 1974. By permission of Macmillan, London and Basingstoke(111).

Groff, Betty and José Wilson, *Good Earth & Country Cooking.* Published by Stackpole Books, Harrisburg, Pennsylvania, 1974. By permission of Stackpole Books(136).

Grumme, Grete, *Danish Food.* © Chr. Erichsens Forlag, Copenhagen. Originally published in Danish under the title *Dansk Mad.* British edition published in 1964 by W. H. Allen, London. By permission of W. H. Allen and Chr. Erichsens Forlag(100).

Guérard, Michel, *Michel Guérard's Cuisine Minceur.* English translation © 1976 by William Morrow and Company, Inc. Originally published in French under the title *La Grande Cuisine Minceur,* © 1976 by Éditions Robert Laffont, S.A. By permission of William Morrow and Company,

Inc.(97).

Hargreaves, Barbara (Editor), *Farmhouse Fare.* Published by Countrywise Books 1946. By permission of the Hamlyn Publishing Group Limited in association with Farmers Weekly, Feltham, Middlesex, England(106—Mrs. Arthur Hurst).

Hawliczkowa, Helena, *Kuchnia Polska.* Copyright by Helena Hawliczkowa. Published by Panstwowe Wydawnictwo Ekonomiczne, Warsaw, 1977. Translated by permission of Agencja Autorska, Warsaw, for the author(95).

Hellermann, Dorothee V., *Das Kochbuch aus Hamburg.* © Copyright 1975 by Verlagsteam Wolfgang Hölker. Published by Verlag Wolfgang Hölker, Münster. Translated by permission of Verlag Wolfgang Hölker(93).

Irish Recipes Traditional and Modern. Published by Mount Salus Press Limited, Dublin. By permission of Mount Salus Press Limited(155).

Isnard, Léon, *La Cuisine Française et Africaine.* Copyright 1949 by Éditions Albin Michel. Published by Éditions Albin Michel, Paris. Translated by permission of Éditions Albin Michel(101, 131). *La Gastronomie Africaine.* Copyright 1930 by Éditions Albin Michel. Published by Éditions Albin Michel, Paris. Translated by permission of Éditions Albin Michel(139, 150).

Jans, Hugh, *Bistro Koken.* © 1973 Unieboek B.V., Bussum, Holland. Published by Van Dishoeck, Bussum. Translated by permission of Unieboek B.V., Bussum(103, 105). *Vrij Nederland, 30 April, 1977* (magazine). Translated by permission of Hugh Jans(146).

Kamman, Madeleine, *The Making of a Cook.* Copyright © 1971 by Madeleine Kamman. Published by Atheneum, New York. Reprinted with the permission of Atheneum Publishers(111, 131).

Karsenty, Irène and Lucienne, *La Cuisine Pied-Noir (Cuisines du Terroir).* © 1974, by Éditions Denoël, Paris. Published by Éditions Denoël, Paris. Translated by permission of Éditions Denoël(121, 133, 162).

Kennedy, Diana, *Recipes from the Regional Cooks of Mexico.* Copyright © 1978 by Diana Kennedy. Reprinted by permission of Harper & Row, Publishers, Inc.(134).

Khawam, René R., *La Cuisine Arabe.* © Éditions Albin Michel, 1970. Published by Éditions Albin Michel, Paris. Translated by permission of Éditions Albin Michel(159).

Koscher, Joseph and Associates, *Les Recettes de la Table Alsacienne.* © Librairie Istra/Saisons d'Alsace, 1969. Published by Société Alsacienne d'Édition et de Diffusion, Strasbourg. Translated by permission of Librairie Istra, Strasbourg(136).

Laasri, Ahmed, *240 Recettes de Cuisine Marocaine.* © 1978, Jacques Grancher, Éditeur. Published by Jacques Grancher, Éditeur, Paris. Translated by permission of Jacques Grancher, Éditeur(88, 112, 122, 124).

Labarre, Irène and Jean Mercier, *La Cuisine du Mouton.* © Solar, 1978. Published by Solar, Paris. Translated by permission of Solar(113, 125).

la Chapelle, Vincent, *The Modern Cook, Vol. III.* London 1733(118, 124, 127).

Lallemand, Roger, *La Vraie Cuisine de l'Auvergne et du Limousin.* Vol. 5 of *La Cuisine de Chez Nous* series. Published by Quartier Latin, La Rochelle, 1973. Translated by permission of Quartier Latin(143).

Lemnis, Maria and Henryk Vitry, *Old Polish Traditions in the Kitchen and at the Table.* © Interpress Publishers, Warsaw, 1979. Published by Interpress Publishers, Warsaw. By permission of the authors, c/o Society of Authors ZAIKS, Warsaw(110, 158).

McNeill, F. Marian, *The Scots Kitchen.* Second edition, 1963. Published by Blackie & Son Ltd., London and Glasgow. By permission of Blackie & Son Ltd.(153).

Marin, *Les Dons de Comus, Vol. 2.* Paris, 1742(140).

Markov, Emil, *Resorts in Bulgaria,* October/November 1979 (magazine from "Culinary Atlas" feature). Published by The State Committee for Tourism, Sofia. By permission of Jusautor Copyright Agency, Sofia, for the author (155).

Mazza, Irma Goodrich, *Accent on Seasoning.* Copyright © 1957 by Irma Goodrich Mazza. Published by Little, Brown and Company, Boston. By permission of Little, Brown and Company(132).

Mehta, Jeroo, *101 Parsi Recipes.* Copyright © 1973 by Vakils, Feffer and Simons Private Ltd. Published by Vakils, Feffer and Simons Private Ltd., Bombay. By permission of the author(86, 122).

Meijer, Berthe, *NRC Handelsblad Menuboek.* Copyright © 1980 by Berthe Meijer. Published by De Bezige Bij, Amsterdam. Translated by permission of the author (89).

Mendes, Helen, *The African Heritage Cookbook.* Copyright © 1971 by Helen Mendes. Published by The Macmillan Company, New York. By permission of The Sterling Lord Agency, Inc., for the author(131, 151).

Menon, *Les Soupers de la Cour, Vol. 1 (ou L'Art de Travailler Toutes Sortes d'Aliments).* Originally published in 1755 by Guillyn, Libraire, Paris. Reprinted in 1978 by Librairie SOETE, Paris(94, 114).

Metzler, Fred and Klaus Oster, *Kochbuch: Aal Blau und Erröthetes Mädchen.* © Walter Hädecke Verlag, Weil der Stadt, 1976. Published by Walter Hädecke Verlag, Weil der Stadt. Translated by permission of Walter Hädecke Verlag(86, 137).

Meyers, Perla, *The Peasant Kitchen.* Copyright © 1975 by Perla Meyers. Published by Harper & Row, Publishers, New York. Reprinted by permission of Harper & Row, Publishers(152).

Monselet, Charles, *Lettres Gourmandes.* Published by Éditions Rabelais, Paris. Translated by permission of Jacques Grancher, Éditeur, Paris(152).

Montagne, Prosper, *New Larousse Gastronomique.* English text copyright © 1977 by The Hamlyn Publishing Group. Used by permission of Crown Publishers, Inc.(164).

Muffoletto, Anna, *The Art of Sicilian Cooking.* Copyright © 1971 by Anna Muffoletto. Reprinted by permission of Doubleday & Company, Inc.(107).

Nignon, Édouard (Editor), *Le Livre de Cuisine de L'Ouest-Éclair.* Published by L'Ouest-Éclair, Rennes, 1924. Translated by permission of Société d'Éditions Ouest-France, Rennes(140).

Nignon, Édouard, *Les Plaisirs de la Table.* Published by the author c. 1920. Reprinted in 1979 by Éditions Daniel Morcrette, Paris. By permission of Éditions Daniel Morcrette(96).

Ojakangas, Beatrice A., *The Finnish Cookbook.* © 1964 by Beatrice A. Ojakangas. Published by Crown Publishers, Inc., New York. By permission of Crown Publishers, Inc.(88).

Olney, Richard, *Cuisine et Vins de France,* July/August 1967 (magazine). Translated by permission of Revue du Vin de France, Paris(158). *Simple French Food.* Copyright © 1974 by Richard Olney. Published by Atheneum, New York. By permission of Atheneum Publishers, New York(124).

Owen, Sri, *Indonesian Food and Cookery.* © Sri Owen, 1976, 1980. Published by Prospect Books, London, 1980. By permission of Prospect Books(129).

Parenti, Giovanni Righi, *La Grande Cucina Toscana.* Published by SugarCo Edizioni S.r.l. Milan, 1976. Translated by permission of SugarCo Edizioni S.r.l.(86, 115, 128).

Peter, Madeleine (Editor), *The Great Women Chefs of France.* Copyright © 1979 by Holt, Rinehart and Winston, New York. Reprinted by permission of Holt, Rinehart and Winston, Publishers(93).

Poulson, Joan, *Old Thames Valley Recipes.* Text © Joan Poulson 1977. Published by Hendon Publishing Co., Ltd., Nelson, Lancashire. By permission of Hendon Publishing Co., Ltd.(90).

Ranhofer, Charles, *The Epicurean.* Originally published by R. Ranhofer, New York, 1893. Republished by Dover Publications, Inc., New York, 1971(116, 151).

Rao, Nguyen Ngoc, *La Cuisine Chinoise à l'Usage des Français.* © 1980 by Éditions Denoël, Paris. Published by Éditions Denoël, Paris. Translated by permission of Éditions Denoël(94, 98).

Read, Jan and Maite Manjón, *Paradores of Spain.* Copyright © 1977 by Jan Read and Maite Manjón. Reprinted by permission of Van Nostrand Reinhold Company Inc., New York(133).

Reige, Odette, *Les Gratins.* © Alain Bouret, Les Loges, Paris 1979. Published by Les Loges, Paris. Translated by permission of Les Loges(91).

Robert, L. S., *L'Art de Bien Traiter.* Published by Jean du Puis, Paris, 1674(113, 143).

Rogers, Ann, *A Basque Story Cook Book.* Copyright © 1968 by Ann Rogers. Published by Charles Scribner's Sons, New York. Reprinted by permission of Curtis Brown, Ltd., New York(98, 102, 122).

Roggero, Savina, *Come Scegliere e Cucinare le Carni.* © Arnoldo Mondadori Editore, 1973. Published by Arnoldo Mondadori Editore, Milan. Translated by permission of the author(104, 109).

Rosciszewska-Stoyanow, Anna (Editor), *Dobra Kuchnia.* Copyright by Anna Rosciszewska-Stoyanow. Published by Wydawnictwo "Watra," Warsaw, 1971. Translated by permission of Agencja Autorska, Warsaw, on behalf of the editor(103, 144).

Roundell, Mrs., *Mrs. Roundell's Practical Cookery Book.* Published by Bickers & Son, London, 1898(102).

Rundell, Mrs., *Modern Domestic Cookery.* Published by Milner and Company, Limited, London(143).

Sastre Rayó, Gabriel and Antonia Ordinas Marí (Editors), *Libre de Cuina de Ca'n Cames Seques (Cocina Mallorquina de Siempre).* Published by Antigua Imprenta Soler, Palma de Mallorca, 1977. Translated by permission of Antonia Ordinas Marí(149).

Schuler, Elizabeth, *Mein Kochbuch.* © Copyright 1948 by Schuler-Verlag, Stuttgart-N, Lenzhalde 28. Published by Schuler Verlagsgesellschaft mbH, Herrsching. Translated by permission of Schuler Verlagsgesellschaft mbH(101, 144).

Schwabe, Calvin W., *Unmentionable Cuisine.* Copyright © 1979 by the Rector and Visitors of the University of Virginia. Published by The University Press of Virginia, Charlottesville. By permission of The University Press of Virginia(107).

Sek-Hiang, Lie, *Indonesian Cookery.* © 1963 by Lie Sek-Hiang. Published by Bonanza Books, a division of Crown Publishers, Inc., New York. By permission of Crown Publishers, Inc.(100).

Sheridan, Monica, *The Art of Irish Cooking.* Copyright © by Monica Sheridan. Reprinted by permission of Doubleday & Company, Inc.(99).

Tante Marguerite, *La Cuisine de la Bonne Ménagère.* Published by Éditions de L'Épi, Paris, 1929(116, 135).

Tendret, Lucien, *La Table au Pays de Brillat-Savarin.* Published by Librairie Dardel, Chambéry, 1934. Translated by permission of Jacques Grancher, Éditeur, Paris(142).

Thuilier, Raymond and Michel Lemonnier, *Les Recettes de Baumanière.* © 1980 by Éditions Stock. Published by Éditions Stock, Paris. Translated by permission of Éditions Stock(93).

Tibbott, S. Minwell, *Welsh Fare.* © National Museum of Wales (Welsh Folk Museum). Published by the National Museum of Wales, 1976. By permission of the publisher(92).

Tobias, Doris and Mary Merris, *The Golden Lemon.* Copyright © 1978 by Doris Tobias and Mary Merris. Published by Atheneum Publishers, Inc., New York, 1978. By permission of Atheneum Publishers, Inc.(110).

Valente, Maria Odette Cortes, *Cozinha Regional Portuguesa.* Published by Livraria Almedina Coimbra, 1973. Translated by permission of Livraria Almedina(142, 145).

Vence, Céline, *Encyclopédie Hachette de la Cuisine Régionale.* © Hachette, 1979. Published by Librairie Hachette, Paris. Translated by permission of Librairie Hachette(126).

Venesz, József, *Hungarian Cuisine.* © The legal successors of József Venesz, 1980. First published by Corvina Press, Budapest. Translated by permission of Artisjus, Agence Littéraire Théatrale et de Musique, Budapest, on behalf of the legal successors of József Venesz(146, 163).

Vergé, Roger, *Roger Vergé's Cuisine of the South of France.* English translation copyright © 1980 by William Morrow and Company, Inc. Originally published in French under the title *Ma Cuisine du Soleil.* © 1979 by Éditions Robert Laffont, S.A. By permission of William Morrow and Company, Inc.(97).

Willinsky, Grete, *Kulinarische Weltreise.* © 1961 by Mary Hahns Kochbuchverlag, Berlin W. Published by Büchergilde Gutenberg, Frankfurt/Main. Translated by permission of Mary Hahns Kochbuchverlag, Munich(104).

Acknowledgments

The indexes for this book were prepared by Karla J. Knight. The editors are particularly indebted to Betsy Crosby, Dr. James E. Harbottle, Dr. Gerald Snyder, United States Department of Agriculture, Washington, D.C.; J. K. Curran, J. R. Ott Ltd., London; Gail Duff, Kent, England; Robert, George and Jean Jacob, The French Market, Washington, D.C.; Sarah S. Kelly, London; Lobel's Meat Market, New York; Ann O'Sullivan, Majorca, Spain; Harold W. Reeves, Beacon Butcher, Alexandria, Virginia;

Dr. R. H. Smith, Aberdeen, Scotland; Caroline Wood, Sussex, England.

The editors also wish to thank: Alison and Mary Attenborough, Essex, England; Susan Campbell, London; Marisa Centis, London; Liz Clasen, London; Lesley Coates, Essex, England; Emma Codrington, Surrey, England; Ardele Dejey, London; Daniel Engeljohn, John McClung, Michael May, Steven Olson, Dr. Calvin Pals, United States Department of Agriculture, Washington, D.C.; Mimi Errington, Nottinghamshire, England; Dr. George J. Flick Jr., Dr. Norman Marriott, Virginia Polytechnic Institute and

State University, Blacksburg; John Francis, The National Live Stock and Meat Board, Chicago; Neyla Freeman, London; Annie Hall, London; Mary Harron, London; Maggi Heinz, London; The International Natural Sausage Casing Association, Chicago; Wanda F. Kemp-Welsh, Oxford, England; Katie Lloyd, London; Pippa Millard, London; Sonya Mills, Kent, England; Wendy Morris, London; Maria Mosby, London; Ernest Roth, Oxford, England; Robert Schuck, London; Stephanie Thompson, London; Fiona Tillett, London; Robert Turner, London; Tina Walker, London; Linda Welch, National Pork Producers Council, Des Moines, Iowa.

Picture Credits

The sources for the pictures in this book are listed below. Credits for each of the photographers and illustrators are listed by page number in sequence with successive pages indicated by hyphens; where necessary, the locations of pictures within pages are also indicated—separated from page numbers by dashes.

Photographs by Tom Belshaw: cover, 8—top left, bottom, 10-11—bottom, 13—top, 16—top and bottom center, 18—bottom, 22—top right, 23—top, 24—top and bottom center, 25—top, 26-27, 30—top left, bottom right, 31—bottom, 34-35—top, 36—bottom right, 38-39—top, 40-41—top, 50—top, 51, 54-55, 64-65, 70-71, 76-77. Other photographs (alphabetically): John Cook, 9—

bottom, 11—top right, 12—top, 13—bottom center, bottom right, 14-15, 17—bottom, 42-43, 48-49—bottom, 52-53—bottom, 56—bottom center, bottom right, 57—bottom, 58-60, 61—top left, top center, 72, 80-81—bottom, 82-84. Alan Duns, 4, 8—top right, 12—bottom, 13—bottom left, 16—bottom right, 17-18—top, 19-20, 25—bottom right, 28, 29—bottom, 30—bottom left, 36—bottom left, bottom center, 44-47, 48—top right, 49—top left, 50—bottom, 52-53—top, 56—top, bottom left, 57—top, 68, 69—top, 80-81—top. John Elliott, 30—top right, 31—top. Louis Klein, 2. Bob Komar, 10—right, 11—top center, 16—bottom left, 24—bottom left, bottom right, 25—bottom left, bottom center, 32, 34-35—bottom, 38-39—bottom, 49—top center, top right, 61—top right, bottom, 66-67, 78—bottom, 79. Aldo Tutino, 9—top, 10—top left, top center, 11—top left, 22—top left, bottom, 23—bottom, 29—top, 36—top, 37, 40-41—

bottom, 48—top left, 62-63, 69—bottom, 74-75, 78—top left.
Illustrations: From The Mary Evans Picture Library and private sources and *Food & Drink: A Pictorial Archive from Nineteenth Century Sources* by Jim Harter, published by Dover Publications, Inc., 1979, 87-167.

Library of Congress Cataloguing in Publication Data
Main entry under title:
Variety meats.
    (The Good cook, techniques & recipes)
    Includes index.
    1. Cookery (Variety meats) I. Time-Life Books.
II. Series.
TX749.V37 1982   641.6'6   82-10380
ISBN 0-8094-2952-7
ISBN 0-8094-2951-9 (lib. bdg.)
ISBN 0-8094-2950-0 (retail ed.)

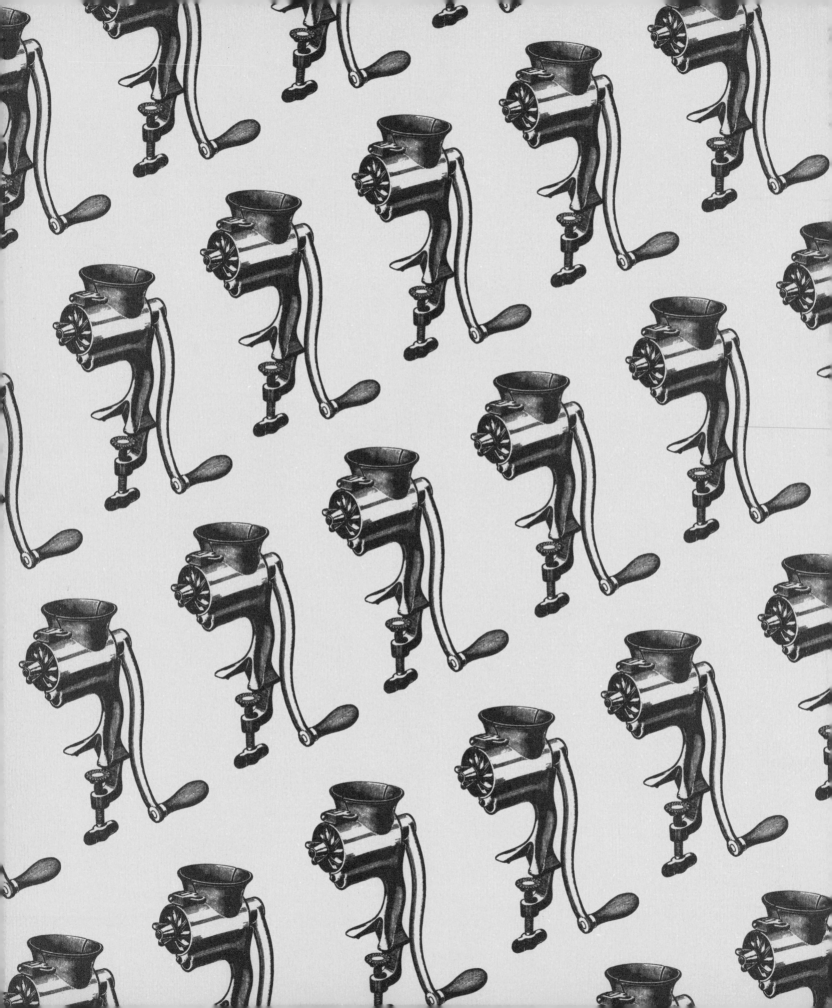